ALSO BY BEVERLY M. ANDERSON (NEMIRO)
AND DONNA M. HAMILTON

The High Altitude Cookbook
The Complete Book of High Altitude Baking
Where to Eat in Colorado
Colorado a la Carte, Series I and II

The New High Altitude Cookbook

The New High Altitude Cookbook

BEVERLY M. ANDERSON
and
DONNA M. HAMILTON

Random House  New York

Library of Congress Gataloging in Publication Data
Nemiro, Beverly Anderson.
The new high altitude cookbook.
Includes material originally included in the author's
The high altitude cookbook and The complete book of
high altitude baking.
Includes index.
1. Cookery. I. Hamilton, Donna Miller, joint
author. II. Title. III. Title: High altitude cook-
book.
TX652.N39   641.5   80–5287
ISBN 0–394–51308–8

Manufactured in the United States of America
23456789B

TO OUR CHILDREN
DEE, GUY AND LEE
JOAN, JOHN, MARK, PAUL AND PETE

FOR THE YEARS OF INSPIRATION,
FAITH, ACTIVE AID, PATIENCE,
ENCOURAGEMENT AND LOVING SUPPORT

Dear Reader,

This cookbook is a collection of high altitude recipes and editorial information that is the result of twenty years' experience, research and testing multiplied by two. Only recipes that require cooking or are affected by altitude are included.

Our first book, *The Complete Book of High Altitude Baking*, drew heavily from our heritage of reliable family heirloom recipes. It was a delightful exercise to change a "lump" of butter to an even tablespoon, a "scant quart of flour" to level cups, and determine the proper equivalent for "four great spoons" of cornmeal. That was 1960.

Nine years later *The High Altitude Cookbook* was published. Four years in the making, it was significantly different from its forerunner in that it addressed the vast differences in cooking as well as baking at high elevations. Questing and testing as we were continually doing, we kept adding to our files, and when the book went into its ninth printing, we felt the time was right for a new and even more comprehensive book, one that would be all-inclusive regarding the exceptionally widespread problems of baking and cooking for those who live 2,500 feet or more above sea level. This area covers more than one-third of the United States.

Our first priority was to include expansive chapters on baking, since that's where the problems are the most visibly dramatic. Then we must include never-before-published material we had gathered, high altitude facts, cooking timetables, charts, and explanatory information in every chapter. And to educate the reader further, we must put in common language the scientific causes why high altitude baking and cooking are different.

When it came to the recipes themselves, the challenge was to select from the enormous collection of old and new that we had created, developed and acquired. Since we had continually tested, it would be important to choose those that would reflect new trends in eating and new products as well as up-to-date appliances. Of course the book just *had* to include some of our time-tested family favorites and old-fashioned classics. From this treasury of heirlooms not yet exhausted, we continued to convert amusing antiquities: butter "the size of a walnut," "twelve 5¢ Hershey bars," "top milk," and "stoned" dates into contemporary terms. After all, a cookbook is a reflection of the times, and ours should represent all that was importantly new as well as tried-and-true.

We present philosophical influences as well. We believe cooked and baked foods are only as good as the ingredients from which they are made. Throughout the book the emphasis is on *fresh*. We recommend only *fresh* cream of tartar, baking powder and yeast; fresh produce, extra-large grade AA eggs, poultry and meat; high-quality products such as pure vanilla extract and chocolate; Japanese soy sauce; top-of-the-line shortening, butter and margarine; natural cheeses, cream and dairy products; the best mayonnaise or brandy; real, not cooking, wines; and, whenever possible, products that are preservative-free and naturally processed.

It is with a feeling of satisfaction that we have our cherished and frequently used jottings, dog-eared pieces of paper, and note cards categorized between hard-bound covers where they are readily accessible and can be shared. At last we have achieved our long-time goal—the first basic and complete all-purpose cookbook for high altitude.

Beverly M. Anderson
Donna M. Hamilton
Denver, Colorado
July 12, 1980

Contents

xii • *Contents*

WHY HIGH ALTITUDE BAKING AND COOKING ARE DIFFERENT

High altitude baking and cooking are *different*. The reason: lower atmospheric pressure due to a thinner blanket of air. As altitude increases, atmospheric pressure decreases, and this in turn causes:

- water to boil at 202.6°F. at an altitude of 5,000 feet rather than at 212°F. as it does at sea level.
- leavening (baking powder, baking soda, cream of tartar) to expand more.
- yeast doughs to rise too rapidly and too high.
- sugar solutions to become more concentrated in frostings, candies, jellies and baked products.
- faster evaporation of liquids in all cooking processes.
- drying out of normal moisture in most food products.

Baking

High altitude has the greatest effects on baking. In baking recipes, each ingredient bears a definite relationship to the others, and the quality of the finished product depends on a delicate balance of ingredients achieved through the proper quantity of each.

The reduction of atmospheric pressure at high altitude allows leavening agents—air, steam and carbon dioxide—to expand more than at sea level. Air can be controlled most easily, simply by not overbeating egg whites. Carbon dioxide and steam, however, get their volume from given weights of their respective sources and depend on existing atmospheric pressure and temperature. One teaspoon of baking powder at 5,000 feet produces 20 percent more volume than at sea level. Bread rises faster and must be watched. At 5,000 feet, steam expands to an approximately 20 percent greater volume than at sea level, causing popovers to puff out too rapidly and thereby lose their steam. Cakes rise excessively, which stretches the cell structure and makes the cake coarse-textured or, worse, breaks the cell walls, causing the cake to fall.

It is important to have a correct ratio of sugar to the other ingredients. Liquids evaporate more quickly at high altitudes, and if a solution contains too much sugar—or not enough liquid—it will become overly concentrated during baking, weakening the cell walls of cakes, desserts, quick breads or cookies.

Shortening, like sugar, can be a problem for the high altitude cook. Too much in a rich cake batter will weaken the cell structure. The substitution of margarine for butter or high-grade hydrogenated or emulsified shortening can noticeably affect the texture in cakes as well as produce an inferior taste.

At high altitude, liquids work in two contradictory ways. On the one hand, their rapid evaporation rate creates the problem of overly concentrated sugar solutions. On the other, they offset the dryness of flour, dilute sugar concentration, dissolve and evenly distribute the other ingredients. Because the high altitude air is a thief of moisture, batter requires a greater proportion of liquid than at sea level.

Unless the cook uses extra-large eggs, the batter will be less stable and the final baked product will not be moist enough. Some cakes, especially angel food and sponge, require a greater number of eggs than at sea level.

Furthermore, unless oven temperatures are increased in baking cakes, yeast or quick breads, the batter will not "set" before the air cells formed by the leavening agent expand too much.

When baking casseroles or roasting meats, standard oven times and temperatures will fail to produce satisfactory results because the boiling point of water in the foods themselves will never exceed 202.6°F. More cooking time and/or higher temperature may be needed.

When baking yeast breads, the cook must carefully watch that the dough does not rise more than double its bulk. Because dough rises faster at high altitudes, flavor doesn't have time to develop. Punching down the dough twice will improve flavor as well as texture.

Cooking

At high altitudes, water boils at lower temperatures than at sea level. (See Boiling Point of Water from Sea Level to 14,000 Feet, page xvi.) At an altitude of 5,000 feet, for example, it will boil at only 202.6°F.—a difference of 9.4°F. from sea level. Foods cooked in or over boiling water —at these lower temperatures—require longer cooking times to become done or tender, and must be cooked according to special timetables and directions. This applies to vegetables, fruits, eggs, poultry, meat, stews, soups, beverages, fish, custards and sauces, as well as canning and preserving. At very high elevations, some boiled foods never become satisfactorily cooked. Oldtime cookbooks warned prospectors going up into the mountains never to cook beans "cuz they don't get done."

The reason for the lower boiling point of water at high altitudes is decreased atmospheric pressure. When a liquid is heated, vapor begins to form. The bubbles of vapor, being lighter than the surrounding liquid, rise upward, but they cannot reach the surface until the pressure within each bubble just exceeds the atmospheric pressure on the surface of the liquid. The temperature at which the bubbles of water vapor break through the surface and escape into the air is called the boiling point. This is why, as altitude increases and atmospheric pressure decreases, the boiling point also decreases, and to compensate for the lower cooking temperature, the cooking time for food must be increased.

You *cannot* cook food more quickly by turning the burner higher. The reason is the distinction between *heat* and *temperature*. The heat flow— from the burner to the saucepan to the water in the saucepan to the food immersed in the water—can be increased *only* until the water starts to boil. Water will not reach a temperature higher than its own boiling point, and consequently the food immersed in it cannot reach a temperature exceeding the boiling point of the water. Turning up the burner after water has started to boil will only boil it away faster.

SOME COMMON PROBLEMS OF COOKING AT HIGH ALTITUDES:

Food is often underdone because the moisture in the food itself and the water in which it is being cooked boils at a lower temperature.

Because of the rapid rate of evaporation, food can easily cook dry.

Unless special adjustments are made in the temperature of cooking oil, deep-fat-fried foods will be overbrowned on the outside, undercooked on the inside.

Because of the lack of moisture in the air, sugar syrups used in making candies, frostings and jellies concentrate much more rapidly than at lower elevations.

Canned fruits, tomatoes and pickled vegetables do not become thoroughly processed because of the lowered boiling point of water, and low-acid foods (vegetables, meat and poultry) can nurture heat-resistant bacteria unless processed longer and at higher poundage in a steam-pressure canner.

In summary, altitude has a great effect on food and food processes. It affects the flavor and taste of food, influencing three of our four basic tastes: sweet, sour and bitter. It affects processing time and moisture content. But there are solutions to the problems facing the high altitude cook. You will find these solutions in each and every chapter of this book, by reading the introductory material, using the guidelines in the charts, and carefully following the directions in the recipes.

BOILING POINT OF WATER FROM SEA LEVEL TO 14,000 FEET

Height above sea level	Boiling point of water (F.)
0	212.0
500	211.0
1000	210.0
1500	209.1
2000	208.2
2500	207.1
3000	206.2
3500	205.3
4000	204.4
4500	203.4
5000	202.6
5500	201.7
6000	200.7
6500	199.8
7000	198.7
7500	198.0
8000	196.9
10000	194.0
12500	189.8
14000	187.3

To determine the boiling point of water where you live:
Find the altitude at which you live on the bottom line. Using a ruler, draw a line from this point upward to meet the slanting line. Mark where your line meets the slanting line. Using the ruler, draw a straight line from the marked point to the Boiling Point of Water scale. Where the line joins the scale indicates the Centigrade and Fahrenheit temperatures of boiling water at your elevation (see example below).

Boiling Point	*of Water*	°C.	100°	96°	95°
90°	85°	°F.	212°	*Elevation* 0	1,000 Feet
205°	203°	200°	194°	4,000	5,000 Feet
190°	185°		10,000 Feet	15,000 Feet	

HIGH ALTITUDE OVEN TEMPERATURE CHART
(Fahrenheit and Centigrade)

Oven	Degrees Fahrenheit	Degrees Centigrade
Slow	300°F. to 325°F.	149°C. to 163°C.
Moderate	340°F. to 375°F.	177°C. to 191°C.
Hot	400°F. to 425°F.	204°C. to 218°C.

HOW TO CONVERT OVEN TEMPERATURES

Fahrenheit into Centigrade:
  Subtract 32, multiply by 5, divide by 9.
    Example: 140°F. − 32 = 108
      108 × 5 = 540
      540 ÷ 9 = 60°C.

Centigrade into Fahrenheit:
  Multiply by 9, divide by 5, add 32.
    Example: 60° C. × 9 = 540
      540 ÷ 5 = 108
      108 + 32 = 140°F.

HOW TO CONVERT TO THE METRIC SYSTEM

Easy Comparisons:
  A liter equals a little more than a quart (1 quart plus 3 tablespoons).
  A kilogram equals a little more than two pounds (2.2 pounds).

Solid Measurements
  Butter in solidly packed standard eight-ounce cups:
              2 cups = 400 grams
              1 cup = 200 grams
              ½ cup = 100 grams
              ¼ cup = 50 grams
  Granulated sugar:
              1 cup = 190 grams
              ⅔ cup = 125 grams
              ½ cup = 95 grams
              ¼ cup = 50 grams
  All-purpose flour:
              1 cup = 140 grams
              ⅔ cup = 100 grams
              ½ cup = 70 grams
              ¼ cup = 35 grams
  Rice:
              1 cup = 150 grams

Liquid Measurements

$$2 \text{ cups} = \frac{1}{2} \text{ liter}$$
$$1 \text{ cup } = \frac{1}{4} \text{ liter}$$
$$\frac{3}{4} \text{ cup } = 1/6 \text{ liter}$$
$$\frac{2}{3} \text{ cup } = 1/7 \text{ liter}$$
$$\frac{1}{2} \text{ cup } = 1/8 \text{ liter}$$
$$\frac{1}{3} \text{ cup } = 1/15 \text{ liter}$$
$$\frac{1}{4} \text{ cup } = 1/16 \text{ liter}$$

HIGH ALTITUDE FACTS ABOUT THE ELECTRIC SLOW COOKER

Because slow cookers use a very low temperature, it is important that the food inside gets hot enough to become properly done, avoiding spoilage and killing health-endangering bacteria. At high altitude, a minimum safe temperature is 200°F. You must take special care to get more heat into the slow cooker, since you are already cooking with a 10-or-more-degree drop in the boiling point.

Since temperature control units on slow cookers vary with each manufacturer's model, you should be careful to select a setting comparable to at least 200°F. Some adjustable heat controls on slow cookers have low temperature settings which should not be used for cooking at all. They are designed for warming. Also, allow for considerably more cooking and baking time at higher elevations.

Dried legumes *cannot* be cooked in a slow cooker at high altitude unless they have been precooked on the stove; then they may be satisfactorily finished and served in the cooker.

Avoid taking the lid off the slow cooker. It takes 20 to 25 minutes to regain the lost steam and temperature. Never remove the cover during the first 2½ to 3 hours when baking in a cooker. Follow high altitude directions for packaged mixes.

Aluminum foil on top of the foods being cooked or between the rim of the cooker and the cover reflects the heat downward into the food and is especially helpful at higher elevations.

Completely thaw all but the quickest-cooking vegetables before cooking them in a crockery pot.

HIGH ALTITUDE FACTS ABOUT ELECTRIC SKILLET AND WOK COOKERY

Successful use of the electric skillet and wok at high altitudes depends on increasing the cooking temperature by about 25°F. When browning a skillet-filling amount of meat or poultry, the cooking temperature may fall off more quickly than at sea level, and you should turn the temperature control up from time to time to keep the heat constant. The same is true when you are cooking large quantities of vegetables.

You should always allow for more cooking time than is called for in accompanying instruction manuals and in sea-level recipes.

You can maintain or increase "cooking power" in ways other than by just turning up the temperature control dial. First, keep the vents tightly closed during cooking to keep all the steam possible inside the skillet or wok. Second, when braising foods that require long cooking times, secure aluminum foil over the skillet's rim, then place the cover on tightly. This optimizes the use of all available heat, reduces heat loss, and helps retain the proper moisture content.

Another way of keeping moisture from being lost to the dry high altitude air is to add water or other liquids in small amounts as needed. This will also prevent scorching.

HIGH ALTITUDE FACTS ABOUT MICROWAVE COOKERY*

High altitude affects most foods cooked in the microwave oven with the exception of vegetables.

Temperature of foods decreases as altitude increases, yet due to more rapid evaporation of liquids in high altitude areas, microwave cooking takes less time than at sea level.

The exceptions are meats and dense, low-moisture foods such as pasta and rice which require the maximum cooking time recommended in manufacturer's instruction manuals and nationally published microwave cookbooks. It is advisable to judge the doneness of the meat by the muscle, not the fat, since fat cooks more quickly than muscle.

Cake batters should stand fifteen minutes before baking to permit some of the leavening gas to escape. Fill baking dish only half full because cakes rise higher and more rapidly in the microwave oven. High altitude directions on package mixes should be followed.

Always to be considered are the variables that can affect cooking time: the temperature, size and shape, and amount of food, plus the power setting of the oven. It is best to underestimate cooking times and check foods during cooking.

* The information in this section has been adapted from materials compiled by Joan Gehle, Home Economist, Denver Public Schools, Emily Griffith Opportunity School.

HIGH ALTITUDE FACTS ABOUT
THE PRESSURE COOKER

Every high altitude cook should own a pressure cooker. When you live at 5,000 feet above sea level, for example, the atmospheric pressure is 18 percent, or 2.1 pounds less than at sea level, and every increase in elevation decreases it further—thereby also decreasing the boiling point of water. By enabling you to increase the pressure inside the cooker to nearer that of sea level, the pressure cooker raises the temperature at which water boils and makes food cook more quickly and thoroughly. In very high areas (7,000 feet and above), the boiling temperatures are so low that the pressure cooker becomes the only means by which dried legumes can be completely cooked. Even at lower altitudes (3,000 feet and above), it is essential for canning, as it inactivates or kills harmful bacteria. And because it shortens the cooking time of foods, it is one of the best ways to prevent them from drying out during the cooking process—an all too frequent problem at high altitudes.

Wherever it is used, the pressure cooker has gained recognition for quick cooking and vitamin-and-energy-saving features, but at high altitudes it provides the additional benefit of accomplishing the otherwise impossible.

Using the Pressure Cooker at High Altitudes

To reach the same boiling temperature as at sea level, the pressure in the cooker must be increased by 1 pound for every 2,000 feet above sea level, and cooking time under pressure should be increased by 5 percent for every 1,000 feet after 2,000 feet above sea level. At sea level, the pressure cooker is normally set to 10 pounds. At higher altitudes (5,000 feet and above), where the atmospheric pressure is so much lower to begin with, the additional 10 pounds will not raise the boiling temperature to as high a point as they do at sea level, and the gauges of most home pressure cookers do not go above 10 pounds. To compensate, it is necessary to lengthen the cooking time recommended for sea level, *or* the gauge from your pressure cooker may be sent to the manufacturer and adjusted to the proper weight for the altitude at which you live.

In addition to altitude, the types of meat and the maturity and size of vegetables must be taken into consideration when determining cooking times under pressure. A 1-to-2-minute increase in cooking time is usually sufficient for most vegetables, except for such bulky roots as potatoes, beets and the like. At an altitude of 5,000 feet, these require an additional 5 minutes of cooking time.

When you are cooking recipes from this book in the pressure cooker, adjustments in cooking time and amounts of liquid will be necessary. Consult the instruction booklet that accompanies your cooker.

To prevent evaporation, reduce heat when desired pressure is attained. This will not reduce the pressure but will help retain moisture.

The New High Altitude Cookbook

Appetizers

HIGH ALTITUDE FACTS ABOUT APPETIZERS

Because of the dry atmosphere at altitudes above 2,500 feet, cold canapés, cheeses, breads, dips, meats, spreads and pastries quickly lose their freshness when left unprotected. To preserve their moistness, cover prepared appetizers with lightly dampened cloth, plastic wrap or aluminum foil. At high altitudes, chafing dishes do not produce enough heat to cook appetizers, nor do candle warmers generate enough heat to keep cocktail tidbits and beverages from cooling. The electric slow cooker is excellent for cooking appetizers and for keeping them piping hot.

AVOCADO WITH HOT SAUCE

4 SERVINGS

2 avocados, cut in half and seeds removed
Juice of 1 lemon
3 tablespoons catsup
3 tablespoons Worcestershire sauce
3 tablespoons chili sauce
6 tablespoons consommé
6 tablespoons tarragon vinegar
½ cup currant or other tart red jelly

1. Arrange avocado halves on crushed ice or lettuce cups in individual serving bowls. Sprinkle with lemon juice.
2. In small saucepan, mix together catsup, Worcestershire sauce, chili sauce, consommé, vinegar and jelly. Bring to boil. Pour into serving bowl.
3. Serve very hot sauce over avocados.

CHILI BEAN DIP

2 CUPS

2 cups canned chili beans in
    chili gravy
1 small clove garlic, minced
¼ cup finely chopped onion

3 tablespoons diced green chilies
½ cup finely grated cheddar
Corn or tortilla chips

1. In top half of double boiler, mash half of beans with wooden spoon until smooth.
2. Add remaining half of beans and all other ingredients. Mix well.
3. Cook, stirring until well blended, over boiling water until cheese is melted. Serve hot with corn or tortilla chips.

NOTE: May be served cold. Keeps well in refrigerator.

CURRIED BEEF OR LAMB PASTIES

2 DOZEN

¼ cup shortening
1 package (3 ounces) cream cheese
½ cup sifted all-purpose flour
1 tablespoon butter
½ pound lean ground beef or lamb
6 green onions and tops, finely
    chopped

1 small clove garlic, minced
¼ teaspoon ground ginger
¼ teaspoon ground cloves
⅛ teaspoon ground cinnamon
2 teaspoons lemon juice
1 teaspoon curry powder
½ teaspoon salt

1. In small bowl, cream together shortening and cheese. Mix in flour. Refrigerate until chilled.
2. Preheat oven to 350°F.
3. On floured board, roll out pastry ⅛ inch thick. Cut into 2-inch circles.
4. In small skillet with cover, melt butter. Cook beef or lamb over medium-high heat, stirring and chopping with wooden spoon into small granules as it browns. Add onions, garlic, ginger, cloves, cinnamon, lemon juice, curry powder and salt. Cover. Simmer 5 minutes.
5. Place 1 teaspoon meat mixture on half of each pastry. Wet edges of pastry with water and fold over filling. Seal edges together.
6. Bake for 20 minutes.

PLANKED BEEF TENDERLOIN AND CANADIAN BACON

▼▼

20 OR MORE SERVINGS

1 *beef tenderloin (about 4 pounds)*	3 *tablespoons water*
¼ *cup firmly packed brown sugar*	20 *Parker House or potato rolls,*
¼ *cup pineapple juice*	*cut in half and buttered*
1 *piece Canadian-type bacon*	
(about 3 pounds)	

1. Preheat oven to 350°F. Have ready 2 shallow baking pans.
2. Trim beef of any fat. Place in baking pan.
3. Mix brown sugar with pineapple juice. Cover Canadian bacon with mixture. Place in second separate pan with water.
4. Place meats in preheated oven. Remove beef after 15 minutes. Allow Canadian bacon to heat through (about 20 minutes).
5. Meanwhile, preheat broiler. Place beef under preheated broiler, turning to brown quickly on all sides, about 5 minutes altogether.
6. Place broiled beef and Canadian bacon side by side on wooden serving plank or heated platter. Slice thinly. Serve 1 slice beef and 1 slice bacon on each buttered roll.

PECAN BRIE IN PUFF PASTRY

▼▼

24 ONE-INCH WEDGES

3 *packages (4½ ounces each) Brie*	1 *egg yolk, beaten*
1 *package (6) frozen patty shells,*	*Pecan halves*
partially thawed but not warm	

1. Preheat oven to 450°F.
2. On lightly floured board or pastry canvas, roll out each patty shell to ⅛ inch thick.
3. Place rounds of Brie in centers of three pastry circles. Top each with pecan halves and one of remaining pastry circles. With fingers crimp edges to seal top and bottom pastries. Brush with egg yolk. Place on cookie sheet.
4. Bake at 450°F. for 10 minutes. *Reduce* heat to 350°F. Bake 20 minutes more. Cut into wedges and serve with crackers or fruit.

NOTE: May be refrigerated or frozen after Step 3.

COCKTAIL BURGERS WITH WATER CHESTNUTS

2 DOZEN

1 *pound lean ground beef*
¼ *pound pork sausage*
⅓ *cup fine dry bread crumbs*
⅓ *cup dry sherry*
¼ *cup cream*
2 *tablespoons finely chopped green onion*
¼ *cup finely chopped water chestnuts*

1 *tablespoon finely chopped parsley*
1 *teaspoon seasoned salt*
½ *teaspoon seasoned pepper*
Shortening or cooking oil
Cocktail-size hamburger buns, or baking powder biscuits
Piquant Sauce, page 166, or sauce of your choice

1. In mixing bowl combine meats, bread crumbs, sherry, cream, onion, water chestnuts, parsley, salt and pepper. Toss together until blended. Shape into thin 1-inch patties.
2. In skillet, sauté patties in shortening or cooking oil until browned on both sides. Drain.
3. Serve in cocktail-size bun, sandwich style, or atop halves of small biscuits, secured with toothpicks. Add dab of Piquant Sauce or other sauce, if desired.

COCKTAIL MEATBALLS: Form meat mixture into 1-inch balls. Sauté as directed and serve on a heated platter or in a chafing dish, with toothpicks for spearing. Serve with Piquant Sauce, page 166, or Barbecue Sauce, page 162.

COCKTAIL CHEESE WAFERS

2 DOZEN

1 *cup sifted all-purpose flour*
1 *teaspoon salt*
Dash cayenne pepper
½ *cup softened butter*

1 *packed cup grated New York sharp cheddar*
Pecan halves, if desired

1. Preheat oven to 425°F. Have ready greased cookie sheet.
2. Mix and sift flour, salt and cayenne pepper together.
3. With two table knives or pastry blender, cut butter into flour until consistency of small grain. Add grated cheese. Mix well.
4. Shape dough into ball. Chill a few minutes if too sticky to roll out.
5. On lightly floured board or pastry canvas, roll out dough ⅛ inch thick. Cut with cookie cutter to desired shape and size. Top each wafer with pecan half, if desired. Place wafers on cookie sheet.
6. Bake for about 15 minutes. Serve piping hot.

NOTE: Delicious accompaniment with soups or salads.

CHILI CON QUESO (CHILI WITH CHEESE)

8 TO 10 SERVINGS

1 cup chopped onion
3 tablespoons butter
1½ cups chopped ripe tomatoes
    or drained and chopped
    canned tomatoes
1 can (4 ounces) chopped
    green chilies

1 teaspoon salt
½ teaspoon pepper
1 pound grated American cheese
    Tomato juice, if necessary
    Toasted tortilla or corn chips

1. In heavy saucepan, sauté onion in butter until limp.
2. Add tomatoes, chilies, salt and pepper. Simmer over low heat for 5 minutes.
3. Add cheese. Stir until melted.
4. Thin with tomato juice, if too thick.
5. Serve hot as a dip for oven-heated tortilla or corn chips.

STUFFED MUSHROOMS

2 DOZEN

24 large mushrooms, washed and
    dried
½ cup melted butter
    Juice of 1 lemon
2 tablespoons minced parsley
2 tablespoons minced onion

¼ cup grated Swiss cheese
½ teaspoon salt
    Dash freshly ground pepper
¾ cup fine bread crumbs
¼ cup sherry

1. Cut stems from mushrooms. Dip caps in ¼ cup melted butter. Sprinkle with lemon juice.
2. Make stuffing: Chop mushroom stems very fine. In skillet, sauté chopped mushroom stems, parsley, and onion in remaining ¼ cup melted butter until limp.
3. Combine grated cheese, salt, pepper, ½ cup bread crumbs, and sherry. Add sautéed vegetables. Toss lightly.
4. Shake lemon juice from mushroom caps. Fill each cap with stuffing. Sprinkle lightly with remaining ¼ cup bread crumbs. Dot with additional butter.
5. Bake at 350°F. for 15 to 20 minutes. Serve piping hot.

NACHOS

12 APPETIZER SERVINGS
4 MAIN-DISH SERVINGS

Cooking oil
12 corn tortillas, cut into sixths
½ pound lean ground beef
½ pound chorizo sausage, removed
    from casing
1 cup chopped onion
2 cans (16 ounces each) refried
    beans

1 can (4 ounces) chopped mild
    green chilies
3 cups grated longhorn cheddar
¾ cup bottled or canned taco sauce
½ cup chopped green onion
1 avocado, peeled, seed removed
    and mashed
1 cup dairy sour cream

1. In heavy saucepan or skillet, heat ¼ inch cooking oil. Cook tortillas until lightly browned and crisp. Remove and drain on paper toweling.
2. Pour off all but 1 tablespoon cooking oil. Add beef, sausage and onion. Cook until meat is lightly browned, stirring constantly.
3. Lightly grease 12 × 8 × 2-inch baking dish. Spread refried beans evenly on bottom. Spread meat and green chilies evenly over beans. Sprinkle with cheese. Drizzle taco sauce over cheese.
4. Bake at 400°F. for 20 to 25 minutes, or until hot. Remove from oven and sprinkle with green onions. Mound mashed avocado in center. Put dollops of sour cream over all. Place fried tortilla pieces around edges of dish and serve. Keep warm on warming tray.

NOTE: May be refrigerated after Step 3 and finished later.

OYSTERS CASINO

4 SERVINGS

1 cup bread crumbs
⅓ cup softened butter
2 tablespoons finely chopped
    green pepper
¼ teaspoon freshly ground
    black pepper
Rock salt

1 clove garlic, finely chopped
12 oysters on the half shell, or
    equivalent fresh or frozen
    oysters, thawed
2 slices bacon, diced and
    partially cooked
Lemon wedges

1. Combine bread crumbs, butter, green pepper and black pepper. Mix thoroughly. Shape into roll about 1 inch thick. Wrap in waxed paper. Chill until firm enough to slice.
2. Arrange bed of rock salt in flat baking pan. Sprinkle garlic over salt.
3. Arrange fresh oysters in shell on rock salt. If using fresh, bulk oysters, drain, place in seafood shells and place filled shells on rock salt.

4. Thinly slice chilled breading. Place slice of breading and bacon bits on top of each oyster or oysters.
5. Broil at least 5 inches from heat for 8 to 12 minutes, being careful to avoid overcooking. Serve with lemon wedges.

RUMAKI

▼▼

2 DOZEN

12 *slices lean bacon, cut in half*
3 *tablespoons Japanese soy sauce*
2 *teaspoons granulated sugar*
¼ *teaspoon fresh finely chopped ginger or ⅛ teaspoon ground ginger*

6 *chicken livers, quartered*
12 *water chestnuts, cut in half*
24 *toothpicks*

1. Cook bacon until half done.
2. Combine soy sauce, sugar and ginger. Pour over chicken livers. Marinate 30 minutes or longer. Drain, reserving marinade.
3. Preheat oven to 450°F.
4. Wrap one-half slice partially cooked bacon around quartered liver and water chestnut half. Secure with toothpick. Place on rack of broiler pan.
5. Bake 10 minutes, turning once, and basting with reserved marinade during cooking.

NOTE: Rumaki may be baked ahead, refrigerated and reheated just before serving.

SPINACH PIE

▼▼

8 APPETIZER SERVINGS
4 MAIN-DISH SERVINGS

1 *package (12 ounces) frozen chopped spinach or 1 pound fresh, washed spinach*
9-inch unbaked pie shell
¼ *cup grated Parmesan*
3 *eggs*
1 *container (8 ounces) cottage cheese*
1 *cup whipping cream*

2 *tablespoons instant onion flakes*
1 *teaspoon caraway seeds*
¼ *teaspoon freshly ground pepper*
¼ *teaspoon ground nutmeg*
¼ *teaspoon Worcestershire sauce*
Few drops liquid hot pepper sauce
1 *tablespoon butter*

1. In medium saucepan, cook spinach, following directions on package. Drain well.

2. Sprinkle pie shell with Parmesan.
3. Bake at 400°F. for 8 minutes. Cool.
4. In bowl, beat eggs just until frothy. Stir in cottage cheese, cream, onion flakes, caraway seeds, pepper, nutmeg, Worcestershire and liquid hot pepper sauces. Mix well.
5. Stir in cooked drained spinach. Spoon into baked, cooled pie shell.
6. In small pan, melt butter. Drizzle over top of spinach.
7. Bake at 375°F. for 30 minutes, or until browned. To serve, cut into wedges.

SPINACH SOUFFLÉ ROLL STUFFED WITH MUSHROOMS

8 TO 10 SERVINGS

¾ cup butter
Bread crumbs
2½ pounds fresh spinach, washed
    and dried
Water
½ teaspoon salt
¼ teaspoon ground pepper
¼ teaspoon ground nutmeg
4 eggs, separated (beat whites
    until stiff, but not dry)

¼ cup grated Parmesan
½ pound mushrooms, washed,
    dried and sliced
½ cup grated Swiss cheese
Paprika
Canned, drained pimiento slices

1. Preheat oven to 350°F.
2. Butter 10½ × 15½ × 1-inch baking pan, using 1 tablespoon butter. Line pan bottom and sides with foil or waxed paper. Butter foil or waxed paper, using 1 tablespoon butter. Sprinkle lightly with bread crumbs.
3. Remove tough and thick stems from spinach.
4. In large saucepan, cook spinach in a little water for about 5 minutes, or until only slightly done. Drain.
5. With sharp knife or scissors, finely chop spinach. Drain again. Spinach should be almost dry.
6. In medium bowl, combine spinach, salt, pepper, nutmeg and 6 tablespoons butter. Beat in egg yolks one at a time. Fold in beaten whites. Carefully spread in prepared pan. Sprinkle with Parmesan.
7. Bake for 12 to 15 minutes, or until soufflé pulls away from sides of pan, but is not dried out. Remove from oven. Cool.
8. In medium skillet, melt 1 tablespoon butter. Sauté mushrooms until limp.
9. Butter sheet of foil large enough to cover baked soufflé. Place over soufflé. Invert soufflé onto buttered foil, using fingers and spatula to remove it if it sticks.
10. Spread mushrooms over spinach.
11. Starting at narrow end, carefully roll up as in making a jelly roll.
12. Sprinkle roll with Swiss cheese and paprika. Decorate with strips of pimiento. Using sharp knife, cut into slices. Serve hot.

Beverages

HIGH ALTITUDE FACTS ABOUT MAKING COFFEE

A longer brewing time is required to compensate for the lower boiling point of water at higher elevations. Coffee brewing involves a heat-activated threshold reaction (the initiation of a chemical process that releases all the coffee's essential oils and flavors). For a good cup of coffee, a high-enough temperature must be reached and held until sufficient infusion takes place. To accomplish this at altitudes above 2,500 feet, set automatic coffeemaker for medium-strong to strong coffee, then adjust to individual preference if too strong, or let coffee brew for a longer period of time over higher heat if using the stove-top method.

Coffee cools more rapidly as elevation increases (see Boiling Point of Water from Sea Level to 14,000 Feet, page xvi). To keep it from quickly becoming disagreeably tepid, we recommend the use of coffee warmers, heavy mugs or insulated cups.

Instant Coffee or Tea

The higher you live, the lower the temperature of boiling water, and the less satisfactory the results obtainable when dissolving instant coffee or tea. Therefore, it is preferable to avoid making coffee or tea in serving cups, since the water will not be hot enough to adequately dissolve the coffee or tea and to release its full flavor.

Use 1 rounded teaspoon instant coffee or tea for each ¾ cup (6 ounces) *furiously* boiling water. Measure the required amount of instant coffee or tea into a stove-top coffeepot or saucepan. Pour the required amount of *furiously* boiling water over the coffee or tea, stirring constantly. Heat over medium-low heat for about 5 minutes. For instant demitasse coffee, use 1 rounded to heaping demitasse spoon instant coffee for each 3 ounces *furiously* boiling water.

Instant coffee and tea will be even more full-bodied when you brew them in an automatic electric percolator, just as you would ground coffee or bulk tea.

Methods for Making Tea

Preheat a glass or earthenware teapot by filling it with boiling water and setting it in a warm place. Since water and containers cool more quickly at elevations above 2,500 feet, preheating the teapot will increase the effectiveness of the steeping process.

Always begin with fresh, cold water; *never* with water that has cooled off and been reheated. Bring water to a *furious* boil.

For 4 cups tea: 3 cups (8 ounces each) water and 4 level teaspoons tea or 4 tea bags. An extra pinch of tea for the pot is often recommended.
For 6 cups tea: 5 cups (8 ounces each) water and 6 level teaspoons tea or 6 tea bags.
For 8 cups tea: 6 cups (8 ounces each) water and 9 level teaspoons tea or 8 tea bags.

1. Pour out water used to preheat pot. Put tea or tea bags in pot. Pour *furiously* boiling water over tea. Cover.
2. Let brew in warm place for 5 to 6 minutes—no less. Stir. If using loose tea, strain into cup or a second heated teapot. Don't rush. The full flavor and fragrance are worth waiting for.

HOT CHOCOLATE

6 SERVINGS

6 *tablespoons cocoa*	1/4 *cup water*
1/8 *teaspoon salt*	5 *cups milk, or 4 cups milk and*
1/2 *cup granulated sugar*	1 *cup half-and-half*

1. In 2-quart saucepan, combine cocoa, salt, sugar, and water.
2. Over low heat, boil gently for 4 minutes, stirring frequently.
3. Add milk, or milk and half-and-half. Heat, but do not boil, until tiny bubbles form around edge, stirring occasionally.

HOT SPICED CHOCOLATE: In Step 1, add ¼ teaspoon ground cinnamon, ⅛ teaspoon each ground cloves and allspice to cocoa mixture. Substitute 2 ounces unsweetened chocolate for cocoa.

MEXICAN CHOCOLATE: In Step 1, add 3 teaspoons instant coffee to chocolate mixture. Add 1 teaspoon vanilla extract just before serving.

HOT SPICED TEA

5 TO 6 CUPS

4 cups water	4 tea bags
8 whole cloves	½ cup granulated sugar
1 stick cinnamon	¼ cup cranberry, lemon or
6 whole allspice	orange juice

1. In saucepan, combine water, cloves, cinnamon, and allspice. Bring to boil. Remove from heat. Add tea bags. Steep 5 minutes.
2. In small saucepan, combine sugar and cranberry, lemon, or orange juice. Bring to boil. Remove from heat. Add to tea mixture. Strain to remove spices. Serve at once.

HOT MULLED BURGUNDY

10 TO 15 SERVINGS

3 cups strong hot tea	2 bottles (⅘ quart each) burgundy
1 cup granulated sugar	Ground nutmeg
2 lemons, sliced	Orange slices
18 whole cloves	Lemon slices
3 sticks (2-inch) cinnamon	Whole cloves

1. In 2-quart saucepan combine hot tea, sugar, lemon slices, cloves and cinnamon. Cook over medium-low heat for 15 minutes. Remove from heat.
2. Strain spiced tea into 4-quart enamel or stainless-steel saucepan. Add burgundy.
3. Heat, but do not boil, over low heat.
4. Serve in punch bowl. Sprinkle top with nutmeg and decorate with orange and lemon slices studded with cloves.

HOT CRANBERRY PUNCH: Substitute 1 quart cranberry-juice cocktail and 1 quart pineapple juice for burgundy.

Quick Breads

HIGH ALTITUDE FACTS ABOUT MAKING
AND BAKING QUICK BREADS

High altitude recipes for biscuits, muffins, coffee cakes, and fruit and nut breads require less leavening and more liquid than do sea-level recipes. To offset the dryness in the air and to produce a uniformly textured, moist product, they often include buttermilk, sour cream and yogurt among the ingredients.

Popovers will not pop to their puffiest unless extra-large eggs are used and shortening is omitted or reduced. The lower boiling point of liquids, which affects the baking temperature of popover batter, requires strict adherence to instructions for preheating popover pans or cups before baking.

Making doughnuts and fritters at high altitudes requires substantial changes, primarily in cooking techniques. The inside of doughnuts and fritters cannot cook as quickly as the outside. Therefore, the temperature of the cooking oil must be lowered to prevent the outside from cracking or burning before the inside is done. The temperature decrease varies according to the type of food being deep-fried, but the rule of thumb is to lower the temperature about 3 degrees for each 1,000 feet of elevation.

BASIC BISCUITS

ABOUT SIXTEEN 2-INCH BISCUITS

2 *cups sifted all-purpose flour*
1 *teaspoon salt*
3 *to 4 teaspoons double-acting baking powder**

6 *tablespoons butter or shortening*
¾ *cup milk*

1. Preheat oven to 450°F. Have ready shallow baking pan.
2. Into mixing bowl, mix and sift flour, salt and baking powder.
3. With two table knives or pastry blender, cut butter or shortening into dry ingredients. Blend until consistency of cornmeal.
4. Make a well in center of dry ingredients. Add small amount of milk. Blend quickly. Add remaining milk. Mix just until moistened.
5. On lightly floured board, roll or pat out dough ¼ to ½ inch thick, handling as little as possible.
6. With unfloured biscuit cutter, cut into desired size rounds. Place in pan.
7. Bake for 12 to 15 minutes.

BACON BISCUITS: In Step 4, add ¼ cup crisply cooked, chopped bacon.

CHEESE BISCUITS: In Step 4, add ⅓ cup grated cheddar, Roquefort, blue, Swiss, Monterey Jack or other natural cheese.

HERB BISCUITS: In Step 4, add 2 teaspoons chopped chives, green onion or parsley, and ½ teaspoon powdered summer savory or thyme.

SCONES: In Step 4, substitute half-and-half for milk. Add 2 well-beaten eggs, reserving 2 tablespoons, and ½ cup raisins. In Step 6, brush scones with remaining egg and sprinkle with sugar.

* Use 4 teaspoons if lighter, fluffier biscuit is desired.

WHEAT-GERM CRACKERS

2½ TO 3 DOZEN

5 *tablespoons cooking oil*
½ *cup water*
1 *tablespoon firmly packed brown sugar*

¾ *cup whole-wheat flour*
½ *cup quick-cooking oats*
¾ *cup wheat germ*
½ *teaspoon salt*

1. Preheat oven to 350°F. Have ready cookie sheet.
2. In large mixing bowl, combine oil, water and sugar. Stir in flour, oats, wheat germ and salt. Shape dough into ball.

3. On lightly floured surface, roll out dough ⅛ inch thick. Dough will crack, but smooths out as it becomes thinner. Using pastry wheel or sharp knife, cut parallel diagonal lines 2 inches apart. Cut across lines to make diamond shapes. Transfer to baking sheet with spatula.

4. Bake about 18 minutes, or until crackers are light golden brown. Cool on rack.

APPLESAUCE OATMEAL BREAD

2 LOAVES

2 cups sifted all-purpose flour	½ teaspoon ground nutmeg
¾ cup firmly packed brown sugar	1½ cups quick-cooking rolled oats
1½ teaspoons baking soda	3 eggs, beaten
1½ teaspoons double-acting baking powder	½ cup cooking oil
½ teaspoon salt	1½ cups applesauce
1 teaspoon ground cinnamon	1 cup chopped nutmeats, dates or raisins

1. Preheat oven to 350°F. Grease two 9 × 5 × 3-inch loaf pans.

2. In large mixing bowl, combine flour, sugar, baking soda, baking powder, salt, cinnamon, nutmeg and oats.

3. In small bowl, blend eggs, oil and applesauce.

4. Make a well in center of dry ingredients.

5. Pour applesauce mixture into well. Mix just until moistened. Add nutmeats, dates or raisins.

6. Pour batter in equal amounts into prepared pans.

7. Bake 1 hour, or until toothpick inserted in center comes out clean.

APRICOT NUT BREAD

3 LOAVES

5 cups sifted all-purpose flour	2 cups chopped nutmeats
5 teaspoons double-acting baking powder	2 cups firmly packed brown sugar
2 teaspoons salt	2½ cups milk
2 packages (12 ounces each) dried apricots, finely chopped	4 eggs, beaten
	½ cup melted butter or margarine

1. Preheat oven to 350°F. Grease and flour three 8 × 4 × 2-inch loaf pans.

2. Into mixing bowl, mix and sift flour, baking powder and salt. Add apricots, nutmeats and brown sugar. Stir to blend ingredients.

3. Combine milk, eggs, and melted butter or margarine. Add liquids to dry ingredients all at once. Mix just until moistened. Batter will not be smooth.

4. Pour batter into prepared pans.

5. Bake for 1 hour, or until toothpick inserted in center comes out clean. Turn out of pans. Cool completely before slicing.

WHOLE-WHEAT BANANA BREAD

▼▼

2 LOAVES

1 *cup shortening*
2 *cups firmly packed brown sugar*
3 *eggs, beaten*
3 *large bananas, mashed*
⅓ *cup water*
2 *cups whole-wheat flour and 1 cup plus 2 tablespoons sifted all-purpose flour, or 1¼ cups wheat germ and 1¼ cups sifted all-purpose flour*

1 *teaspoon salt*
2 *teaspoons baking soda*
2 *teaspoons double-acting baking powder*
1 *cup chopped nutmeats*

1. Preheat oven to 350°F. Grease two 9 × 5 × 3-inch loaf pans.

2. In large mixing bowl, cream shortening and sugar until light and fluffy. Add eggs, bananas and water. Mix well.

3. Mix flours or wheat germ and flour, salt, baking soda and baking powder together.

4. Combine dry ingredients with liquid mixture, stirring only until blended. Add nutmeats, stirring only until blended.

5. Pour batter into prepared pans.

6. Bake 1 hour, or until toothpick inserted in center comes out clean. Cool in pan.

CORN BREAD OR MUFFINS

▼▼

ONE 9 × 9 × 2-INCH PAN OR 12 MUFFINS

1 *egg, slightly beaten*
2 *to 4 tablespoons granulated sugar*
¼ *cup melted butter or shortening*
1 *cup milk*
1 *cup sifted all-purpose flour*

1 *cup cornmeal*
3 *teaspoons double-acting baking powder*
½ *teaspoon salt*

1. Preheat oven to 400°F. Grease 9 × 9 × 2-inch baking pan or 2½ × 1¼-inch muffin pan cups.

2. In mixing bowl, blend egg, sugar, melted butter or shortening, and milk together.

3. Mix and sift together flour, cornmeal, baking powder and salt.
4. Make a well in center of dry ingredients. Add small amount of liquid mixture. Blend quickly. Add remaining liquid mixture, using as few strokes as possible to blend two together.
5. Pour batter into prepared baking pan or muffin pan cups.
6. Bake bread for 25 minutes, muffins about 20 minutes.

SOUR CREAM OR BUTTERMILK CORN BREAD: In Step 1, increase oven temperature to 425°F. In Step 2, substitute 1 cup dairy sour cream or buttermilk for milk. In Step 3, reduce baking powder to 1 teaspoon and add ½ teaspoon baking soda.

CRANBERRY ORANGE BREAD

1 LOAF

1 egg, beaten
2 tablespoons melted butter
1 cup milk
3 cups sifted all-purpose flour
1 teaspoon salt
4 teaspoons double-acting baking
    powder

½ cup granulated sugar
Grated rind of 1 orange
½ cup chopped nutmeats
1 cup chopped cranberries

1. Preheat oven to 350°F. Grease 9 × 5 × 3-inch loaf pan.
2. In mixing bowl, blend beaten egg, melted butter and milk.
3. Mix and sift flour, salt, baking powder and ¼ cup sugar together. Add grated orange rind and nutmeats.
4. Combine dry ingredients with liquid mixture, stirring only until blended.
5. Mix remaining ¼ cup sugar with chopped cranberries. Fold into batter.
6. Pour batter into prepared pan.
7. Bake about 1 hour, or until toothpick inserted in center comes out clean. Bread will slice best if cooled overnight.

WHITE GINGERBREAD (SOUR MILK GINGERBREAD)

8 SERVINGS

4 cups sifted all-purpose flour
1 cup softened butter
2 cups granulated sugar
2 eggs, beaten
1 cup sour milk

½ teaspoon ground cinnamon
1 teaspoon ground nutmeg
1 teaspoon ground ginger
1 teaspoon baking soda
½ teaspoon salt

1. Preheat oven to 350°F. Butter 12 × 8 × 2-inch baking pan.
2. Put sifted flour in mixing bowl. With mixer or hands, combine flour with butter to make crumblike mixture. Add sugar. Blend well. Set aside 2 cupfuls.
3. To remaining crumbed mixture, add beaten eggs, sour milk, cinnamon, nutmeg, ginger, soda and salt. Blend thoroughly.
4. Spread 1 cup reserved crumbed mixture on bottom of prepared pan. Pour batter over crumbs. Top batter with remaining 1 cup crumbed mixture.
5. Bake for 35 to 40 minutes, or until toothpick inserted in center comes out clean.

PINEAPPLE MACADAMIA OR CASHEW BREAD

1 LOAF

½ cup plus 1 tablespoon butter
1½ cups finely chopped macadamia
   or cashew nuts
¾ cup plus 1 tablespoon
   granulated sugar
1 egg, beaten
1¼ cups undrained, crushed
   pineapple

¼ cup milk
1 teaspoon vanilla extract
½ teaspoon grated lemon peel
2½ cups sifted all-purpose flour
2 teaspoons double-acting baking
   powder
1 teaspoon salt
½ teaspoon baking soda

1. Preheat oven to 375°F. Butter 9 × 5 × 3-inch loaf pan with 1 tablespoon butter. Sprinkle with ¼ cup macadamia or cashew nuts and 1 tablespoon sugar.
2. In large mixing bowl, cream remaining ½ cup butter with remaining ¾ cup sugar. Beat in egg, pineapple, milk, vanilla extract and lemon peel.
3. Mix and sift flour, baking powder, salt and soda together.
4. Combine dry ingredients with liquid mixture. Mix just until moistened. Add remaining macadamia or cashew nuts, stirring only until blended.
5. Pour batter into prepared pan.
6. Bake about 1 hour, or until toothpick inserted in center comes out clean. Cool in pan. To serve, invert on plate. Crunchy layer becomes top of bread.

PUMPKIN BREAD

3 LOAVES

3 cups granulated sugar
1½ teaspoons salt
2 teaspoons baking soda
1 teaspoon ground cinnamon
1 teaspoon ground nutmeg
¼ teaspoon ground ginger
3½ cups sifted all-purpose flour

1 cup cooking oil
4 eggs, beaten
⅔ cup water
1 teaspoon vinegar
2 cups cooked mashed pumpkin
1 cup chopped walnut or
   pecan meats

1. Preheat oven to 350°F. Grease three 9 × 5 × 3-inch loaf pans.
2. In large mixing bowl, combine sugar, salt, baking soda, cinnamon, nutmeg, ginger and flour. Make a well in center of dry ingredients.
3. Pour oil, beaten eggs, water, vinegar and pumpkin into well. Mix just until moistened. Add nutmeats, stirring only until blended.
4. Pour batter into prepared pans.
5. Bake 1¼ hours, or until toothpick inserted in center comes out clean.

ZUCCHINI RAISIN BREAD

2 LOAVES

3 eggs, beaten
1 cup granulated sugar
1 cup firmly packed brown sugar
1 cup cooking oil
1 tablespoon vanilla extract
2 cups shredded or ground
    zucchini
3 cups sifted all-purpose flour

2 teaspoons baking soda
1 teaspoon double-acting baking
    powder
1½ teaspoons salt
1 teaspoon ground cinnamon
1 teaspoon ground nutmeg
1 cup chopped nutmeats
1 cup raisins

1. Preheat oven to 350°F. Grease two 9 × 5 × 3-inch loaf pans.
2. In large mixing bowl, blend eggs, sugars, oil and vanilla extract. Add zucchini. Mix well.
3. Mix and sift flour, baking soda, baking powder, salt, cinnamon and nutmeg together.
4. Combine dry ingredients with liquid mixture. Mix just until moistened. Add nutmeats and raisins, stirring only until blended.
5. Pour batter into prepared pans.
6. Bake about 1 hour, or until toothpick inserted in center comes out clean. Cool in pans.

PEACH BREAD: In Step 2, substitute 2 cups peeled, mashed peaches for zucchini. Reduce vanilla extract to 1 teaspoon. In Step 4, omit raisins.

GRANDMOTHER'S COFFEE CAKE

6 TO 9 SERVINGS

¼ cup butter
½ cup granulated sugar
1 egg, beaten
1½ cups sifted all-purpose flour
1½ teaspoons double-acting
    baking powder

½ teaspoon salt
⅔ cup milk
Cinnamon
Brown sugar

1. Preheat oven to 350°F. Grease and flour 9 × 9 × 2-inch baking pan.
2. In mixing bowl, cream butter with sugar until light and fluffy. Add egg. Beat well.
3. Mix and sift flour, baking powder and salt together.
4. Add dry ingredients alternately with milk, mixing thoroughly after each addition.
5. Pour batter into prepared pan. Sprinkle top with cinnamon and brown sugar.
6. Bake for about 30 to 35 minutes, or until cake center springs back when pressed with fingertip.

SOUR-CREAM COFFEE CAKE

ABOUT **16** SERVINGS

½ cup softened butter
½ cup shortening
1¼ cups granulated sugar
2 eggs
½ teaspoon baking soda
1 cup dairy sour cream

2 cups sifted cake flour
½ teaspoon salt
1 teaspoon double-acting
    baking powder
1 teaspoon vanilla extract
Streusel Topping, page 115

1. Preheat oven to 350°F. Grease and flour 10 × 4-inch tube pan.
2. Cream butter and shortening with sugar until light and fluffy. Add eggs one at a time, beating well after each addition.
3. Dissolve soda in sour cream.
4. Mix and sift flour, salt and baking powder together.
5. Add dry ingredients alternately with sour cream to the creamed mixture, mixing well after each addition. Add vanilla extract. Mix well.
6. Pour batter into prepared pan. Sprinkle with Streusel Topping.
7. Bake 1 hour, or until cake center springs back when pressed with fingertip.

DUMPLINGS

4 TO **6** SERVINGS

Experienced cooks will immediately notice the increased amounts of liquid and cooking time required for higher elevations. Use ample broth in which to cook dumplings, don't overcrowd the cooking pan, and don't peek during cooking.

1 cup sifted all-purpose flour
2 teaspoons double-acting baking
    powder
½ teaspoon salt

½ cup milk
1 egg, beaten
6 to 8 cups stock, bouillon or broth

1. Into mixing bowl, mix and sift flour, baking powder and salt.
2. Make well in center of dry ingredients. Add small amount of milk. Add beaten egg. Blend quickly. Add remaining milk, using as few strokes as possible to blend two together.
3. Heat stock, bouillon or broth in wide-topped, deep kettle with cover. Drop batter by tablespoonfuls into boiling liquid, rinsing spoon in water to keep dough from sticking, if necessary. Cover. Cook over low heat without raising cover for 20 minutes, or until toothpick inserted in center of dumpling comes out clean.

FLAVORFUL ADDITIONS TO DUMPLINGS:

¼ cup chopped fresh parsley
¼ teaspoon dried basil, oregano or thyme
2 teaspoons curry powder
Paprika sprinkled over ready-to-cook batter
1 teaspoon grated onion
2 tablespoons finely chopped green pepper
2 tablespoons grated cheese
1 teaspoon poppy or sunflower seeds

CAKE DOUGHNUTS

3 DOZEN DOUGHNUTS

Doughnuts made from sea-level recipes are frequently cracked and have a hard brown crust. This recipe has the correct balance of leavening, fat and sugar to avoid these characteristics. See High Altitude Facts about Making and Baking Quick Breads, page 14.

1 *cup granulated sugar*	4 *teaspoons double-acting*
3 *eggs, well beaten*	*baking powder*
2½ *tablespoons melted butter*	1 *teaspoon salt*
¾ *cup milk*	¼ *teaspoon ground cinnamon*
3½ *cups sifted all-purpose flour*	¼ *teaspoon ground nutmeg*

1. In mixing bowl, gradually add sugar to beaten eggs. Blend in melted butter and milk.
2. Mix and sift flour, baking powder, salt, cinnamon and nutmeg together.
3. Add dry ingredients to liquid mixture. Stir until blended.
4. If too sticky, dough may be chilled until manageable.
5. In large cooking pan or electric deep-fat fryer, heat cooking oil or shortening to 350°F. Have sufficient oil or shortening to float doughnuts, or at least 1½ inches deep.
6. On well-floured surface, roll out dough ⅜ inch thick. Cut with doughnut cutter. Cut-out doughnuts that are dried for 15 minutes before cooking absorb less fat during cooking.

7. Drop doughnuts into hot cooking oil or shortening. Brown on one side. Fry only 3 or 4 doughnuts at a time. Turn and brown on other side, or about 3 minutes in all. Drain on paper toweling.

8. Roll in powdered sugar or sprinkle with mixture of 2 teaspoons cinnamon and ⅔ cup granulated sugar. Doughnuts may be shaken in paper bag containing either of these coatings.

CHOCOLATE CAKE DOUGHNUTS: In Step 1, add 1½ ounces melted unsweetened chocolate and 1 teaspoon vanilla extract. In Step 2, reduce flour to 3¼ cups.

ORANGE CAKE DOUGHNUTS: In Step 1, substitute ¼ cup orange juice for milk. Add 1 tablespoon grated orange rind.

SOUR-CREAM CAKE DOUGHNUTS: In Step 1, omit butter. Substitute dairy sour cream for milk. In Step 2, reduce baking powder to 1½ teaspoons. Add 1 teaspoon baking soda.

VEGETABLE, MEAT OR FISH FRITTERS

4 TO 6 SERVINGS

2 eggs, separated (beat whites
    until stiff, but not dry)
1 tablespoon melted butter
⅔ cup milk or flat beer
1½ cups sifted all-purpose flour
1½ teaspoons double-acting
    baking powder

1 teaspoon salt
½ teaspoon ground pepper
1½ to 2 cups chopped or diced
    cooked vegetables, meat or
    seafood

1. In mixing bowl, beat egg yolks. Blend in butter and milk or beer.
2. Mix and sift 1¼ cups flour, baking powder, salt and pepper together.
3. Blend dry ingredients with liquid mixture. Stir well. Cover. Refrigerate for 2 or more hours.
4. In large cooking pan or electric deep-fat fryer, heat cooking oil or shortening to 350° to 360°F. Have sufficient oil or shortening to float fritters, or at least 1½ inches deep.
5. Beat batter until smooth. With pliable rubber scraper or whisk, fold in stiffly beaten egg whites.
6. Dredge meat, vegetables or seafood in remaining ¼ cup flour. Fold into batter.
7. Drop by spoonfuls into hot cooking oil or shortening. Fry a few at a time until golden brown on all sides. Drain on paper toweling.

NOTE: Using too-hot cooking fat will result in a disappointingly over-browned fritter with an underdone middle. A thermometer will help to keep cooking oil or shortening properly heated to 350° to 360°F.

MUFFINS

1 egg
¼ cup granulated sugar
3 tablespoons melted butter
   or shortening
1¼ cups milk

2¼ cups sifted all-purpose flour
3½ teaspoons double-acting
   baking powder
¾ teaspoon salt

1. Preheat oven to 425°F. Grease and flour 3 × 1½-inch muffin pan cups.
2. In mixing bowl, beat egg. Blend in sugar, butter or shortening, and milk.
3. Into large mixing bowl, mix and sift flour, baking powder and salt.
4. Make a well in center of dry ingredients. Add small amount of liquid mixture. Blend quickly. Add remaining liquid mixture, using as few strokes as possible to blend the two together completely.
5. Fill prepared muffin pan cups ⅔ full.
6. Bake for 25 to 30 minutes.

APPLE MUFFINS: In Step 3, add ½ teaspoon each ground cinnamon and nutmeg. In Step 4, add 1 cup peeled finely chopped apples and ½ cup chopped nutmeats.

BLUEBERRY MUFFINS: In Step 3, increase baking powder to 5 teaspoons. In Step 4, add 1 cup fresh, frozen, or well-drained canned blueberries.

HONEY-BRAN MUFFINS: In Step 2, add 3 tablespoons honey and increase shortening to ⅓ cup. In Step 3, reduce flour to 1¼ cups and add 1¼ cups all-bran cereal.

CREPES

1 cup sifted all-purpose flour
⅛ teaspoon salt
3 eggs

1½ cups milk
Butter or margarine

1. Combine all ingredients in blender and blend until smooth, *or*, in medium mixing bowl, combine flour and salt. With electric mixer, add eggs one at a time, beating well after each addition. Gradually add milk, beating until smooth. Batter should be consistency of heavy cream. Cover with plastic wrap. Refrigerate 1 to 2 hours.
2. For upside-down crepe pans or electric crepe makers, cook according to manufacturer's directions, allowing a little more time for high altitude. Or, place 6- or 7-inch crepe pan or skillet on medium heat. When a few drops

water sprinkled on hot cooking surface bounce and sputter, the temperature is right. Add ¼ teaspoon butter or margarine. Swirl to coat surface. Pour in about 2 tablespoons batter. Quickly tilt pan in all directions, allowing batter to flow over entire surface. As crepe begins to brown, loosen edges with spatula. Turn over. Cook until light golden brown. Turn out onto plate. Cool. Stack as additional crepes are made.

PANCAKES

BATTER TO SERVE 4

This recipe is truly family- and time-tested. The ingredients are perfectly balanced for high altitudes.

5 tablespoons granulated sugar	2 cups milk
3 eggs, beaten	2½ cups sifted all-purpose flour
4 tablespoons melted butter	1 teaspoon salt
½ teaspoon vanilla extract, if desired	1 teaspoon double-acting baking powder

1. Preheat very lightly greased griddle, skillet or electric skillet.
2. Add sugar to beaten eggs. Blend in melted butter, vanilla extract if desired, and milk.
3. Into pitcher or mixing bowl that pours, mix and sift flour, salt and baking powder.
4. Make a well in center of dry ingredients. Add small amount of liquid mixture. Blend quickly. Add remaining liquid mixture, using as few strokes as possible to blend the two together completely.
5. When few drops of water sprinkled on hot cooking surface bounce and sputter, the temperature is right (about 400°F. on electric skillet). Pour or spoon batter onto cooking surface in amount for desired size pancakes. When top of pancake is well covered with bubbles beginning to burst, turn pancake. *Turn only once.* Serve immediately.

BLUEBERRY PANCAKES: In Step 4, fold in ¾ cup fresh or well-drained canned blueberries.

CHOCOLATE OR CAROB CHIP PANCAKES: In Step 4, fold in ¾ cup semisweet chocolate or carob pieces.

PECAN OR WALNUT PANCAKES: In Step 4, fold in ¾ to 1 cup chopped pecan or walnut meats.

COCONUT PEANUT BUTTER PANCAKES: In Step 4, add ¼ cup peanut butter and 2 tablespoons flaked coconut.

BUCKWHEAT PANCAKES

BATTER TO SERVE 4

1 tablespoon granulated sugar
or molasses
1 egg, beaten
2 tablespoons melted shortening
or butter
2¼ cups milk

1 cup sifted all-purpose flour and
1 cup buckwheat flour, or
½ cup sifted all-purpose flour
and 1½ cups buckwheat flour
4 teaspoons double-acting
baking powder
½ teaspoon salt

1. Preheat very lightly greased griddle, skillet or electric skillet.
2. Add sugar or molasses to beaten egg. Blend in melted shortening or butter and milk.
3. Into pitcher or mixing bowl that pours, place flours, baking powder and salt. Mix very well.
4. Make a well in center of dry ingredients. Add small amount of liquid mixture. Blend quickly. Add remaining liquid mixture, using as few strokes as possible to blend the two together completely.
5. When few drops of water sprinkled on hot cooking surface bounce and sputter, the temperature is right (about 400°F. on electric skillet). Pour or spoon batter onto cooking surface in amount for desired size pancakes. When top of pancake is well covered with bubbles beginning to burst, turn pancake. *Turn only once.* Serve immediately.

OATMEAL PANCAKES: In Step 3, substitute quick-cooking rolled oats for buckwheat flour.

POPOVERS

Popovers made by sea-level recipes will expand too rapidly at altitudes over 2,500 feet, thereby losing their steam before a crust can form: thus a stronger batter is needed at high elevations. This recipe is time- and family-tested, and success depends on following it to the letter. Be sure to have the oven preheated to 450°F. and the pans well buttered. Do not peek during baking!

FOR 8 POPOVERS:
2 extra-large eggs
1 cup milk

1 cup sifted all-purpose flour
½ teaspoon salt

FOR 16 POPOVERS:
5 extra-large eggs
2 cups milk

2 cups sifted all-purpose flour
1 teaspoon salt

1. Preheat oven to 450°F. Grease very generously muffin pan cups, glass custard cups or cast-iron popover pan.
2. In mixing bowl, beat eggs and combine with milk.
3. Mix and sift flour and salt together. Add dry ingredients to liquids. Beat well.
4. Heat pans 3 minutes in oven.
5. Pour batter into preheated cups, filling half full.
6. Bake on lowest shelf of oven at 450°F. for 15 minutes. *Reduce* temperature to 350°F. and bake 20 minutes more. Do not open oven door during baking.

WHOLE-WHEAT POPOVERS

6 TO 8 POPOVERS

Safflower or other cooking oil
1 *cup sifted 100% whole-wheat*
  flour
½ *teaspoon salt*

3 *extra-large eggs, beaten*
1½ *cups milk*
3 *tablespoons melted margarine*
  or butter*

1. Preheat oven to 450°F. Place 1 teaspoon oil in bottom of muffin-pan cups, glass custard cups or cast-iron popover-pan cups. Place on cookie sheet.
2. Mix and sift flour and salt together.
3. Place eggs, milk and flour mixture in electric blender and whirl 30 seconds at medium speed, or beat for 1½ minutes. Add melted margarine or butter.
4. Heat pans 3 minutes in oven.
5. Pour batter into preheated cups, filling each cup three-fourths full.
6. Bake on lowest shelf of oven at 450°F. for 15 minutes. *Reduce* heat to 350°F. Bake 25 minutes more. Do not open oven door during baking.

* Use only the oily part, discarding the milky substance at the bottom of the pan used to melt the butter.

YORKSHIRE PUDDING

3 TO 6 SERVINGS

1 *cup plus 2 tablespoons sifted*
  all-purpose flour
½ *teaspoon salt*
2 *eggs, beaten*

1 *cup milk*
2 *tablespoons cold water*
  Hot beef pan drippings or
  melted butter

1. Into mixing bowl, mix and sift flour and salt.
2. Make well in center of dry ingredients. Pour beaten eggs, milk and water into center. Beat well until batter is smooth and bubbly. Refrigerate 2 to 3 hours.

3. Preheat oven to 450°F. Cover bottom of 9 × 9 × 2-inch baking pan with hot beef drippings or melted butter ¼ inch deep.
4. Beat batter vigorously. Pour into hot drippings or butter.
5. Bake 30 minutes.

PERFECT WAFFLES

▼▼▼

BATTER TO SERVE 6

2 eggs, separated (beat whites
    until stiff, but not dry)
2 tablespoons granulated sugar
½ cup melted butter or shortening
1¾ cups milk

2 cups sifted all-purpose flour
½ teaspoon salt
4 teaspoons double-acting
    baking powder

1. Preheat waffle iron.
2. Beat egg yolks until thick and lemon-colored. Add sugar to beaten egg yolks. Blend in melted butter or shortening and milk.
3. Into pitcher or mixing bowl that pours, mix and sift flour, salt and baking powder.
4. Make a well in center of dry ingredients. Add small amount of liquid mixture. Blend quickly. Add remaining liquid mixture, using as few strokes as possible to blend the two together completely.
5. With pliable rubber scraper or whisk, gently fold in stiffly beaten egg whites.
6. Fill waffle iron two-thirds full. Bake approximately 5 minutes. Serve immediately.

BUTTERMILK WAFFLES: In Step 2, substitute 1¼ cups buttermilk for milk. In Step 3, reduce all-purpose flour to 1¾ cups, *or* substitute 2 cups sifted cake flour. Reduce baking powder to 2 teaspoons. Add ½ teaspoon baking soda.

CHOCOLATE WAFFLES: In Step 2, increase sugar to 3 tablespoons and add 2 ounces melted unsweetened chocolate. In Step 3, substitute cake flour for all-purpose flour.

PECAN WAFFLES: In Step 2, increase sugar to 3 tablespoons. In Step 3, substitute cake flour for all-purpose flour. In Step 5, add ¾ cup chopped pecan meats.

STONE-GROUND WHEAT WAFFLES

1¼ cups stone-ground whole-wheat
    flour
½ cup instant dry milk
1 teaspoon salt
3 teaspoons double-acting
    baking powder
2 cups milk, buttermilk or yogurt

2 tablespoons honey, molasses
    or sugar
⅔ cup vegetable oil
1 cup wheat germ
3 eggs, separated (beat whites
    until stiff, but not dry)

1. In pitcher or mixing bowl that pours, mix together flour, dry milk, salt and baking powder.
2. Blend together milk, buttermilk or yogurt; honey, molasses or sugar; oil, wheat germ and egg yolks.
3. Make well in center of dry ingredients. Add small amount of liquid mixture. Blend quickly. Add remaining liquid mixture with as few strokes as possible to blend together completely. With pliable rubber scraper or whisk, gently fold in stiffly beaten egg whites.
4. Fill preheated waffle iron two-thirds full. Bake approximately 5 minutes.

Yeast Breads

HIGH ALTITUDE FACTS ABOUT MAKING AND BAKING YEAST BREADS

Knowing the way yeast dough should look and feel can come only from experience. It is very important, yet equally difficult to describe. One old cookbook advised, "Add flour until the dough is soft like a baby's bottom." Because of the dried air at altitudes over 2,500 feet, it is often necessary to use less flour and more liquids. A rainy day, on the other hand, usually dictates the need for more flour.

Yeast dough rises more rapidly at higher elevations because there is less atmospheric pressure. It must be watched carefully to make sure that it rises only until it is just doubled in bulk.

To begin and to stabilize the leavening action and to get better yeast bread, increase oven temperature for 10 minutes at the beginning of the baking time. An increase of 20 to 25 degrees is the general rule, but this varies from recipe to recipe.

Quick-Mix Method for Making Yeast Breads

1. Measure liquid ingredients into saucepan, including honey, molasses and the like. Add shortening, butter or margarine, sugar and salt. Heat over low heat until liquids are warm and temperature has reached about 125°F. Stir until well-mixed.
2. In bowl large enough to accommodate raised dough, mix *undissolved* yeast with one-third of flour.

3. Gradually add liquid mixture to flour and yeast with electric mixer set on low speed. If recipe calls for eggs, add them at this step. With mixer set on high speed, beat two minutes more, or until batter is smooth and satiny, scraping bowl sides with rubber spatula. Add remaining flour gradually, changing from mixer or spoon to hands as required by individual recipe being followed. Proceed with completion according to recipe directions.

How to Shape Loaves

Form dough into smooth, round ball. With sharp knife, cut into equal portions, one for each loaf desired. Lift the dough by the ends and stretch it lengthwise. Place lengthened piece of dough on lightly floured bread board. Fold right third of dough over center third, then left third over the right. Press out air bubbles. Seal open edges by gently pressing together. Start with narrow edge and roll into loaf, pressing out air bubbles and sealing edges. Place loaf, with sealed edge down, in greased loaf pan. Brush with melted butter or shortening, or cooking oil.

FRENCH OR VIENNA BREAD: Roll dough under palms of hands to 14-inch long loaf. *Or* stretch dough lengthwise to 14 inches as directed for loaves and roll up, beginning with wide side of rectangle, pressing out air bubbles and sealing edges. With sharp knife, cut diagonal slashes in top of loaf about every two inches. Place on greased cookie sheet. Brush with mixture of egg white and water.

How to Braid Bread

Divide dough into three equal parts. Roll or pat each part into a 12 × 3-inch strip. Place strips side by side on bread board. Starting from the middle, braid toward alternate sides of each end. Pinch the ends to prevent separation. Braids may be baked in 9 × 5 × 3-inch loaf pans or on cookie or baking sheet.

FAVORITE WHITE BREAD OR ROLLS

2 LOAVES

1 package active dry yeast or 1 fresh cake compressed yeast	2 tablespoons granulated sugar 2 teaspoons salt
1¼ cups lukewarm water	6 to 6½ cups sifted all-purpose
1 cup scalded milk	flour
1 tablespoon melted shortening	Melted butter or shortening or
1 tablespoon melted butter	cooking oil

1. In bowl large enough to accommodate raised dough, sprinkle dry yeast or crumble compressed yeast into ¼ cup lukewarm water. Stir to dissolve.

2. Into scalded milk mix melted shortening, melted butter, sugar, salt and remaining 1 cup water. Stir until dissolved. Cool to lukewarm. Add to yeast mixture.

3. Add one-third of sifted flour. With electric mixer set at low speed, or with a spoon, beat batter until smooth and satiny. Add remaining flour gradually, changing from mixer or spoon to hands as the dough becomes stiffer.

4. Turn dough onto floured board. Knead until elastic (tight-feeling), smooth and no longer sticky enough to adhere to board; or continue to knead in mixing bowl until all flour and dough are cleaned from sides of bowl by kneading process.

5. Grease same bowl and replace dough in it. Brush exposed surface with melted butter, shortening or cooking oil. Cover with damp cloth, leaving edges outside bowl. Let rise in warm place (about 80°F.) until doubled in bulk.

6. Punch down dough. Work the edges to center, turn bottom side up and knead very lightly. Lightly grease top, re-cover with damp cloth and let rise again until almost doubled in bulk.

7. Preheat oven to 425°F. Grease two 9 × 5 × 3-inch loaf pans.

8. Punch down dough, knead lightly and divide into two equal parts. Shape into loaves. Place in prepared pans. Brush tops with melted butter, shortening or cooking oil. Re-cover with damp cloth. Let rise until center of dough is well rounded above pan, or until just doubled in bulk.

9. Bake at 425°F. for 15 minutes. *Reduce* temperature to 350°F. Bake 30 to 35 minutes longer or until done. (Bread is done when it shrinks from pan sides and sounds hollow when thumped on sides.) Turn out immediately to cool on wire rack or across top of pans. Brush with melted butter, if desired.

CHEESE BREAD: Follow directions for Favorite White Bread. In Step 3, add 2 ounces grated sharp cheddar or Swiss cheese after adding one-third of flour.

CINNAMON BREAD: Follow directions for Favorite White Bread. In Step 2, increase sugar to ½ cup and shortening to ¼ cup. Add 2 teaspoons grated lemon rind, if desired. In Step 8, after second rising, roll out dough into two rectangles. Combine ½ cup granulated sugar with 1 teaspoon ground cinnamon. Spread half over each rectangle. Sprinkle 1½ teaspoons water over each rectangle. Roll rectangle as for jelly roll. Cut in half and place in prepared pans. Let rise and bake as directed for Favorite White Bread.

GRAHAM BREAD: Follow directions for Favorite White Bread. In Step 2, substitute ⅓ cup honey, light molasses or firmly packed brown sugar for granulated sugar. In Step 3, reduce all-purpose flour to 3 cups. Add 3 cups graham flour.

HEALTH BREAD: Follow directions for Favorite White Bread. In Step 2, substitute 1 cup water for scalded milk and ½ cup light molasses for granulated sugar. In Step 3, reduce all-purpose flour to 3 cups. Add 1 cup rye flour and 1 cup cornmeal.

HERB BREAD: Follow directions for Favorite White Bread. In Step 2, reduce water to ¼ cup. Use to dissolve yeast. Increase milk to 1½ cups, sugar to ¼ cup, and shortening to ½ cup. Omit butter. Add 2 beaten eggs. In Step 3, increase total flour by ½ to 1 cup. Add 1 teaspoon each dried sage, marjoram and thyme leaves, *or* ½ teaspoon ground nutmeg, 1 teaspoon ground sage and 2 teaspoons celery seed.

ORANGE BREAD: Follow directions for Favorite White Bread. In Step 2, reduce water to ¾ cup and substitute 1¼ cups *lukewarm* orange juice for milk. Increase melted shortening to ¼ cup and sugar to ½ cup. Add 3 tablespoons grated orange rind, and a few drops orange food coloring, if desired.

PAN ROLLS: Follow directions for Favorite White Bread. In Step 6, shape dough into 1½-inch balls. Place close together in two greased 8 × 8 × 2-inch pans. Cover with damp cloth. Let rise until doubled in bulk. Bake in oven preheated to 400°F. for 15 to 20 minutes.

RAISIN BREAD: Follow directions for Favorite White Bread. In Step 2, increase sugar to ½ cup and shortening to ¼ cup. In Step 3, add 2 cups golden or dark raisins. In Step 8, shape dough into four small loaves. Bake at 375°F. for 25 to 30 minutes. Drizzle with Powdered Sugar Glaze, page 114, while still warm.

WHOLE-WHEAT BREAD: Follow directions for Favorite White Bread. In Step 2, substitute 4 tablespoons molasses or firmly packed brown sugar for granulated sugar. In Step 3, reduce all-purpose flour to 2 cups and add 3 cups whole-wheat flour, *or* omit all-purpose flour and add 4⅔ to 5 cups whole-wheat flour.

WHOLE-WHEAT BREAD WITH SUNFLOWER SEEDS: Follow directions for Whole-Wheat Bread. In Step 3, add ½ to 1 cup shelled sunflower seeds and ½ cup chopped walnut meats, if desired.

BRIOCHES

ABOUT 18 BRIOCHES

1 *package active dry yeast or*
   1 *fresh cake compressed yeast*
¾ *cup lukewarm water or ¼ cup*
   lukewarm water and ½ cup
   scalded milk, cooled
4 *cups sifted all-purpose flour*
3 *eggs*

1 *egg, separated*
½ *teaspoon lemon extract or*
   1 *teaspoon grated lemon rind*
⅔ *cup softened butter*
½ *cup granulated sugar*
1 *teaspoon salt*

1. In large mixing bowl, sprinkle dry yeast or crumble cake yeast into luke-warm water, or into water and milk mixture. Stir to dissolve. Add 1 cup flour.
2. With electric mixer set at low speed, beat until smooth. Add 3 eggs and 1 egg yolk, one at a time, beating well between additions. Add lemon extract or rind, butter, sugar, salt and 1 cup flour. Beat 10 minutes at medium speed. Blend in remaining flour, mixing until smooth.
3. Scrape dough from sides of bowl. Cover with damp cloth, leaving edges outside bowl. Let rise until doubled in bulk.
4. Stir down dough. Cover with waxed paper or plastic wrap and re-cover with damp cloth. Refrigerate overnight, or for 12 hours.
5. Preheat oven to 375°F. Grease well a muffin pan with 3-inch cups.
6. Divide dough into two parts, one part to be two-thirds of the dough, the other to be one-third. Divide the larger piece into 18 equal parts. Roll each into a ball and place in a prepared muffin cup. Make a thumbprint in top of each. Divide remaining dough into 18 small balls and place one on top of each brioche. Brush tops with remaining egg white beaten lightly with 1 tablespoon water. Cover with damp cloth. Let rise until just doubled in bulk.
7. Bake 15 to 20 minutes, or until rolls shrink from muffin cup sides and are golden brown.

CROISSANTS

40 CROISSANTS

1 *package active dry yeast or*	¾ *teaspoon salt*
1 *fresh cake compressed yeast*	1 *tablespoon granulated sugar*
¼ *cup lukewarm water*	3½ *cups sifted all-purpose flour*
1 *cup ice-cold milk*	1 *cup cold butter*
1 *cold egg*	

1. In bowl large enough to accommodate raised dough, sprinkle dry yeast or crumble cake yeast into lukewarm water. Let stand 5 minutes.
2. Mix together milk, egg, salt and sugar. Add to yeast mixture.
3. Stir flour into yeast mixture. Knead dough in bowl, or on lightly floured pastry cloth or board, until smooth and elastic. Cover dough with damp cloth, leaving edges outside bowl. Let rise until doubled in bulk, then refrigerate until thoroughly chilled.
4. On very lightly floured board, roll out dough into a 10 × 20-inch rectangle about ¼ inch thick. Dot half the dough with butter, leaving a half-inch rim around dough edge. Fold other half of dough over butter. With rolling pin, roll out dough into rectangle. Fold dough into thirds and turn around with narrow end toward you. Roll out again, fold and turn as before and roll out again. Fold again, wrap in waxed paper and refrigerate for 2 or more hours.
5. Roll out dough into 10 × 20-inch rectangle. Cut dough in half length-wise and cut each strip crosswise into 10 pieces. Cut each piece diagonally, making 40 triangles. Beginning with the wide side, roll up each triangular

piece, stretching it slightly; shape into a crescent. Place with points underneath, about 1½ inches apart on greased cookie sheets.

6. Cover with damp cloth. Let rise for 2 hours or until almost doubled in bulk, in cool place.

7. Preheat oven to 400°F. Bake 15 to 20 minutes, or until golden brown.

FRENCH BREAD OR ROLLS

1 LARGE LOAF OR 18 ROLLS

1 package active dry yeast or
  1 fresh cake compressed yeast
1¼ cups lukewarm water
1 tablespoon granulated sugar
1½ teaspoons salt
2 tablespoons melted shortening

4 cups sifted all-purpose flour
Melted butter
White cornmeal or farina
1 egg white, beaten with
  1 tablespoon cold water

1. In bowl large enough to accommodate raised dough, sprinkle active dry or crumble compressed yeast into ¼ cup *lukewarm* water. Stir to dissolve.
2. In remaining 1 cup water, dissolve sugar and salt. Blend in melted shortening. Add to yeast mixture.
3. Add one-third of sifted flour. With electric mixer set at low speed, or spoon, beat batter until smooth and satiny. Add remaining flour gradually, changing from mixer or spoon to hands as the dough becomes stiffer.
4. Turn dough onto floured board. Knead until elastic (tight-feeling), smooth and no longer sticky. *Or* continue to knead in mixing bowl until all flour and dough are cleaned from sides of bowl by kneading process (about 10 minutes).
5. Grease bowl. Put dough in it. Brush exposed surface with melted butter. Cover bowl with damp cloth, leaving edges outside bowl. Let rise in warm place (about 80°F.) until doubled in bulk.
6. Punch down dough. Work the edges to center, turn bottom side up and knead very lightly. Lightly grease, re-cover with damp cloth and let rise again until almost doubled in bulk.
7. Preheat oven to 375°F. Grease cookie or baking sheet.
8. Punch down dough. Cover and let rest 10 minutes.
9. FOR FRENCH BREAD. Form dough into 14 × 2-inch loaf. Sprinkle prepared cookie or baking sheet with cornmeal or farina. Place dough on cornmeal or farina. Using a very sharp knife, make diagonal cuts in top every 2 inches.
FOR FRENCH ROLLS: Divide dough into 18 portions. Cover and let rest 15 minutes. Form into French shape (oval) rolls. Place 2½ inches apart on cookie or baking sheet prepared as directed. Brush bread or rolls with egg white and water mixture. Re-cover with damp cloth. Let rise until doubled in bulk.
10. Place a shallow pan of boiling water on bottom of oven, which will heat and steam to produce crustiness.
11. Bake bread at 375°F. for 10 minutes. *Reduce* temperature to 350°F. and

bake 10 minutes. Brush bread again with egg white mixture. Bake 25 to 35 minutes longer. Turn out immediately to cool on wire rack. *Or* bake rolls at 375°F. for 35 to 45 minutes, brushing with egg white mixture after 15 minutes.

OATMEAL BREAD

2 LOAVES

1 cup cooked, thick oatmeal
2 cups hot potato water
¼ cup mashed potatoes
¼ cup dark molasses
2 tablespoons melted shortening
1 package active dry yeast or
    1 fresh cake compressed yeast

¼ cup lukewarm water
6 cups sifted all-purpose flour
½ cup less 2 teaspoons granulated sugar
1½ teaspoons salt
    Melted butter or shortening

1. In bowl large enough to accommodate raised dough, mix together oatmeal, potato water, mashed potatoes, molasses and melted shortening. Let stand 1 hour.
2. Sprinkle dry yeast or crumble fresh yeast into lukewarm water. Stir to dissolve. Add to oatmeal mixture.
3. Add one-third of sifted flour and all of sugar and salt to oatmeal mixture. With electric mixer set at low speed, or with a spoon, beat batter until smooth and satiny. Add remaining flour gradually. Beat until elastic.
4. Brush surface of dough with melted butter or shortening. Cover with damp cloth, leaving edges outside bowl. Let rise in warm place (about 80°F.) until doubled in bulk.
5. Punch down dough with a wooden spoon. Beat vigorously. Grease lightly, re-cover with damp cloth, and let rise again until almost doubled in bulk.
6. Preheat oven to 350°F. Grease two 9 × 5 × 3-inch loaf pans.
7. Punch down dough, beat well and divide into two equal parts. Shape into loaves. Place in prepared pans. Brush tops with melted butter or shortening. Re-cover with damp cloth. Let rise until center of dough is well rounded above pan, or until just doubled in bulk.
8. Bake for 1 hour, or until loaf shrinks from pan sides.

SOPAPILLAS

2 DOZEN

1 package active dry yeast or
    1 fresh cake compressed yeast
¼ cup lukewarm water
1¾ cups milk
  6 tablespoons granulated sugar

1 teaspoon salt
2 tablespoons butter
1 egg, beaten
3 cups sifted all-purpose flour
    Cooking oil

1. In bowl large enough to accommodate raised dough, sprinkle dry yeast or crumble cake yeast into lukewarm water. Let stand.
2. In medium saucepan, combine milk, sugar and salt. Bring to boil. Remove from heat. Stir in butter. Cool until lukewarm. Add to yeast mixture.
3. Add egg. Beat well.
4. Gradually add 2½ cups flour, beating well after each addition. Add the remaining ½ cup flour with hands to make dough soft, but not sticky. Dough will not be stiff.
5. Cover dough with damp cloth, leaving edges outside bowl. Let rise 1½ hours. Punch down dough.
6. Turn dough onto floured board and knead until smooth. Cover. Let rest 10 minutes.
7. Roll out dough ¼ inch thick. Cut into twenty-four 2 × 3-inch rectangles.
8. In deep-fat dryer or heavy saucepan, add cooking oil to depth of 2 inches. Heat to 350°F.
9. Add strips of dough a few at a time. Deep-fry 3 minutes, or until golden brown, turning once when puffed and brown on underside.

SWEDISH LIGHT RYE BREAD

2 LOAVES

1 package active dry yeast or
   1 fresh cake compressed yeast
1 cup lukewarm water
1 cup sifted rye flour
1 cup firmly packed dark brown
   sugar
2 tablespoons butter or margarine
2 teaspoons salt

2 tablespoons caraway seed
1 cup boiling water
4½ to 5½ cups sifted all-purpose
   flour or half all-purpose and
   half rye flour
Melted butter, shortening or
   cooking oil

1. Make sponge in bowl large enough to accommodate raised dough. Sprinkle active dry or crumble compressed yeast in lukewarm water. Blend in rye flour. Let sponge rise overnight, or let rise and fall.
2. In small saucepan, dissolve sugar, butter or margarine, salt and caraway seed in boiling water. Cool.
3. With electric mixer set at low speed, or spoon, alternately add brown-sugar mixture and flour to rye sponge, changing from mixer or spoon to hands as the dough becomes stiffer.
4. Turn dough onto lightly floured board. Knead until elastic (tight-feeling), and no longer sticky enough to adhere to board. *Or* continue to knead in mixing bowl until all flour and dough are cleaned from sides of bowl by kneading process (about 20 minutes).
5. Grease bowl. Put dough in it. Brush exposed surface with melted butter, shortening or cooking oil. Cover with damp cloth, or greased plastic, leaving edges outside bowl. Let rise in warm place (about 80°F.) until doubled in bulk.

6. Preheat oven to 350°F. Grease two 9 × 5 × 3-inch loaf pans.

7. Punch down dough. Work the edges to center, turn bottom side up and knead. Divide dough into two equal parts. Shape into loaves. Place in prepared pans. Brush tops with melted butter, shortening or cooking oil. Re-cover with damp cloth or greased plastic. Let rise until rounded above pan or doubled in bulk.

8. Bake 35 to 45 minutes. Turn out immediately to cool on wire rack or across top of pans. Brush with melted butter, if desired. Bread is done when it shrinks from pan sides and sounds hollow when thumped on sides.

FOUNDATION SWEET YEAST DOUGH

3½ TO 4 DOZEN ROLLS OR
3 COFFEE-CAKE BRAIDS, RINGS OR BUNS

Before you begin, read through the variations and fillings to choose from the exciting assortment of flavors, shapes and special-occasion touches that may be made from this one delicious recipe. Don't be intimidated by the long instructions.

2 packages active dry yeast or
2 fresh cakes compressed yeast
1 cup lukewarm water
½ cup plus 1 tablespoon
granulated sugar
1 cup scalded milk
6 tablespoons melted butter or
shortening

2 teaspoons salt
3 eggs, beaten
7 cups sifted all-purpose flour
Melted butter
Filling of choice, pages 115 to
117, or see suggestions
following directions
Frosting or glaze of choice

1. In bowl large enough to accommodate raised dough, sprinkle active dry yeast or crumble compressed yeast into *lukewarm* water. Add 1 tablespoon sugar. Stir to dissolve.

2. Into scalded milk, mix melted butter or shortening, ½ cup sugar, and salt. Cool to *lukewarm*. Add to yeast mixture.

3. Add beaten eggs. Mix well. Add one-third of sifted flour. With electric mixer set at low speed, or spoon, beat batter until smooth and satiny. Add remaining flour gradually, changing from mixer or spoon to hands as the dough becomes stiffer. Knead for a few minutes. Grease exposed surface. Cover bowl with damp cloth, leaving edges outside bowl. Let rise in warm place (about 80°F.) until doubled in bulk.

4. Preheat oven. Select and prepare filling, or fillings. Determine shapes and sizes of rolls, cake, braid, ring or buns.

5. Punch down dough.

ALMOND RING: Follow directions for Foundation Sweet Yeast Dough. Use one-half of raised and punched-down dough. Grease cookie sheet.

Mix together 1 can (12 ounces) almond cake and pastry filling, ¼ cup softened butter, 3 tablespoons granulated sugar, and 2 tablespoons water. Roll out dough into 20 × 10-inch rectangle. Spread with filling. Roll rectangle as for jelly roll. Place one end in center of cookie sheet. Coil roll loosely around center, making a snail shape. Tuck end under. Cover with damp cloth. Let rise until dough is doubled in bulk. Brush with 1 tablespoon water beaten with 1 egg. Bake at 375°F. for about 30 minutes. Frost or glaze. Sprinkle with sliced almonds.

APPLE COFFEE CAKE: Follow directions for Foundation Sweet Yeast Dough. Use one-third of dough. Grease 13 × 9 × 2-inch oblong pan. Spread dough in pan. Arrange 3 cups pared, sliced apples over dough, covering top completely. Combine 1 cup granulated sugar, ½ teaspoon ground cinnamon and 2 tablespoons softened butter. Reserve 2 tablespoons. Sprinkle remainder over apples. Cover with damp cloth. Let rise until dough is doubled in bulk. Bake in oven preheated to 375°F. for 20 to 25 minutes. Blend 1 beaten egg and ⅓ cup half-and-half together. Pour over coffee cake. Bake about 15 minutes longer. Remove from oven. Sprinkle with remaining cinnamon and sugar. Serve warm.

CARAMEL BUNS: Follow directions for Foundation Sweet Yeast Dough. Roll out dough into 20 × 10-inch rectangle. Spread with softened butter. Cream additional ½ cup softened butter and ½ cup firmly packed brown sugar together. Spread over rolled-out, buttered dough. Sprinkle dough with 1 cup finely chopped nutmeats. Roll rectangle as for jelly roll. With sharp knife cut into ½-to-¾-inch slices. Place in well-greased oblong pan or on greased cookie sheet. Let rise about 30 minutes, or until almost doubled in bulk. Bake at 375°F. for 20 to 25 minutes. Frost or glaze, if desired.

CINNAMON ROLLS: Follow directions for Foundation Sweet Yeast Dough. Roll out dough, on well-floured board, in one large rectangle, ¼ inch thick. Brush generously with melted butter. Sprinkle generous amounts of brown sugar and ground cinnamon over butter. Raisins and/or chopped nutmeats may be sprinkled over dough, if desired. Roll rectangle as for jelly roll, starting with wide side. With sharp knife, cut into ½-to-¾-inch slices. Place in well-greased oblong pan, or on greased cookie sheet. Cover with damp cloth. Let rise about 30 minutes, or until dough is almost doubled in bulk. Bake at 375°F. for 20 to 25 minutes. Frost or glaze, if desired.

CHRISTMAS RINGS OR TWISTS: Follow directions for Foundation Sweet Yeast Dough. In Step 3, add 1¼ teaspoons ground cardamom seeds, 1½ cup golden raisins, 1 cup chopped citron and 1 cup chopped almonds, if desired. Cover with damp cloth. Let rise in warm place (about 80°F.) until doubled in bulk. Punch down dough. Knead well. Divide dough in three equal parts. On floured board, roll each in long sausage-like roll.

Twist into pretzel shape. Place on greased cookie or baking sheet. *Or,* grease two 10 × 4-inch tube plans. Divide dough in half. Roll enough to shape for placement in bottom of pan. Cover twists or rings with damp cloth. Let rise until almost doubled in bulk. Brush with melted butter. Bake at 400°F. for 45 minutes to 1 hour. Sprinkle with powdered sugar or frost with Powdered Sugar Glaze, page 114.

EUROPEAN COFFEE BRAID: Follow directions for Foundation Sweet Yeast Dough. In Step 3, add 3 egg yolks, 1 teaspoon vanilla extract and 2 teaspoons grated lemon rind. Punch down raised dough. Divide into six equal parts. Combine 1 cup finely chopped golden raisins, ½ cup finely chopped candied cherries, 1 cup finely chopped walnut meats and 3 tablespoons lemon juice. On floured board, roll out dough into 10 × 3-inch strips. Brush with melted butter. Spread one-sixth of filling on each. Braid three strips together, sealing strips at each end. Grease two 10-inch round or square casseroles. Place one braid in each. Cover with damp cloth. Let rise until doubled in bulk. Brush with remaining egg whites. Bake 10 minutes at 400°F. Reduce temperature to 350°F. Bake for 30 to 35 minutes more.

HOT CROSS BUNS: Follow directions for Foundation Sweet Yeast Dough. In Step 3, add ⅔ cup currants or raisins, ½ teaspoon ground cinnamon and ¼ teaspoon ground allspice; *or* ½ teaspoon ground mace, ⅓ cup candied orange peel or cherries, and 3 tablespoons finely chopped citron. *To Shape:* Using palms of hands to roll dough, shape dough into 12-inch roll. Cut roll into nine pieces. Roll each piece into ball. Place in greased 8 × 8 × 2-inch baking pan. Flatten each ball with hand. Brush with beaten egg yolk. Let rise until doubled in bulk. Bake in oven preheated to 400°F. for 15 minutes. Cool. Drizzle Powdered Sugar Glaze, page 114, over each bun in shape of cross.

KOLACHES (SOUR-CREAM SWEET YEAST ROLLS)

2 TO 3 DOZEN ROLLS

1 package active dry yeast or
   1 fresh cake compressed yeast
¼ cup lukewarm water
1 cup scalded dairy sour cream
2 tablespoons melted shortening
¼ cup granulated sugar
½ teaspoon salt

⅛ teaspoon baking soda
1 egg, beaten
3 cups sifted all-purpose flour
   Melted butter
   Fruit Filling for Sweet Yeast
    Rolls, page 116

1. Preheat oven to 375°F. Grease cookie sheet.
2. In bowl large enough to accommodate raised dough, sprinkle dry yeast or crumble cake yeast into lukewarm water. Stir to dissolve.

3. Into scalded cream, stir shortening, sugar, salt and soda. Cool to lukewarm. Add to yeast mixture.

4. Add beaten egg. Mix well. Add one-third of sifted flour. With a spoon, or electric mixer set at low speed, beat batter until smooth and satiny. Add remaining flour gradually, changing from mixer or spoon to hands, if necessary, as dough becomes stiffer.

5. Turn dough onto floured board and knead for a few minutes. Cover with damp cloth for 5 minutes.

6. Roll out dough ¼ inch thick. Brush generously with melted butter. Spread with Fruit Filling for Sweet Yeast Rolls. Cut into 3-inch squares. Roll squares up like small jelly rolls. Place on prepared cookie sheet, seams down.

7. Bake 15 to 20 minutes, or until golden brown.

APRICOT SOUR-CREAM ROLLS: In Step 6, substitute 1 can (12 ounces) apricot cake and pastry filling for Fruit Filling for Sweet Yeast Rolls.

WHOLE-WHEAT OR GRAHAM FLOUR GRIDDLE CAKES

TEN 4-INCH GRIDDLE CAKES
4 TO 6 SERVINGS

2 *cups scalded milk*
2 *tablespoons butter or margarine*
1 *tablespoon granulated sugar*
1 *teaspoon salt*
½ *package active dry yeast or*
   ½ *fresh cake compressed yeast*

1 *cup whole-wheat or graham flour*
1 *cup sifted all-purpose flour*
¼ *teaspoon baking soda*
2 *tablespoons water*

1. Pour scalded milk into large mixing bowl. Add butter or margarine, sugar and salt. Cool to lukewarm. Sprinkle yeast into lukewarm milk. Stir to dissolve.

2. In pitcher or mixing bowl that pours, mix together wheat or graham and all-purpose flour. Make well in center of dry ingredients. Add small amount of yeast mixture. Beat well. Add remainder of yeast mixture. Blend thoroughly. Cover bowl with damp cloth, leaving edges on outside of bowl. Refrigerate overnight.

3. Preheat very lightly greased griddle, skillet or electric skillet.

4. Add baking soda dissolved in water to batter.

5. When a few drops of water sprinkled on the hot cooking surface bounce and sputter, the temperature is right (about 400°F. on electric skillet). Pour or spoon batter onto grill in amount for desired size pancake.

6. When top of pancake is well covered with bubbles beginning to burst, turn pancake and bake until underside is done. Turn only once. Serve immediately.

Cakes

HIGH ALTITUDE FACTS ABOUT MAKING AND BAKING CAKES

High altitude has the greatest effect on cake making and baking. An ingredient-balanced, altitude-adjusted, time- and family-tested recipe is the best way to bake a perfect cake at elevation over 2,500 feet. Many elements in a recipe can be adjusted to produce a moist and fine-textured cake at high altitudes, but not all the adjustments possible need be made in any individual recipe.

The first adjustment is to decrease the amount of leavening agent: baking powder, baking soda, cream of tartar, and the air beaten into egg whites. The lower atmospheric pressure at high altitudes allows leavening agents to expand faster during baking and to push cake batter higher—often too high. The result is a fallen, coarse and crumbly cake. For suggested reductions in the amount of leavening agents, see High Altitude Adjustments for Sea-Level Cake Recipes, page 45.

Fresh cream of tartar and *fresh* baking powder work best at high altitudes. Double-acting baking powder (sodium aluminum sulfate) was used in testing the recipes in this collection. It is recommended for high altitude use because it reacts in two stages, and therefore more slowly: only slightly in the batter, then releasing its leavening power during the actual baking. Substitute 1½ teaspoons of any other type baking powder (tartrate or calcium phosphate) for 1 teaspoon double-acting baking powder.

When the egg is the leavening agent, avoid too much beating of the whole eggs, yolks or whites. Beat egg whites just until stiff and satiny, but not dry. Egg whites resembling soap suds will dry out the cake and toughen its texture. In some recipes, too much air beaten into egg whites can cause the cake to fall.

The second adjustment in high altitude cake baking is to increase the liquid. Additional liquid offsets the rapid evaporation that causes cakes to dry out. It also compensates for the dryness of flour, dilutes sugar concentrations, and properly dissolves and distributes the other ingredients. Buttermilk, sour cream and soured milk add much needed moisture and vitality to cakes baked at elevations over 2,500 feet.

The third suggested adjustment is a reduction in the amount of sugar. (This, however, is applicable only when a recipe calls for the maximum amount of sugar relative to the other ingredients.) Too much sugar makes a coarse and crumbly cake because the sugar becomes too concentrated in the cake batter, weakening the cell structure. See High Altitude Adjustments for Sea-Level Cake Recipes, page 45.

Pioneer cooks relied on eggs to solve their high altitude cake-baking problems. One early cookbook recommended the addition of an egg as the only change in converting a sea-level recipe for high altitude. Today, the recommendation is to always use extra-large eggs in all baking. The protein in the eggs strengthens the cell structure and makes up for dryness in the air, creating velvety, moist cakes.

Very rich cake batters sometimes call for large amounts of shortening, butter or margarine. Like sugar, these fats can become too concentrated at high altitudes, weakening the cell structures and causing a tough, crumbly cake. For successful high altitude cakes it is often necessary to decrease the fats in sea-level recipes by 1 or 2 tablespoons.

Some ingredients perform better at high altitude than others. Cake flour is preferable to all-purpose flour for cakes. Self-rising flour should not be used for cakes at increased elevations because of the overexpansion of their leavening agents. "Wonder" flours that have been moistened, heated and dried to a powder produce adverse results.

The substitutions of margarine for butter or shortening can negatively affect the texture and the taste in cakes and other baked products. Only high-grade margarines should be used. Always use high-quality emulsified or hydrogenated-type shortenings (finest all-vegetable), which are also interchangeable cupful for cupful with butter. When a recipe calls for shortening, use half shortening and half butter for extra flavor.

Though more expensive, pure vanilla extract, peppermit oil and other natural flavorings should never be replaced with imitations. Substitutes for real chocolates, other than carob exchanges, fail to satisfy.

The handling of ingredients is as important in high altitude baking as adjusting their amounts. Do not undercream shortening and sugar. Too little creaming results in a coarse-textured cake. If eggs are overbeaten at high altitude, the cake will be dry. Excessive mixing when adding flour and liquids or after adding them will dry out the cake and toughen its texture. Remember, the retention of moisture is crucial to successful high altitude baking.

Low altitude recipes often require a temperature adjustment. It is recommended that the baking temperature be increased by 25°F. so as to set the batter before the cells formed by the leavening agent have a chance to expand too much.

Use the correct size of cake pans and generously grease or line them with waxed paper to prevent sticking. The minute cakes are turned out onto a rack they begin to dry out quickly, so cool cakes in pans, then frost immediately to preserve moisture.

Angel Food and Sponge Cakes

When making angel food or sponge cakes, do not overbeat eggs, yolks or whites. Use a little less leavening if any other than air is included in the recipe. The addition of an extra egg often strengthens and stabilizes these delicate, light batters. Have eggs at room temperature before beginning to mix a sponge or angel food cake.

Cupcakes

Cake batters make excellent cupcakes, especially creamed cake batters. Keep cupcakes from sticking to the pan by generously greasing muffin pan cups or, even better, by using paper baking cups. Fill each muffin pan cup one-half to two-thirds full. A standard-size ice cream dipper usually holds the correct amount of batter and is a handy tool for neatly and accurately filling cups. Bake cupcakes according to directions for each cake recipe, reducing baking time to about 20 minutes and pressing the center lightly with fingertip to test for doneness. An average cake-batter recipe yields about 2 to 3 dozen cupcakes.

High Altitude Adjustments for Cake Mixes

The special directions for high altitude on packaged cake mixes should always be followed. These usually include extra additions of flour and liquid. After making the recommended adjustments, add 2 tablespoons cooking oil to small packages of cake or brownie mix and 4 tablespoons to larger packages. Adding an egg yolk will also improve the texture and quality of packaged mixes.

HIGH ALTITUDE ADJUSTMENTS FOR SEA-LEVEL CAKE RECIPES

Decrease each measurement the lesser amount at the lowest altitude and the larger amount at highest altitude within the given range.

Adjustment	At 2,000 to 3,500 feet	At 3,500 to 5,000 feet	At 5,000 to 6,500 feet	At 6,500 to 8,000 feet
For each teaspoon of baking powder, baking soda, or cream of tartar, decrease by:	¼ to ⅓ tea-spoon	⅓ to ½ tea-spoon	½ to ⅔ tea-spoon	⅔ to ¾ teaspoon
For each cup of sugar, decrease by:	1 to 1½ table-spoons	1½ to 2½ table-spoons	2½ to 3 table-spoons	3 to 3½ table-spoons
For each cup of liquid, increase by:	0 to 2 table-spoons	2 to 3 table-spoons	3 to 4 table-spoons	4 to 6 table-spoons
Increase cake flour by:	—	1 table-spoon	2 table-spoons	3 table-spoons
Increase baking tem-perature by:	—	15° to 25°F.	15° to 25°F.	25°F.

Begin adjustment for your altitude by reducing baking powder, baking soda, or cream of tartar. Liquid and flour adjustments may not be necessary after adjusting the leavening; this can be determined by experience. Very rich cake batters may be better if shortening is decreased 1 to 2 tablespoons.

HIGH ALTITUDE LEAVENING (BAKING POWDER AND BAKING SODA) ADJUSTMENTS FOR SEA-LEVEL CAKE RECIPES

Recipes Used Above 2,000 Feet

Use larger amount of leavening at lower altitude.
Use smaller amount of leavening at higher altitude.

Sea-Level Measurement	At altitudes 2,000 to 3,500 reduce to:	At altitudes 3,500 to 5,000 reduce to:	At altitudes 5,000 to 6,500 reduce to:	At altitudes 6,500 to 8,000 reduce to:
1 teaspoon	¾ to ⅔	⅔ to ½	½ to ⅓	⅓ to ¼
1½ teaspoons	1¼ to 1	1 to ¾	¾ to ⅔	⅔ to ½
2 teaspoons	1¾ to 1½	1½ to 1¼	1¼ to 1	1 to ¾
2½ teaspoons	2 to 1¾	1¾ to 1½	1½ to 1¼	1¼ to 1
3 teaspoons	2¼ to 2	2 to 1½	1½ to 1¼	1¼ to 1
3½ teaspoons	3 to 2½	2½ to 2	2 to 1½	1½ to 1
4 teaspoons	3 to 2½	2½ to 2	2 to 1½	1½ to 1

Assorted Cream Cakes

COLLECTOR'S COCOA OR CAROB CAKE

ABOUT 12 SERVINGS

½ cup butter
1½ cups granulated sugar
3 eggs, beaten
½ cup cocoa or carob powder
    dissolved in ⅓ cup hot water
1 teaspoon baking soda
1 cup milk

1¾ cups sifted cake flour
½ teaspoon double-acting
    baking powder
½ teaspoon salt
1 teaspoon vanilla extract
Chocolate Buttercream
    Frosting, page 110

1. Preheat oven to 350°F. Grease and flour, or line with waxed paper and grease two 9-inch layer pans.
2. Cream butter with sugar until light and fluffy. Add beaten eggs. Beat well. Blend in cocoa or carob powder dissolved in water.
3. Dissolve soda in milk.
4. Mix and sift flour, baking powder and salt together.
5. Add dry ingredients alternately with milk, mixing thoroughly after each addition. Add vanilla extract. Mix very well. Batter will seem thin.
6. Pour batter into prepared pans.
7. Bake for 30 to 35 minutes or until cake center springs back when lightly pressed with fingertip. Cool.
8. Fill and frost with Chocolate Buttercream Frosting.

PRIZE CHOCOLATE CAKE

3 ounces unsweetened chocolate
½ cup plus 2 tablespoons
   shortening
1 cup granulated sugar
1 cup firmly packed brown sugar
4 eggs, separated (beat whites
   until stiff, but not dry)
1 teaspoon baking soda

1½ cups milk or 1 cup buttermilk
3 cups sifted cake flour
½ teaspoon salt
1 teaspoon vanilla extract
  Creamy Chocolate
   Frosting, page 111

1. Preheat oven to 350°F. Grease and flour three 9-inch layer pans, or line with waxed paper and grease.
2. Melt chocolate over simmering water. Cool.
3. Cream shortening with sugars until light and fluffy. Add egg yolks. Beat well. Blend in melted chocolate.
4. Dissolve soda in milk or buttermilk.
5. Mix and sift flour and salt together.
6. Add dry ingredients alternately with milk or buttermilk to chocolate mixture, mixing thoroughly after each addition. Add vanilla extract.
7. With pliable rubber scraper or whisk, gently fold in stiffly beaten egg whites.
8. Pour batter into prepared pans.
9. Bake 30 to 35 minutes, or until cake center springs back when pressed with fingertip. Cool.
10. Fill and frost with Creamy Chocolate Frosting.

GERMAN CHOCOLATE CAKE

4 ounces German chocolate
½ cup water
1 cup softened butter, margarine
   or shortening
2 cups less 2 tablespoons
   granulated sugar
4 eggs, separated (beat whites
   until stiff, but not dry)

1 teaspoon baking soda
1 cup buttermilk
2½ cups sifted cake flour
½ teaspoon salt
1 teaspoon vanilla extract
  Coconut-Nut Frosting, page 111

1. Preheat oven to 375°F. Line with waxed paper and grease three 8- or 9-inch layer pans.
2. Melt chocolate with water over simmering water. Cool.
3. Cream butter, margarine or shortening with sugar until light and fluffy. Beat in egg yolks one at a time. Blend in melted chocolate.

4. Dissolve soda in buttermilk.
5. Mix and sift flour and salt together.
6. Add dry ingredients alternately with buttermilk, mixing thoroughly after each addition. Add vanilla extract. Mix very well.
7. With pliable rubber scraper or whisk, gently fold in stiffly beaten egg whites.
8. Pour batter into prepared pans.
9. Bake about 35 minutes, or until cake center springs back when pressed with fingertip. Cool.
10. Fill and frost with Coconut-Nut Frosting.

THE ULTIMATE CHOCOLATE CAKE

12 TO 16 SERVINGS

3½ *ounces unsweetened chocolate*
½ *cup softened butter*
1½ *cups granulated sugar*
4 *eggs, separated (beat whites until stiff, but not dry)*
2 *cups sifted cake flour*
3 *teaspoons double-acting baking powder*

½ *teaspoon salt*
1¼ *cups milk*
1 *teaspoon vanilla extract*
Creamy Chocolate Frosting, page 111

1. Preheat oven to 375°F. Grease and flour, or line with waxed paper and grease, three 9-inch layer pans.
2. Melt chocolate over simmering water. Cool.
3. Cream butter with sugar until light and fluffy. Add egg yolks. Beat well. Blend in chocolate.
4. Mix and sift flour, baking powder and salt.
5. Add dry ingredients alternately with milk, mixing thoroughly after each addition. Add vanilla extract. Blend well.
6. With pliable rubber scraper or whisk, gently fold in stiffly beaten egg whites.
7. Pour batter into prepared pans.
8. Bake layers 30 to 35 minutes, or until cake center springs back when pressed with fingertip. Cool.
9. Fill and frost with Creamy Chocolate Frosting.

PETITE FUDGE CAKE

6 SERVINGS

½ cup softened butter	½ teaspoon salt
1 cup granulated sugar	½ cup milk
3 tablespoons cocoa	1 teaspoon vanilla extract
2 eggs, beaten	½ cup chopped nutmeats
1 cup sifted cake flour	
½ teaspoon double-acting baking powder	

1. Preheat oven to 350°F. Grease and flour 8 × 8 × 2-inch pan.
2. Cream butter with sugar and cocoa until light and fluffy.
3. Add beaten eggs. Beat well.
4. Mix and sift flour, baking powder and salt together.
5. Add dry ingredients alternately with milk, mixing thoroughly after each addition. Add vanilla extract. Blend well. Stir in nutmeats.
6. Pour batter into prepared pan.
7. Bake 30 to 35 minutes, or until cake center springs back when pressed with fingertip.

CHOCOLATE CHOCOLATE-CHIP CAKE: In Step 5, add ½ cup semisweet chocolate pieces with nutmeats.

CARROT CAKE

ABOUT 12 SERVINGS

1½ cups granulated sugar	2 teaspoons ground cinnamon
4 eggs	½ teaspoon ground allspice
1 teaspoon vanilla extract	3½ cups peeled, grated carrots
1½ cups cooking oil	1 cup chopped nutmeats
2 cups sifted all-purpose flour	Cream Cheese Frosting,
2 teaspoons baking soda	page 111
1 teaspoon salt	

1. Preheat oven to 350°F. Grease and flour 13 × 9 × 2-inch pan.
2. In large mixing bowl, beat sugar and eggs until thick and lemon-colored. Add vanilla extract and oil. Beat well.
3. Mix and sift flour, soda, salt, cinnamon and allspice together.
4. Gradually add dry ingredients to egg mixture, mixing thoroughly after each addition. Fold in carrots and nutmeats.
5. Pour into prepared pan.
6. Bake about 45 minutes, or until cake center springs back when pressed with fingertip. Cool.
7. Frost with Cream Cheese Frosting.

SACHER TORTE

8 TO 12 SERVINGS

7 ounces semisweet chocolate
¾ cup softened butter
¾ cup granulated sugar
¼ teaspoon salt
½ teaspoon vanilla extract
8 egg yolks

1 cup sifted all-purpose flour
10 egg whites, beaten until stiff
but not dry
½ cup apricot jam
Chocolate Glaze, page 113
1 cup whipping cream, whipped

1. Preheat oven to 325°F. Generously grease and flour 8-inch springform pan.
2. Melt chocolate over simmering water. Cool.
3. In mixing bowl, cream butter with sugar until light and fluffy. Blend in salt, chocolate and vanilla extract.
4. Add egg yolks one at a time. Beat well after each addition. Gradually add sifted flour to chocolate mixture.
5. With pliable rubber scraper or whisk, gently fold stiffly beaten egg whites into batter.
6. Spread batter evenly in prepared pan.
7. Bake for 50 to 55 minutes. Cool cake for 15 minutes. Remove pan sides and bottom. Invert cake on wire rack. Let stand until completely cooled.
8. In saucepan, heat apricot jam, stirring frequently until boiling. Remove from heat. Press through fine sieve.
9. Place cake, bottom-side up, on serving plate. Brush top and sides of cake with strained apricot jam. Let stand about 1 hour to allow glaze to set.
10. Frost top and sides with Chocolate Glaze. Refrigerate until frosting has hardened. Top each serving with a generous dollop of whipped cream.

GINGERBREAD WITH CREAM CHEESE AND DATE FILLING

8 TO 12 SERVINGS

½ cup shortening
½ cup granulated sugar
½ cup light molasses
2 eggs
2 teaspoons baking soda

1 cup boiling water
2½ cups sifted all-purpose flour
½ teaspoon salt
1 teaspoon ground ginger
½ teaspoon ground cloves

1. Preheat oven to 350°F. Grease and flour 8- or 9-inch square pan.
2. Cream shortening with sugar until light and fluffy. Blend in molasses. Add eggs one at a time, beating well after each addition.
3. Dissolve soda in boiling water.
4. Mix and sift flour, salt, ginger and cloves together.
5. Add dry ingredients alternately with water to creamed mixture, mixing thoroughly after each addition.

6. Pour batter into prepared pan.
7. Bake for 35 to 40 minutes, or until cake center springs back when pressed with fingertip. Cool.
8. Split in half and fill.

FILLING

2 packages (3 ounces each) cream cheese
¼ cup half-and-half

1 cup pitted, finely chopped dates
¼ cup chopped nutmeats

Combine all ingredients. Spread between layers of cooled gingerbread.

MOCHA CAKE

ABOUT 10 SERVINGS

½ cup shortening
1 cup granulated sugar
2 eggs, separated (beat whites until stiff, but not dry)
2¼ cups sifted all-purpose flour
2 teaspoons double-acting baking powder

½ teaspoon salt
1 cup cold coffee
1 teaspoon vanilla extract
½ cup chopped walnut meats, if desired
Caramel Buttercream Frosting, 110

1. Preheat oven to 375°F. Grease and flour, or line with waxed paper and grease, two 9-inch layer pans.
2. Cream shortening with sugar until light and fluffy. Add egg yolks. Beat well.
3. Mix and sift flour, baking powder and salt together.
4. Add dry ingredients alternately with coffee to creamed mixture, mixing thoroughly after each addition. Add vanilla extract. Mix very well. Add walnut meats, if desired.
5. With pliable rubber scraper or whisk, gently fold in stiffly beaten egg whites.
6. Pour batter into prepared pans.
7. Bake for 25 to 30 minutes, or until cake center springs back when pressed with fingertip. Cool.
8. Fill and frost with Caramel Buttercream Frosting.

CHESTNUT CAKE: In Step 4, omit walnut meats. In Step 8, to one-third of frosting, add 1 cup canned, drained, puréed chestnuts. Use as filling between cake layers. Use remaining two-thirds to frost top and sides of cake.

PEACH OR PINEAPPLE UPSIDE-DOWN CAKE

6 TO 8 SERVINGS

¼ cup butter
¼ cup firmly packed brown sugar
6 to 9 canned peach halves or
    pineapple slices (reserve
    syrup)

6 to 9 maraschino cherries

1. Preheat oven to 360°F.
2. In small saucepan, melt butter and brown sugar together over low heat.
3. Arrange peach halves (cut side down) or pineapple slices on bottom of ungreased 8 × 8 × 2-inch pan, putting cherry in center of each.
4. Cover with brown-sugar mixture.

BATTER

3 eggs, separated (beat whites
    until stiff, but not dry)
1 cup granulated sugar
1½ cups sifted all-purpose flour
1 teaspoon double-acting
    baking powder

½ teaspoon salt
½ cup syrup from canned peaches
    or pineapple
Sweetened whipped cream,
    if desired

1. In large mixing bowl, beat egg yolks well. Gradually add sugar. Beat until blended.
2. Sift flour again. Mix and sift flour with baking powder and salt.
3. Add dry ingredients alternately with syrup to batter, mixing thoroughly after each addition.
4. With pliable rubber scraper or whisk, gently fold in stiffly beaten egg whites.
5. Pour batter over fruit.
6. Bake 45 minutes, or until cake center springs back when pressed with fingertip.
7. Let stand at least 15 minutes. Turn onto plate, fruit side up, to cool.
8. Serve with sweetened whipped cream, if desired.

PUMPKIN CAKE

ABOUT 12 SERVINGS

½ cup butter
1¼ cups granulated sugar
2 eggs
1 cup canned pumpkin
2¼ cups sifted all-purpose flour
1 teaspoon salt
3 teaspoons double-acting
   baking powder
½ teaspoon baking soda

3½ teaspoons pumpkin pie spice,
   or ½ teaspoon ground
   cinnamon, ¼ teaspoon
   ground cloves and ¼
   teaspoon ground nutmeg
¾ cup milk
   Blue Ribbon Butter Frosting,
   page 110, if desired

1. Preheat oven to 350°F. Grease and flour 12 × 8 × 2-inch pan.
2. Cream butter with sugar until light and fluffy. Add eggs one at a time, beating well after each addition. Blend in pumpkin.
3. Mix and sift flour, salt, baking powder, soda and pumpkin pie spice together.
4. Add dry ingredients alternately with milk to creamed mixture, mixing thoroughly after each addition.
5. Pour batter into prepared pans.
6. Bake for about 50 minutes, or until cake center springs back when pressed with fingertip. Cool.
7. Frost with Blue Ribbon Butter Frosting, if desired.

APPLESAUCE CAKE: In Step 2, substitute unsweetened applesauce for pumpkin. In Step 3, substitute 1 teaspoon ground cinnamon and ½ teaspoon ground nutmeg for pumpkin pie spice. In Step 4, add 1 cup seedless raisins and 1 cup chopped nutmeats.

RED VELVET CAKE

ABOUT 12 SERVINGS

½ cup shortening
1½ cups granulated sugar
3 eggs, separated (beat whites
   until stiff, but not dry)
2 ounces red food coloring
2 tablespoons cocoa
2 cups plus 3 tablespoons sifted
   all-purpose flour or 2½ cups
   sifted cake flour

1¼ cups buttermilk
3 teaspoons cherry extract
1 teaspoon almond extract
1 teaspoon salt
1½ teaspoons baking soda dissolved
   in 1 tablespoon vinegar
   Blue Ribbon Butter Frosting,
   page 110

1. Preheat oven to 350°F. Line with waxed paper and grease two 9-inch layer pans or a 12 × 8 × 2-inch pan.
2. In mixing bowl, cream shortening with sugar until light and fluffy. Add egg yolks one at a time, beating very well after each addition. Add food coloring and cocoa. Beat well.
3. Add sifted flour alternately with buttermilk to creamed mixture, beginning and ending with flour. Add cherry and almond extracts, salt, and baking soda dissolved in vinegar. Beat well. With pliable rubber scraper or whisk, gently fold in stiffly beaten egg whites.
4. Pour batter into prepared pans.
5. Bake 20 to 25 minutes for layers, 30 to 35 minutes for sheet cake, or until cake center springs back when lightly pressed with fingertip. Cool.
6. Fill and frost with Blue Ribbon Butter Frosting.

SPICE CAKE

ABOUT 12 SERVINGS

¾ cup shortening
1½ cups firmly packed brown sugar
3 eggs
2½ cups sifted cake flour
¾ teaspoon baking soda
1 teaspoon salt
1 teaspoon ground cinnamon
½ teaspoon ground nutmeg

½ teaspoon ground allspice
1¼ cups sour milk or buttermilk
1 cup finely chopped nutmeats
1 cup raisins, cooked, drained and cut up
Seafoam Frosting, page 109, or frosting of choice

1. Preheat oven to 350°F. Line with waxed paper and grease 13 × 9 × 2-inch pan or two 9-inch layer pans.
2. Cream shortening with brown sugar until light and fluffy. Add eggs one at a time, beating well after each addition.
3. Mix and sift flour, soda, salt, cinnamon, nutmeg and allspice together.
4. Add dry ingredients alternately with sour milk or buttermilk to creamed mixture, mixing thoroughly after each addition. Stir in nutmeats and raisins.
5. Pour batter into prepared pans.
6. Bake sheet cake for 45 to 50 minutes, layers about 25 minutes, or until cake center springs back when pressed with fingertip. Cool.
7. Frost with Seafoam Frosting or frosting of choice.

COCONUT CAKE

ABOUT 12 SERVINGS

1 cup shredded coconut
2 tablespoons milk
¾ cup butter or margarine
1¾ cups minus 1 tablespoon
   granulated sugar
2¾ cups sifted all-purpose flour
2½ teaspoons double-acting
   baking powder

½ teaspoon salt
1 cup plus 2 tablespoons water
1 teaspoon lemon extract
4 egg whites, beaten until stiff,
   but not dry
Seven-Minute Frosting,
   page 113

1. Preheat oven to 375°F. Grease and flour two 9-inch layer pans.
2. Soak coconut in milk for 5 to 10 minutes.
3. Cream butter or margarine with sugar until light and fluffy.
4. Mix and sift flour, baking powder and salt together.
5. Add dry ingredients alternately with water to creamed mixture, mixing thoroughly after each addition. Add lemon extract and coconut-milk mixture. Blend very well.
6. With pliable rubber scraper or whisk, gently fold in stiffly beaten egg whites.
7. Pour batter into prepared pans.
8. Bake for 25 to 30 minutes, or until cake center springs back when pressed with fingertip. Cool.
9. Fill and frost with Seven-Minute Frosting. Sprinkle top with additional coconut, if desired.

KLARA'S POPPY-SEED CAKE

ABOUT 10 SERVINGS

¼ to ½ cup poppy seeds
1 cup milk
⅔ cup butter
1½ cups granulated sugar
2 cups plus 2 tablespoons sifted
   cake flour
2 teaspoons double-acting
   baking powder

½ teaspoon salt
½ teaspoon vanilla extract
4 egg whites, beaten until stiff,
   but not dry
Frosting of choice

1. Soak poppy seeds in milk for at least 5 hours in refrigerator.
2. Preheat oven to 375°F. Grease and flour two 9-inch layer pans.
3. Cream butter with sugar until light and fluffy.
4. Mix and sift flour, baking powder and salt together.
5. Add dry ingredients to creamed mixture alternately with milk and poppy-

seed mixture, mixing thoroughly after each addition. Add vanilla extract. Mix very well.

6. With pliable rubber scraper or whisk, gently fold in stiffly beaten egg whites.

7. Pour batter into prepared pans.

8. Bake for about 25 to 30 minutes, or until cake center springs back when pressed with fingertip. Cool.

9. Fill and frost with frosting of choice.

EDELWEISS WHITE CAKE

ABOUT 12 SERVINGS

½ cup butter
1 cup granulated sugar
2 cups sifted cake flour
2½ teaspoons double-acting
    baking powder
¼ teaspoon salt

1 cup milk
1 teaspoon vanilla extract
3 egg whites, beaten until stiff
    but not dry
    Buttercream Frosting, page 109

1. Preheat oven to 350°F. Grease and flour two 8- or 9-inch layer pans.

2. Cream butter with sugar until light and fluffy.

3. Mix and sift flour, baking powder and salt together.

4. Add dry ingredients alternately with milk to creamed mixture, mixing thoroughly after each addition. Add vanilla extract. Mix very well.

5. With pliable rubber scraper or whisk, gently fold in stiffly beaten egg whites.

6. Pour batter into prepared pans.

7. Bake for 25 to 30 minutes, or until cake center springs back when lightly pressed with fingertip. Cool.

8. Fill and frost with any flavor Buttercream Frosting.

LADY BALTIMORE WHITE CAKE

ABOUT 12 SERVINGS

½ cup butter
1½ cups granulated sugar
3 cups sifted cake flour
4 teaspoons double-acting
    baking powder
½ teaspoon salt
1 cup water
1 teaspoon vanilla extract, or
    ½ teaspoon vanilla extract
    and ¼ teaspoon almond
    extract

4 egg whites, beaten until stiff,
    but not dry (egg yolks may be
    used in Three-Layer Yellow
    Cake opposite)
1 cup ground walnut meats,
    if desired
    Lady Baltimore Frosting,
    page 109

1. Preheat oven to 350°F. Grease and flour, or line with waxed paper and grease, three 8-inch layer pans.
2. Cream butter with sugar until light and fluffy.
3. Mix and sift flour, baking powder and salt together.
4. Add dry ingredients alternately with water, mixing thoroughly after each addition.
5. Add vanilla extract, or vanilla and almond extracts. Mix very well.
6. With pliable rubber scraper or whisk, gently fold in stiffly beaten egg whites. Fold in walnut meats, if desired.
7. Pour batter into prepared pans.
8. Bake for 25 to 30 minutes, or until cake center springs back when lightly pressed with fingertip. Cool.
9. Fill and frost with Lady Baltimore Frosting.

THREE-LAYER YELLOW CAKE

12 TO 16 SERVINGS

1 cup softened butter or
    margarine
1½ cups granulated sugar
4 eggs, separated (beat whites
    until stiff, but not dry)
3 cups sifted cake flour
2½ teaspoons double-acting
    baking powder

½ teaspoon salt
1 cup plus 2 tablespoons milk
2 teaspoons vanilla extract or
    1 teaspoon grated lemon rind
Frosting of choice

1. Preheat oven to 375°F. Grease and flour, or line with waxed paper and grease, three 8-inch layer pans.
2. Cream butter or margarine with sugar until light and fluffy. Add egg yolks. Beat well.
3. Mix and sift flour, baking powder and salt together.
4. Add dry ingredients alternately with milk to creamed mixture, mixing thoroughly after each addition. Add vanilla extract or grated lemon rind. Mix very well.
5. With pliable rubber scraper or whisk, gently fold in stiffly beaten egg whites.
6. Pour batter into prepared pans.
7. Bake for 25 to 30 minutes, or until cake center springs back when lightly pressed with fingertip. Cool.
8. Fill and frost with frosting of choice.

TWO-LAYER YELLOW CAKE

8 TO 10 SERVINGS

½ cup shortening or softened
    butter
1 teaspoon vanilla extract
1 cup milk
2¼ cups sifted all-purpose flour
1½ cups granulated sugar

3 teaspoons double-acting
    baking powder
½ teaspoon salt
2 eggs
Frosting of choice

1. Preheat oven to 350°F. Grease and flour two 8-inch layer pans.
2. Mix shortening or butter, vanilla extract and ⅔ cup milk until well blended.
3. Mix and sift flour with sugar, baking powder and salt.
4. Add dry ingredients to shortening and milk mixture a little at a time, mixing thoroughly after each addition. Beat in eggs. Add remaining ⅓ cup milk. Beat very well.
5. Pour batter into prepared pans.
6. Bake for 25 to 30 minutes, or until cake center springs back when lightly pressed with fingertip.
7. Fill and frost with frosting of choice.

DESSERT RING

ABOUT 12 SERVINGS

¾ cup softened butter
1½ cups granulated sugar
2 eggs
1 cup dairy sour cream
1 teaspoon vanilla extract

2 cups sifted cake flour
1 teaspoon double-acting
    baking powder
¼ teaspoon salt
Cocoa Pecan Topping (below)

1. Preheat oven to 350°F. Grease and flour 9 × 4-inch tube pan.
2. Cream butter with sugar until light and fluffy.
3. Add eggs one at a time, beating well after each addition. Blend in sour cream and vanilla extract.
4. Mix and sift flour, baking powder and salt together.
5. Add dry ingredients a little at a time to creamed mixture, mixing thoroughly after each addition.
6. Spoon batter into prepared pan. Sprinkle Cocoa Pecan Topping over top.
7. Bake for 50 to 60 minutes, or until cake center springs back when lightly pressed with fingertip.

COCOA PECAN TOPPING

2 tablespoons firmly packed
    brown sugar
1 teaspoon instant cocoa mix or
    ½ teaspoon cocoa and
    ½ teaspoon sugar

½ teaspoon ground cinnamon
½ cup chopped pecan meats

In small mixing bowl, mix all ingredients thoroughly.

POUND CAKE

ABOUT 12 SERVINGS

¾ cup softened butter
1 cup granulated sugar
4 eggs, separated (beat whites of
    2 eggs until stiff, but not dry)
1¾ cups sifted cake flour
½ teaspoon double-acting
    baking powder

½ teaspoon salt
¼ teaspoon ground nutmeg or
    mace, if desired
1 teaspoon vanilla extract
2 tablespoons brandy, if desired
2 teaspoons powdered sugar

1. Preheat oven to 350°F. Line with waxed paper and grease 10 × 4-inch tube pan, or 10 × 5 × 3-inch loaf pan.
2. Cream butter with sugar until light and fluffy.
3. Add 2 whole eggs and 2 egg yolks one at a time, beating well after each addition.
4. Mix and sift flour together with baking powder, salt and nutmeg or mace, if desired.
5. Add dry ingredients to creamed mixture a little at a time, beating thoroughly after each addition. Add vanilla extract. Blend in brandy, if desired. If dough seems too stiff, a very small additional amount of brandy may be added.
6. Add powdered sugar to stiffly beaten egg whites. With pliable rubber scraper or whisk, gently fold in egg whites.
7. Pour batter into prepared pans.
8. Bake about 1¼ hours, or until cake tester inserted in center comes out clean.

Sponge Cakes

ANGEL FOOD CAKE DELUXE

It is the air beaten into the egg whites that makes angel food cakes rise. At high elevations, care must be taken not to beat too much air into the whites, as this will make the cake fall. Gradually fold in sifted flour and sugar to guard against overmixing and produce a fine-textured, moist cake. Egg yolks may be used for Yellow Angel Food Cake.

1¼ cups egg whites (about 10)
½ teaspoon salt
1½ teaspoons fresh cream of tartar
1 teaspoon vanilla extract or
    ½ teaspoon vanilla extract
    and ½ teaspoon almond
    extract

1½ cups less 1 tablespoon
    granulated sugar, sifted twice
1¼ cups sifted cake flour
    Seven-Minute Frosting,
    page 113, if desired

1. Preheat oven to 325°F. Have ready ungreased, *spotlessly clean* 10 × 4-inch tube pan.
2. Beat egg whites until foamy. Add salt, cream of tartar and vanilla extract or vanilla and almond extracts. Continue beating until egg whites form stiff but moist peaks.
3. Using rubber scraper or whisk, gradually fold in ¾ cup sifted sugar 1 tablespoon at a time.
4. Mix and sift flour with remaining sugar three times.
5. Sift ¼ cup flour and sugar mixture over batter. Rotating bowl, gently fold it in with pliable rubber scraper or whisk, using 12 to 15 strokes for each

addition. Repeat until all the flour and sugar are folded into the egg whites.

6. Pour batter into pan. Cut through batter several times with scraper or knife, to break up air bubbles.

7. Bake for 45 to 50 minutes, or until cake is delicately brown and center top springs back when lightly pressed with fingertip. Invert pan on wire rack or inverted funnel until cold. Remove from pan.

8. Frost with Seven-Minute Frosting, if desired.

YELLOW ANGEL FOOD CAKE

12 TO 16 SERVINGS

12 eggs yolks, beaten
½ cup hot water
1 cup granulated sugar, sifted
   twice
1 cup sifted cake flour
2 teaspoons double-acting
   baking powder

¼ teaspoon salt
1 teaspoon lemon extract or
   1 teaspoon vanilla extract or
   ½ teaspoon grated lemon or
   orange rind

1. Preheat oven to 325°F. Have ready ungreased, *spotlessly clean* 10 × 4-inch or 9 × 3½-inch tube pan.

2. Beat egg yolks until thick and lemon-colored. Beat in hot water. Beat in sifted sugar.

3. Mix and sift flour, baking powder and salt together three times.

4. With pliable rubber scraper or whisk, fold dry ingredients into egg mixture a little at a time, mixing thoroughly. Blend in lemon or vanilla extract, or grated lemon or orange rind.

5. Pour batter into pans. Cut through batter several times with knife or scraper to break up air bubbles.

6. Bake for about 50 minutes, or until lightly browned and cake center springs back when lightly pressed with fingertip. Cool.

CHOCOLATE ROLL

ABOUT 8 TO 10 SERVINGS

6 eggs, separated (beat whites
   until stiff, but not dry)
1 teaspoon vanilla extract
2 tablespoons sifted all-purpose
   flour
2 tablespoons cocoa
1 cup plus 3 tablespoons sifted
   powdered sugar

½ teaspoon salt
2 cups whipping cream
½ cup finely chopped nutmeats or
   crushed peppermint candy
   Fudge Sauce, page 112

1. Preheat oven to 400°F. Line with waxed paper and grease 15 × 10 × 1-inch jelly roll pan or cookie sheet.
2. Beat egg yolks until thick and lemon-colored. Add vanilla extract.
3. Mix and sift flour, cocoa, 1 cup sugar and salt together.
4. Add dry ingredients to egg yolks a little at a time, stirring thoroughly after each addition.
5. With pliable rubber scraper or whisk, gently fold in stiffly beaten egg whites.
6. Spread batter onto prepared pan.
7. Bake for 15 minutes. Watch carefully that edges do not get too done.
8. Turn onto clean towel coated with additional powdered sugar. Remove waxed paper from bottom. Cut off hard edges. Roll up cake and towel into jelly-roll shape. Shape and cool for 10 minutes.
9. Whip cream. When nearly the consistency for spreading, add remaining 3 tablespoons powdered sugar. Whip until consistency for spreading. Fold in nutmeats, or crushed peppermint candy.
10. Unroll cake. Remove towel. Spread cake with whipping cream.
11. Serve with Fudge Sauce.

SPONGE CAKE

ABOUT 16 SERVINGS

Do not overbeat egg whites or yolks. Addition of an extra egg often strengthens and stabilizes batter.

8 *extra large* or 9 *medium eggs, separated*	1 *tablespoon almond extract or amaretto liqueur*
1½ *cups less 2 tablespoons granulated sugar, sifted 5 times*	1½ *cups cake flour, sifted 5 times* *French Custard Filling, page 115*
½ *teaspoon salt*	

1. Preheat oven to 275°F. Have ready an ungreased, *spotlessly clean* 10 × 4-inch tube pan.
2. Beat egg whites just until soft peaks form. Gradually beat in ¾ cup sugar. Add salt and almond extract or amaretto liqueur.
3. In large separate mixing bowl, beat egg yolks until lemon colored. Gradually add remaining sugar. Continue to beat until very light in color.
4. With a pliable rubber scraper or whisk, gently fold egg yolks into egg whites. Gently fold sifted flour into egg mixture a little at a time.
5. Pour batter into prepared pan. Cut through batter several times with a knife or scraper to break up air bubbles.
6. Bake at 275°F. for 45 minutes, then *increase* temperature to 325°F. and bake 15 minutes more, or until lightly browned and cake center springs back when pressed with fingertip.
7. Invert on wire rack or inverted funnel until cold. Remove from pan.
8. Split and fill with any flavor French Custard Filling. Sprinkle top with powdered sugar.

Fruitcakes

NEW ENGLAND FRUITCAKE

FOUR 9 × 5-INCH LOAVES OR TWO 10-INCH TUBE CAKES

1½ cups chopped candied pineapple
1 cup chopped candied cherries
3 cups raisins
1½ cups currants
2 cups chopped pecan meats
1½ cups chopped almonds
1 cup rum
1 cup softened butter
2 cups granulated sugar
6 eggs
2½ cups sifted all-purpose flour

2 teaspoons double-acting
  baking powder
½ teaspoon baking soda
1½ teaspoons ground ginger
1½ teaspoons ground mace
1 tablespoon ground nutmeg
1 tablespoon ground cinnamon
1 cup orange juice
2 cups flaked coconut
1½ cups apricot preserves

1. In large mixing bowl, combine pineapple, cherries, raisins, currants, pecan meats and almonds with rum. Cover. Refrigerate overnight.
2. Preheat oven to 275°F. Line with waxed paper and grease four 9 × 5 × 3-inch or two 10-inch tube pans.
3. In very large kettle or crock, cream butter with sugar until light and fluffy. Add eggs one at a time, beating well after each addition.
4. Mix and sift flour, baking powder, soda, ginger, mace, nutmeg and cinnamon together.
5. Add dry ingredients alternately with orange juice to creamed mixture. Fold in candied fruits, coconut and apricot preserves. Mix very well.
6. Spread batter in prepared pans.
7. Bake for about 3 hours, or until toothpick inserted in center comes out clean. Cool. Wrap in plastic wrap or foil. Will keep in refrigerator for several weeks.

INDIVIDUAL FRUITCAKES: In Step 6, spoon batter into paper-lined muffin pan cups filling each cup two-thirds full. Top each with cherry or pecan half. Bake in oven preheated to 300°F. for 1 hour.

CHOCOLATE FRUITCAKE: In Step 1, substitute chopped dates for currants. In Step 3, add 4 ounces unsweetened chocolate, melted.

WHITE FRUITCAKE

THREE 9 × 5-INCH LOAVES OR ONE 10-INCH TUBE CAKE

1 cup softened butter	1 pound golden raisins
1 cup granulated sugar	1 cup halved candied cherries
6 eggs	½ cup chopped candied pineapple
½ cup orange juice	½ cup chopped candied
2½ cups sifted all-purpose flour	orange peel
¼ teaspoon baking soda	1 cup chopped pecan meats
½ teaspoon salt	

1. Preheat oven to 275°F. Line with waxed paper and grease three 9 × 5 × 3-inch loaf pans or one 10-inch tube pan.
2. In large mixing bowl, cream butter with sugar until light and fluffy. Add eggs one at a time, beating well after each addition. Add orange juice.
3. Mix and sift flour, baking soda and salt together.
4. Mix a little flour with raisins, cherries, pineapple, orange peel and pecan meats. Gradually add remaining flour to creamed mixture, mixing thoroughly after each addition. Add fruit mixture.
5. Pour batter into prepared pans.
6. Bake for about 2 hours, or until toothpick inserted in center comes out clean. Cool. Wrap in plastic wrap or foil. Will keep in refrigerator for several weeks.

Candies

HIGH ALTITUDE FACTS ABOUT MAKING CANDIES

Candies should be cooked for a shorter amount of time at high altitudes than at sea level because of the more rapid evaporation of liquids. If sea-level directions are followed for candy-making, the syrup will become too concentrated by the time the prescribed temperature is reached, and the candy will be too done, or hard. The cold-water test is the surest way to determine the correct amount of cooking of candies: Have ready a cup of very cold water. Drop ½ teaspoon of boiling syrup into it. The *soft-ball stage* has been reached when the syrup can be picked up and formed with the fingers into a soft ball, but then flattens. The *firm-ball stage* is reached when the syrup can be formed with the fingers into a solid, but not hard, ball that holds its shape unless pressed. The *hard-ball stage* is the last stage where a ball can still be formed. The *soft-crack stage* is reached when the syrup separates into hard, but not brittle, threads. In the *hard-crack stage*, the syrup separates into hard and brittle threads, or breaks like glass when hit against the side of the cup.

HIGH ALTITUDE TEMPERATURE GUIDE FOR CANDY-MAKING

Type of Candy	Cold-water test	Candy thermometer reading for:		
		2,000 feet	5,000 feet	7,500 feet
Creams	Soft-ball stage	230°F. to	224°F. to	219°F. to
Fudges		236°F.	230°F.	225°F.
Fondants				

HIGH ALTITUDE TEMPERATURE GUIDE FOR CANDY-MAKING
(CONTINUED)

		Candy thermometer reading for:		
Type of Candy	Cold-water test	2,000 feet	5,000 feet	7,500 feet
Caramels	Firm-ball stage	238°F. to 244°F.	232°F. to 238.5°F.	227°F. to 233°F.
Divinities Taffies Caramel popcorn	Hard-ball stage	246°F. to 264°F.	240°F. to 258°F.	235°F. to 253°F.
Butterscotch English toffees	Soft-crack stage	266°F. to 286°F.	260°F. to 286°F.	255°F. to 275°F.
Brittles	Hard-crack stage	296°F. to 306°F.	290°F. to 300°F.	285°F. to 295°F.

ALMOND BUTTER CRUNCH

▼▼▼

1½ TO 2 POUNDS

Variations in altitude and sudden barometric changes have a noticeable effect on candy-making.

1 *cup butter*
1⅓ *cups granulated sugar*
2 *tablespoons light corn syrup*
3 *tablespoons water*
¼ *teaspoon salt*
1 *cup coarsely chopped blanched almonds, toasted*

16 *ounces semisweet chocolate pieces*
1 *cup finely chopped blanched almonds, toasted*

1. Butter a 13 × 9 × 2-inch pan. Have ready 2 sheets of aluminum foil or waxed paper.
2. Melt butter in heavy 2-quart saucepan. Add sugar, corn syrup, water and salt. Cook over low heat, stirring occasionally, until a small quantity dropped into cold water reaches the hard-crack stage, or until correct reading for your elevation is reached on a candy thermometer (see table above). (Watch carefully after temperature reaches 270°F. to prevent scorching.) Remove from heat. Quickly stir in coarsely chopped nutmeats.
3. Spread in prepared pan. Cool completely.
4. In top of double boiler over simmering water, melt chocolate, stirring fast and steadily so it melts evenly. Set aside.
5. Turn cooled candy onto aluminum foil or waxed paper. Coat top with half of melted chocolate. Sprinkle with half of finely chopped almonds.
6. Cover closely with aluminum foil or waxed paper. Invert quickly. Peel off foil or waxed paper. Spread with remaining chocolate and sprinkle with remaining almonds.
7. Refrigerate until firm. Break into pieces and store in airtight container.

CARAMEL NUT CORN

▼▼▼

ABOUT 3 QUARTS

2 *cups firmly packed brown sugar*	½ *teaspoon baking soda*
1 *cup light molasses*	12 *cups popped popcorn*
2 *tablespoons vinegar*	2 *cups salted peanuts*
1 *tablespoon butter*	

1. In 3-quart heavy saucepan, combine sugar, molasses, vinegar and butter. Cook over low heat, without stirring, to 250.5°F. on candy thermometer, or until a small quantity dropped into cold water is slightly brittle.
2. Remove from heat. Add baking soda. Beat well.
3. In large bowl, mix together popped popcorn and peanuts. Slowly pour syrup over mixture, tossing until coated. If desired, form into balls.

CARAMELS WITH NUTS

▼▼▼

ABOUT 1½ POUNDS

2 *cups granulated sugar*	1½ *cups chopped pecan meats,*
1¾ *cups light corn syrup*	*hazelnuts or walnuts*
½ *cup butter*	½ *teaspoon salt*
2 *cups half-and-half*	1 *teaspoon vanilla extract*

1. Butter 8-inch square pan.
2. In heavy 4-quart saucepan combine sugar, corn syrup, butter and 1 cup cream. Cook over low heat until mixture boils. Add remaining 1 cup cream gradually without interrupting boiling. Cook, stirring constantly with wooden spoon, until a small quantity dropped into cold water forms a firm ball, or until correct reading for your elevation is reached on candy thermometer (see table opposite). Remove from heat. Stir in nutmeats, salt and vanilla extract.
3. Pour into prepared pan to depth of ¾ to 1 inch. Cool.
4. When firm, cut into squares. Wrap individually in plastic wrapping or waxed paper.

CHOCOLATE CARAMELS: In Step 2, substitute 1 cup firmly packed brown sugar for granulated sugar. Add 3 ounces unsweetened chocolate.

DIVINITY

3 cups granulated sugar
1 cup water
1 cup light corn syrup
¼ teaspoon salt

3 egg whites
1 cup chopped nutmeats
½ teaspoon vanilla or
    almond extract

1. Grease cookie sheet for divinity patties, or 9 × 5 × 3-inch loaf pan for divinity fudge.
2. In 4-quart heavy saucepan, combine sugar, water, corn syrup and salt. Cook over low heat, stirring constantly, until sugar is dissolved.
3. With damp cloth, wipe all sugar grains from pan sides. Cook gently, without stirring, to 250.5°F. on candy thermometer, or until a small quantity dropped into cold water forms hard ball.
4. While candy is cooking, in large bowl, beat egg whites with electric mixer until stiff, but not dry. Slowly pour cooked syrup over egg whites, beating until mixture loses gloss and small amount dropped from spoon holds its shape, but do not overbeat. Stir in nutmeats and vanilla or almond extract.
5. Drop by teaspoonfuls onto prepared cookie sheet, or pour into loaf pan. Do not scrape pan sides. Cool. Store in airtight container.

MAPLE DIVINITY: In Step 2, substitute 1 cup maple syrup for corn syrup. In Step 4, omit vanilla or almond extract.

PENUCHE

2 cups firmly packed brown
    sugar and 1 cup granulated
    sugar or 3 cups firmly packed
    brown sugar
1 cup half-and-half or
    evaporated milk

¼ teaspoon salt
1 tablespoon butter
1½ teaspoons vanilla extract
¾ cup chopped pecan or
    walnut meats

1. Lightly butter 9 × 5 × 3-inch loaf pan.
2. In heavy 3-quart saucepan, cook sugar, cream or evaporated milk, and salt over low heat, stirring constantly, until a small quantity dropped into cold water forms a soft ball, or until correct reading for your altitude is reached on candy thermometer (see table, page 65). Remove from heat.
3. Add butter; do not stir. Set aside and cool to lukewarm. Add vanilla extract.
4. With wooden spoon, beat until thick and creamy. Add nutmeats. Turn into prepared pan.

5. When completely cooled, cover pan and let stand overnight at room temperature. Cut into squares. Store in airtight container.

PEANUT PENUCHE: In Step 4, substitute peanuts for pecan or walnut meats.

OLD-FASHIONED CHOCOLATE FUDGE

ABOUT 1¼ POUNDS

2 ounces unsweetened chocolate
2 cups granulated sugar
½ cup milk
2 tablespoons light corn syrup

¼ teaspoon salt
2 tablespoons butter
½ teaspoon vanilla extract
½ to 1 cup chopped nutmeats

1. Butter 8 × 8 × 2-inch square pan.
2. In 3-quart heavy saucepan, combine chocolate, sugar, milk, corn syrup and salt. Stir over low heat until sugar dissolves. Cook, stirring as little as possible, to 228.5°F. on candy thermometer, or until small quantity dropped into cold water forms a soft ball. Add butter, but do not stir. Cool until lukewarm.
3. Add vanilla extract and chopped nutmeats. Beat until the mixture is creamy and loses gloss. Pour into prepared pan. Do not scrape pan sides, as scraping may make candy sugary. When the candy is firm, cut into squares.

NEVER-FAIL FUDGE

ABOUT 3 POUNDS

4½ cups granulated sugar
¼ teaspoon salt
1 can (13 ounces) evaporated
   milk
1 package (10½ ounces)
   miniature marshmallows

1 12-ounce package and 1 6-ounce
   package semisweet chocolate
   pieces
3 ounces unsweetened chocolate
3 tablespoons butter
2 teaspoons vanilla extract
1½ to 2 cups chopped nutmeats

1. Butter 13 × 9 × 2-inch pan.
2. In 4-quart heavy saucepan, combine sugar, salt and evaporated milk. Stir over low heat until sugar dissolves. When mixture comes to full, rolling boil, cook 5 minutes, stirring occasionally.
3. Turn off heat. Add marshmallows, chocolate pieces, unsweetened chocolate and butter. Gently stir until all ingredients are completely dissolved and combined. Beat with electric mixer until fudge begins to thicken.
4. Add vanilla extract. Beat until well blended. Add nutmeats.
5. Pour into prepared pan. Do not scrape pan sides, as scraping may make candy sugary. When firm, cut into squares. Store in tightly covered container.

PEANUT OR CASHEW BRITTLE

ABOUT 2 POUNDS

2 *cups granulated sugar*
1 *cup light corn syrup*
½ *cup water*
1 *tablespoon honey*
3 *cups raw Spanish peanuts or*
     raw cashew nuts

1 *tablespoon butter*
1 *teaspoon vanilla extract*
1¾ *teaspoons baking soda*

1. Butter cookie sheet or broiling pan very well.
2. In 4-quart heavy saucepan, combine sugar, corn syrup, water and honey. Cook to 290.5°F. on candy thermometer, or until a small quantity dropped into cold water is very brittle and cracks or shatters like glass when hit against side of cup. Remove from heat.
3. Add peanuts or cashews and butter. Cook until syrup is slightly brown. Remove from heat. Add vanilla extract and baking soda. Beat well.
4. Pour onto prepared pan, spreading candy out as thinly as possible. Cool. Break into small pieces.

Canning
and Freezing

HIGH ALTITUDE FACTS ABOUT CANNING

In canning, all fruits and nonacidic vegetables are first heat-processed in a boiling-water bath so as to destroy or inactivate such microorganisms as molds, yeasts and bacteria (including the life-threatening botulinus organism) that are present at all times in the air, the water and the soil. Beginning at 1,000 feet above sea level, the lower boiling temperature of water necessitates an increase in this processing time and extra caution must be taken *never* to underprocess; if anything, it is better to *over-process* fruits and vegetables. The general rule is to add 1 minute to the processing time for each 1,000 feet above sea level if the processing time is 20 minutes or less, and to increase the time by 2 minutes for every 1,000 feet if the processing time is *more* than 20 minutes. (See High Altitude Time Corrections for Canning in Boiling-Water Bath, page 72.)

To prevent the temperature from dropping during processing—thus underprocessing the product—water must be kept *furiously* boiling for the full cooking time.

Acidic foods such as fruits, tomatoes and pickled vegetables may be canned in a boiling-water bath. The high degree of acidity will help to safely control any harmful organisms. Low-acid foods, such as most vegetables, meats, fish and poultry, *must be* processed at 240°F., and this requires the use of a pressure cooker. The pressure should be increased 1 pound for each 2,000 feet above sea level. The cooking time should be increased 5 percent for every 1,000 feet above the first 2,000 (15 percent at 5,000 feet). (See High Altitude Time Corrections for Canning in Pressure Cooker, page 73.)

Caution: Before tasting or serving any home-canned meat, fish or vegetable, bring food to a full, rolling boil for at least:

13 minutes at 2,500 feet
15 minutes at 5,000 feet
20 minutes at 8,000 feet or above
20 minutes for spinach and corn at all altitudes.

Sterilizing Jars and Glasses

Wash jars or glasses in soapy water. Sterilize by placing them on a rack or heavy cloth in hot water. Fill each jar or glass three-fourths full with water. Bring water to *furious* boil. Sterilize 15 to 20 minutes. Fill immediately with properly prepared fruit or vegetables.

High Altitude Time Corrections for Canning

Standard instructions for canning foods in a boiling-water bath or in a pressure cooker must be adjusted for high altitudes, as shown in the following tables.

HIGH ALTITUDE TIME CORRECTIONS FOR CANNING IN BOILING-WATER BATH

Elevation	If time called for is less than 20 minutes, add:	If time called for is greater than 20 minutes, add:
1,000 feet	1 minute	2 minutes
2,000 feet	2 minutes	4 minutes
3,000 feet	3 minutes	6 minutes
4,000 feet	4 minutes	8 minutes
5,000 feet	5 minutes	10 minutes
6,000 feet	6 minutes	12 minutes
7,000 feet	7 minutes	14 minutes
8,000 feet	8 minutes	16 minutes
9,000 feet	9 minutes	18 minutes
10,000 feet	10 minutes	20 minutes

HIGH ALTITUDE TIME CORRECTIONS FOR CANNING IN PRESSURE COOKER

Elevation	Pressure	Increase in Cooking Time
2,500 feet	15 pounds	10%
5,000 feet	15 pounds	15%
7,500 feet	15 pounds	20%
10,000 feet	15 pounds	35%

Canning Fruits Without Sugar

Fruits, fruit purées and juices may be canned without sugar, although they will not hold their color, flavor or shape as well. Unsweetened canned fruit is especially useful for pie-making.

Fruits with more juice, such as berries, cherries, currants and plums, should be canned in their own juices rather than in water when no sugar is used. The juice from the riper fruits can be extracted by crushing, heating and then straining. Place the remaining fruits in the juice, tightly pack them into glass jars without preheating, and add enough boiling juice to cover the fruit. Partially seal the jars. Process them in a hot-water bath according to the timetable on pages 74–76, then seal tightly.

Another canning method is to precook the fruit at simmering temperature for two to four minutes and then pour immediately into sterilized containers. Partially seal and process according to timetable, then seal tightly.

SYRUPS FOR CANNING AND FREEZING FRUIT

Syrup	Sugar	Water	Yield
Thin	2 cups	4 cups	5 cups
Medium	3 cups	4 cups	5½ cups

Add sugar to boiling water, stirring to dissolve. Cool. Add Solution to Prevent Darkening of Fruits, below.

Solution to Prevent Darkening of Fruits

Add ½ teaspoon ascorbic acid crystal to each quart cooled syrup. *Or* place whole fruits, such as peaches, pears, plums and apricots in 5 cups water mixed with the juice of 1 lemon.

HIGH ALTITUDE TIMETABLE FOR WATER-BATH CANNING

See High Altitude Time Corrections for Canning in Boiling-Water Bath, page 72; Solution to Prevent Darkening of Fruits, page 73; and Syrups for Canning and Freezing Fruit, page 73.

Fruit	Preparation	Method	Minutes (5,000 feet)
Apples	Pare and core apples, cut in pieces, drop into Solution to Prevent Darkening of Fruits. Drain, then boil 5 minutes in thin syrup or water.	Pack hot fruit to ½ inch of jar top. Cover with hot syrup or water, leaving ½ inch space at top of jar. Adjust jar lids. Process following Method for Water-Bath Canning below.	20
Applesauce	Make applesauce, sweetened or unsweetened. Heat through, stirring to keep from sticking to pan.	Pack hot to ¼ of jar top. Adjust lids. Process following Method for Water-Bath Canning below.	15
Apricots	Follow method for peaches. Peeling may be omitted.		25 to 27
Berries	Wash berries and drain well.	Fill jars to ½ inch of top. Shake while filling for a full pack. Cover with boiling syrup, leaving ½ inch space at top. Adjust lids. Process following Method for Water-Bath Canning below.	20
Cherries	Follow method for firm berries, adding a little water when heating unpitted cherries to keep them from sticking to the pan.		20
Fruit juices	Heat to simmer. Add sugar, if desired, ½ to 1 cup to gallon of juice.	Fill hot to jar top. Adjust jar lids. Process in water bath with water at simmering temperature (below boiling), following Method for Water-Bath Canning below.	25 to 27

HIGH ALTITUDE TIMETABLE FOR WATER-BATH CANNING
(CONTINUED)

Fruit	Preparation	Method	Minutes (5,000 feet)
Fruit purées	Use sound, ripe fruit. Wash and remove pits, if desired. Cut large fruit in pieces. Simmer until soft, adding a little water if needed to keep fruit from sticking. Press through a sieve or food mill. Add sugar to taste. Heat again to simmering.	Pack hot to ½ inch of jar top. Adjust lids. Process following Method for Water-Bath Canning below.	25 to 27
Peaches (hot pack)	Wash peaches. Dip in boiling water, then quickly in cold water. Remove skins, cut peaches in halves, remove pits. Slice if desired. Drop in Solution to Prevent Darkening of Fruits. Drain just before heating or packing cold. Heat peaches through in hot syrup. If fruit is very juicy, heat with sugar, adding no liquid.	Pack hot fruit to ½ inch of jar top. Cover with boiling liquid, leaving ½ inch space at top of jar. Adjust jar lids. Process following Method for Water-Bath Canning below.	25 to 27
Peaches (cold pack)	Prepare peaches as directed above.	Pack raw fruit to ½ inch of jar top. Cover with boiling syrup, leaving ½ inch space at top of jar. Adjust lids. Process following Method for Water-Bath Canning below.	35 (pint jars) 45 (quart jars)
Pears	Wash pears. Peel, cut in halves and core. Continue as with peaches, either hot or cold pack.	Process following Method for Water-Bath Canning below.	35 (pint jars)

HIGH ALTITUDE TIMETABLE FOR WATER-BATH CANNING
(CONTINUED)

Fruit	Preparation	Method	Minutes (5,000 feet)
Plums	Wash plums. To can whole, prick skins. Freestone varieties may be halved and pitted. Heat to boiling in syrup or juice. If fruit is very juicy, heat with sugar, adding no liquid.	Pack hot fruit to ½ inch of jar top. Cover with boiling liquid, leaving ½ inch space at top of jar. Adjust jar lids. Process following Method for Water-Bath Canning below.	20
Rhubarb	Wash rhubarb and cut into ½-inch pieces. Add ½ cup sugar to each quart of rhubarb and let it stand to draw out juice. Bring to boiling.	Pack hot to ½ inch of jar top. Adjust jar lids. Process following Method for Water-Bath Canning below.	15
Tomatoes (hot pack)	Use only perfect, ripe tomatoes. To loosen skins, dip into boiling water for about ½ minute; then dip quickly into cold water. Cut out stem ends and peel tomatoes.	Quarter peeled tomatoes. Bring to boil, stirring often. Pack hot in glass jars to ½ inch of top. Add ½ teaspoon salt to pints; 1 teaspoon to quarts. Adjust lids. Process following Method for Water-Bath Canning below.	15
Tomatoes (cold pack)	Leave tomatoes whole or cut in halves or quarters.	Pack tomatoes to ½ inch of jar top, pressing gently to fill spaces. Add no water. Add ½ teaspoon salt to pints; 1 teaspoon to quarts. Adjust lids.	45 (pint jars) 55 (quart jars)
Tomato juice	Use ripe, juicy tomatoes. Wash, remove stem ends, cut into pieces. Simmer until softened, stirring often. Press through sieve. Add 1 teaspoon salt to each quart of juice. Reheat at once just to boiling.	Pack boiling hot juice to ¼ inch of jar top. Adjust lids. Process following Method for Water-Bath Canning below.	20

METHOD FOR WATER-BATH CANNING

1. Before preparing fruit or vegetables, set water-bath canner with rack on stove. Add water to half full. Start heating. Also, begin to heat additional water to use after filled jars are placed in canner.

2. Prepare and pack fruit or vegetables following High Altitude Timetable for Water-Bath Canning, pages 74–76.

3. After each jar is filled, gently work blade of spatula or knife around inside filled jar to eliminate air. Add more boiling liquid, if necessary. Wipe off rim of jar with warm, damp cloth. Prepare lids following manufacturer's directions. Tightly screw down lid. As each jar is filled and sealed, place on canner rack with jar lifter or tongs.

4. When canner is filled with jars, add hot water to 2 inches above jars. Cover. Bring water to *furious* boil. Cook, following High Altitude Time Corrections for Canning in Boiling-Water Bath, page 72.

5. When processing time is finished, transfer hot jars to heatproof surface that is draft-free, separating jars to allow air to circulate among them. Test two-part jar lids for seal by pressing center. If the dip in the lid holds, the jar is sealed. One-part lids are sealed when jar does not leak when tipped.

Jellies, Jams, Preserves, Fruit Butters and Pickles

HIGH ALTITUDE FACTS ABOUT MAKING JELLY

The jellying point is reached more quickly at high altitudes. Because of the lower atmospheric humidity and rapid evaporation rate, the sugar and juice mixture concentrates in a shorter amount of time than at sea level.

For good results, reduce the finish temperature of jelly by 1.90°F. for each 1,000 feet in elevation (220°F. at sea level would be adjusted to 210.5°F. at 5,000 feet). See High Altitude Facts About Making Candies, page 65. If you prefer not using a thermometer (and many prefer not to), you can make sure the jelly is properly done by letting it cook until it forms two distinct drops when poured from the side of a metal spoon, then runs together into one drop or "sheet."

APPLE, CRABAPPLE OR QUINCE JELLY

ONE PINT OF FRUIT JUICE WITH SUGAR ADDED YIELDS ABOUT
THREE 8-OUNCE OR FOUR 6-OUNCE GLASSES

1 quart tart red apples, crabapples or quinces, stemmed, washed and quartered
1 cup water

¾ cup granulated sugar for each 1 cup apple or quince juice
2 2-inch sticks cinnamon, if desired

1. Place fruit and water in large enamel or stainless-steel saucepan.
2. Cook over low heat, stirring occasionally, until moisture begins to be drawn from the fruit. Increase heat to medium-low. Cook until fruit is soft, or about 20 minutes.
3. Remove from heat. Pour cooked fruit into dampened jelly bag or sieve or colander lined with cheesecloth.
4. Measure no more than 4 cups juice into large heavy saucepan. Bring juice to boil. Skim off froth. Add ¾ cup sugar for each 1 cup juice. Add cinnamon sticks, if desired. Stir over medium-low heat until sugar is dissolved. Heat to boiling. Cook without stirring. See High Altitude Facts About Making Jelly to determine point of jelling. Remove cinnamon.
5. Pour into hot sterilized glasses (see Sterilizing Jars and Glasses, page 72). Seal with thin layer of paraffin and/or lids.

APPLE AND BLACKBERRY JELLY: In Step 1, use half apples and half black-berries.

HERB JELLY: In Step 4, while sugar and juice are cooking, wash and tie in a bunch fresh, unsprayed mint, basil, tarragon, lemon verbena or rose geranium leaves. When syrup reaches point of jelling, remove from heat. Hold the stem ends and swish the leaves through the jelly several times, until the desired amount of flavoring is reached.

CONCORD GRAPE JELLY

Three parts just-ripe and 1 part slightly underripe grapes make the best jelly.

ONE PINT OF FRUIT JUICE WITH SUGAR ADDED YIELDS ABOUT
THREE 8-OUNCE OR FOUR 6-OUNCE GLASSES

4 cups grapes, washed and stemmed
¼ cup water

1 cup granulated sugar for each 1 cup grape juice

1. Crush a layer of grapes in bottom of large enamel or stainless-steel sauce-pan. Add remaining grapes.
2. Cook over low heat, stirring occasionally, until moisture begins to be drawn from the fruit. Increase heat to medium-low. Cook until fruit is soft, or about 5 to 10 minutes.
3. Remove from heat. Pour cooked fruit into dampened jelly bag or sieve or colander lined with cheesecloth.
4. Measure no more than 4 cups juice in large heavy saucepan. Bring juice to boiling. Skim off froth. Add 1 cup granulated sugar for each cup grape juice. Stir over medium-low heat until sugar is dissolved. Heat to boiling. Cook without stirring. See High Altitude Facts About Making Jelly, opposite, to determine point of jelling.

5. Pour into hot sterilized glasses (see Sterilizing Jars and Glasses, page 72). Seal with thin layer of paraffin and/or lids.

SPICED GRAPE JELLY: In Step 4, add four 2-inch sticks cinnamon and 24 whole cloves. In Step 5, remove cinnamon before pouring.

PORT WINE JELLY

ABOUT SIX 6-OUNCE GLASSES

3 cups sugar
2 cups port
6 tablespoons liquid fruit pectin

¼ teaspoon crumbled dried
   rosemary, if desired

1. In large enamel or stainless-steel saucepan, combine sugar and wine.
2. Heat, stirring constantly, until sugar is dissolved. Increase heat and bring to full, rolling boil. Boil 1 minute, stirring constantly. Add liquid pectin and rosemary, if desired. Bring again to full, rolling boil. Boil 1 minute. Remove from heat. Skim off froth.
3. Pour through fine sieve into hot, sterilized glasses (see Sterilizing Jars and Glasses, page 72). Seal with thin layer of paraffin and/or lids.

CRANBERRY PORT WINE JELLY: In Step 1, reduce port to 1 cup. Add 1 cup cranberry juice. In Step 2, substitute ¼ teaspoon cinnamon for rosemary.

GRAPE PORT WINE JELLY: In Step 1, reduce port to 1 cup. Add 1 cup grape juice. In Step 2, omit rosemary. Add ¼ teaspoon each cinnamon and nutmeg.

CHAMPAGNE JELLY: In Step 1, substitute pink champagne for port. In Step 2, omit rosemary.

CRANBERRY-CIDER JELLY: In Step 1, substitute 1 cup cranberry juice cocktail and 1 cup apple cider for wine. Add 1 cinnamon stick. Remove cinnamon before pouring.

MINT OR BASIL JELLY

SEVEN 8-OUNCE GLASSES

2 cups water
1 cup white vinegar
1 cup fresh mint or basil leaves
6½ cups granulated sugar

6 drops green food coloring
1 bottle (6 ounces) liquid
   fruit pectin

1. In large enamel or stainless-steel saucepan, combine water, vinegar, mint or basil leaves, sugar and food coloring.

2. Heat, stirring constantly, until sugar is dissolved. Increase heat and bring to full, rolling boil. Boil 1 minute, stirring constantly. Add liquid pectin. Bring again to full, rolling boil. Boil 1 minute. Remove from heat. Skim off froth.

3. Pour into hot, sterilized glasses (see Sterilizing Jars and Glasses, page 72). Seal with thin layer of paraffin and/or lids.

GREEN CHILI JELLY

SIX 8-OUNCE GLASSES

1 green pepper, washed, seeded
   and finely chopped
2 cans (4 ounces each) whole
   green chilies, seeded

1¼ cups white vinegar
5 cups granulated sugar
1 bottle (6 ounces) fruit pectin
   Green food coloring

1. In blender or food processor, purée green pepper, green chilies and ¼ cup vinegar.

2. In heavy enamel or stainless-steel saucepan, combine pepper purée with sugar and remaining 1 cup vinegar. Bring to full rolling boil, stirring constantly. Add fruit pectin. Bring to full rolling boil. Boil 1 minute. Remove from heat. Skim off foam.

3. Pour into hot, sterilized glasses (see Sterilizing Jars and Glasses, page 72). Seal with thin layer of paraffin and/or lids.

HOT PEPPER JELLY: In Step 1, omit green chilies. Do not purée green peppers. In Step 2, add chopped peppers to sugar and vinegar.

PINEAPPLE PEPPER JELLY: Omit Step 1 and green peppers and chilies. In Step 2, substitute ¾ cup apple cider vinegar for white vinegar. Add 2¼ cups pineapple juice and 1 teaspoon crumbled, dried red peppers.

BERRY JAM

FOUR CUPS BERRIES YIELD ABOUT THREE 8-OUNCE OR
SIX 6-OUNCE JARS OR GLASSES

4 cups berries (blackberries,
   loganberries, elderberries,
   strawberries, red or black
   raspberries), washed and
   drained

¼ cup water
¾ to 1 cup granulated sugar for
   each 1 cup berries
   Juice of 1 lemon

1. Crush all or part of berries depending on individual preference for smooth or chunky jam. Measure. Place in large enamel or stainless-steel saucepan. Add water. Warm berries over low heat. Add ¾ to 1 cup sugar for each 1 cup berries, depending on the tartness of berries. Stir until sugar is dissolved. Add lemon juice.

2. Cook over medium-low heat, stirring frequently to prevent scorching, until berries are thickened, clear and a spoonful dropped on a dish will hold shape. Remove from heat. Skim off foam.

3. Pour into hot sterilized jars or glasses (see Sterilizing Jars and Glasses, page 72). Seal with thin layer of paraffin and/or lids.

PLUM AND NECTARINE PRESERVES

SIX 8-OUNCE JARS OR GLASSES

4 cups diced, unpeeled plums
½ cup water
2 cups peeled, diced nectarines
2 tablespoons lime juice

1 package (1¾ ounces)
   powdered fruit pectin
6½ cups granulated sugar

1. In large heavy saucepan with tight-fitting cover, combine plums and water. Cover. Cook over low heat for 5 minutes. Add nectarines, lime juice and fruit pectin. Bring to full rolling boil, stirring constantly. Add sugar. Bring to full rolling boil. Boil 1 minute, stirring constantly. Remove from heat. Skim off foam.

2. Pour into hot, sterilized glasses or jars (see Sterilizing Jars and Glasses, page 72). Seal with thin layer of paraffin and/or lids.

CRANBERRY PINEAPPLE PRESERVES: In Step 1, substitute 1 pound fresh cranberries for plums, substitute 1 can (1 pound, 4 ounces) crushed pineapple for nectarines and reduce sugar to 5½ cups.

STRAWBERRY JAM OR PRESERVES

FIVE 6-OUNCE OR FOUR 8-OUNCE JARS OR GLASSES

4 cups strawberries, washed
   and drained
8 cups boiling water

4 cups granulated sugar
1½ teaspoons vinegar or lemon
   juice

1. Place strawberries in colander. Set colander in bowl. Pour boiling water over berries. Let stand 1 minute. Drain well.

2. Place berries in large enamel or stainless-steel saucepan. Crush all or part of berries, depending on individual preference for smooth or chunky jam or preserves.

3. Bring to full rolling boil over medium heat. Boil 2 minutes. Add 2 cups sugar, stirring constantly. Bring to full rolling boil. Boil 3 minutes. Add remaining 2 cups sugar and vinegar. Boil 4 to 5 minutes. Remove from heat. Skim off foam.

4. Pour into hot sterilized jars or glasses (see Sterilizing Jars and Glasses, page 72). Seal with thin layer of paraffin and/or lids.

PINEAPPLE-APRICOT JAM

FOUR 8-OUNCE JARS OR GLASSES

2 cups dried apricots, rinsed
and drained
2½ cups water

2 cups canned crushed pineapple
and juice
½ lemon, sliced
4 cups granulated sugar

1. Place apricots and water in large enamel or stainless-steel saucepan. Cover. Simmer over low heat until tender.
2. Mash apricots. Add pineapple and juice, lemon slices and sugar.
3. Cook over medium-low heat, stirring frequently to prevent scorching, until thickened and clear. Remove from heat. Skim off foam.
4. Pour into hot sterilized jars or jelly glasses (see Sterilizing Jars and Glasses, page 72). Seal with a thin layer of paraffin and/or lids.

OLD-FASHIONED PLUM PRESERVES

THREE 8-OUNCE OR SIX 6-OUNCE JARS OR GLASSES

4 cups plums, washed, cut in half
and pitted

4 cups granulated sugar
1 orange, ground

1. Place plums in large enamel or stainless-steel saucepan. Stir in sugar. Cover. Let stand overnight to extract juices. Add ground orange.
2. Warm plums over low heat, gently stirring with wooden spoon. Cook over medium heat, stirring frequently to prevent scorching, until plums and syrup are thickened, clear and a spoonful dropped on a dish will hold shape. Remove from heat. Skim off foam.
3. Pour into hot sterilized jars or jelly glasses (see Sterilizing Jars and Glasses, page 72). Seal with a thin layer of paraffin and/or lids.

CHERRY PRESERVES: Substitute cherries for plums, being careful to save all juice during pitting process. If cherries are sweet, reduce sugar to 3 cups.

APPLE BUTTER

ABOUT FIVE 8-OUNCE JARS OR GLASSES

5 *pounds tart apples*
Water or apple cider
½ *cup granulated sugar for each*
  1 cup apple pulp
6 *tablespoons lemon juice*
2 *teaspoons grated lemon rind*

1½ *teaspoons ground* or *2 2-inch*
  sticks cinnamon
½ *teaspoon ground* or *1 teaspoon*
  whole cloves
½ *teaspoon ground* or *1 teaspoon*
  whole allspice

1. Wash, core and cut apples into quarters. Measure fruit. Place in large heavy enamel or stainless-steel saucepan.
2. Add 1 cup water or apple cider for each cup apples. Cook over medium-low heat, stirring frequently, until fruit is soft.
3. Press cooked apples through sieve or food mill.
4. Measure pulp into same saucepan. Add ½ cup sugar for each cup pulp. Stir until sugar is dissolved. Add lemon juice and rind. Add ground spices or whole spices tied in a cheesecloth bag. Cook over medium-low heat, stirring frequently, until thickened, or until a rim of liquid does not separate from butter when a small quantity is dropped on a cold dish.
5. Pour into hot sterilized jars or glasses (see Sterilizing Jars and Glasses, page 72). Seal with thin layer of paraffin and/or lids.

PEAR BUTTER: Substitute pears for apples. In Step 2, reduce water to ½ cup for each cup pears.

PEACH OR APRICOT BUTTER

ABOUT FIVE 8-OUNCE JARS OR GLASSES

Whole spices tied in cheesecloth bag will not darken the fruit butter as much as ground spices.

4 *pounds peaches or apricots*
⅔ *cup granulated sugar for each*
  1 cup pulp
4 *tablespoons lemon juice*
1 *teaspoon grated lemon rind*
½ *teaspoon ground* or *2 2-inch*
  sticks cinnamon

½ *teaspoon ground* or *1 teaspoon*
  whole cloves
½ *teaspoon ground* or *1 whole*
  nutmeg, cracked

1. Immerse peaches or apricots in boiling water for 1 minute, or until skins slip off easily. Remove skins and pits. Place in large enamel or stainless-steel saucepan. Crush fruit.
2. Cook over medium-low heat, stirring frequently, until fruit is soft.
3. Press cooked fruit through sieve or food mill.

4. Measure pulp into same saucepan. Add ⅔ cup sugar for each cup pulp. Stir until sugar is dissolved. Add lemon juice and rind. Add ground spices or whole spices tied in bag. Cook over medium-low heat, stirring frequently, until thickened, or until a rim of liquid does not separate from butter when a small quantity is dropped on a cold dish.

5. Pour into hot sterilized jars or glasses (see Sterilizing Jars and Glasses, page 72). Seal with a thin layer of paraffin and/or lids.

FROZEN SPICED CRABAPPLES

16 APPLES

16 small ripe crabapples with stems
1 cup granulated sugar
1 cup water
6 whole cloves
½ cup red cinnamon candies
¼ teaspoon ground ginger
¼ teaspoon salt
3 strips (1½ × ¼ inch) lemon peel

1. Remove blossom end of apples, but do not remove stems or peel. Prick in several places with fork.

2. In large heavy saucepan with tight-fitting cover, combine remaining ingredients. Bring to boil. Place apples stem side up in syrup. Cover. Cook over low heat for 10 minutes. Remove from heat. Cool completely.

3. Lifting apples by stems, place in airtight freezer containers. Strain syrup over apples. Seal. Label and freeze. Thaw 1 to 2 hours before serving.

CHILI SAUCE

ABOUT TWENTY 8-OUNCE JARS

20 pounds ripe tomatoes, washed
   Boiling water
2 pounds onions, peeled
1 dozen medium green peppers,
   washed and seeded
8 cups granulated sugar
1 cup salt
1 tablespoon ground allspice
1 tablespoon ground cinnamon
1 tablespoon ground cloves
1 tablespoon ground red pepper
8 cups vinegar

1. Immerse tomatoes in boiling water for 1 minute or until skins slip off easily. Remove skins.

2. Finely chop tomatoes, onions and green peppers. Place in large enamel or stainless-steel saucepan with tight-fitting cover. Add sugar and salt. Cover. Boil 30 minutes.

3. Add spices and vinegar to vegetable mixture.

4. Cook over low heat, stirring frequently, until thickened, or about 2 to 3 hours depending on the juice in the tomatoes.

5. Pour into sterilized jars (see Sterilizing Jars and Glasses, page 72). Seal.

PEACH OR OTHER FRUIT CHUTNEY

ABOUT EIGHT 8-OUNCE JARS

8 cups peaches, apricots, nectarines
 or mangoes, peeled, pitted and
 chopped
1 lime, seeded and chopped
1 cup seedless raisins
½ cup chopped candied ginger
1 cup finely chopped onion
1 teaspoon salt

1 teaspoon ground cinnamon
½ teaspoon ground cloves
1 teaspoon mustard seed
½ teaspoon ground allspice
½ teaspoon cayenne pepper
2 cups firmly packed brown sugar
1 cup apple cider vinegar
1 cup finely chopped walnut meats

1. In large heavy saucepan with tight-fitting cover, combine all ingredients except walnut meats. Bring to boil, stirring constantly. Cover. Cook over low heat for 2 hours, stirring frequently. Add walnut meats.
2. Spoon into hot sterilized jars (see Sterilizing Jars and Glasses, page 72). Seal.

BLUE RIBBON DILL PICKLES

FOUR 1-QUART JARS

Do not pack cucumbers too tightly in jars, as each quart must have at least 1½ cups of vinegar mixture to keep pickles from spoiling.

30 to 40 cucumbers (3-inch size)
12 sprigs fresh dill, with seeds
12 small hot red peppers
 4 cloves garlic

½ teaspoon powdered alum
2 quarts cider vinegar
1 quart water
1 cup coarse salt

1. Have hot sterilized jars ready (see Sterilizing Jars and Glasses, page 72).
2. Scrub cucumbers. Do not cut off ends.
3. Place sprig of dill in bottom of each jar. Pack cucumbers into jars, distributing among them 3 red peppers and 1 clove garlic to each jar. Place another sprig of dill in center of cucumbers and another on top. Add ⅛ teaspoon alum to each jar.
4. In large enamel or stainless-steel saucepan, combine vinegar, water and salt. Bring to boil. Fill jars with boiling vinegar mixture. Seal. Pickles are better if allowed to ripen several weeks before serving.

Freezing

PREPARATION OF VEGETABLES FOR FREEZING

Choose garden-fresh, young, tender vegetables that are uniform in size and in prime condition. Peas, corn and lima beans should be slightly immature. Salad vegetables (cucumbers, lettuce, sprouts, radishes and cabbage) are not recommended for freezing. A few vegetables, such as squash, celery and sweet potatoes, will require precooking. Water-blanching (scalding) or steam-blanching is necessary for all vegetables in order to inactivate enzymes that bring about chemical changes causing nutritional loss and undesirable flavors. Blanching also makes vegetables more pliable and easier to handle.

TO PREPARE VEGETABLES: Vegetables are prepared for freezing in the same way they are prepared to appear on the table. They must be washed, peeled and cut up. Cleanliness is important because freezing does not kill bacteria but only retards growth.

TO WATER-BLANCH VEGETABLES: In large kettle with cover, bring 4 quarts water to a *furious* boil. Place 1 pound prepared vegetables in steaming basket or colander. Plunge vegetables into boiling water. Cover. Begin timing. See Preparing and Processing Vegetables for Freezing at High Altitude, pages 88–90, for exact time to blanch each vegetable. At end of blanching period, remove vegetables, and chill promptly by putting basket or colander with vegetables into very cold or ice water. This water will have to be changed frequently to maintain the cold temperature. Peas, beans and other vegetables cool in about 2 minutes; larger vegetables require up to 4 minutes or more. The vegetables should feel cold. Drain well on several thicknesses of paper toweling or terry-cloth towel. Pack immediately. Quick-freeze at once.

TO STEAM-BLANCH VEGETABLES: In large kettle with cover, bring 6 quarts water to *furious* boil. Place 1 pound prepared vegetables in steaming basket or colander on rack in kettle. Cover. When steam begins to escape under cover, begin timing. See Preparing and Processing Vegetables for Freezing at High Altitudes, below, for exact length of time to steam-blanch vegetables. Remove vegetables immediately when steaming time is up. Cool quickly in very cold or ice water. Drain well on several thicknesses of paper toweling or terry-cloth towel. Pack in freezing containers to within ½ inch of top. Quick-freeze at once.

PREPARING AND PROCESSING VEGETABLES FOR FREEZING AT HIGH ALTITUDES

This table is for elevations up to 5,000 feet. At elevations of 5,000 or more feet, allow 1 minute longer processing time.

| | | Processing Time to: | |
| | | Water-Blanch | |
Vegetable	Preparation	(*scald*)	Steam-Blanch
Asparagus	Wash. Cut off woody bases, remove scales, if sandy, and sort according to size of stalk.	Small stalks, 2 minutes Large stalks, 4 minutes	2½ minutes 4 minutes
Beans (green or wax)	Wash. Remove ends and strings. Sort according to size and cut lengthwise, slantwise or crosswise; or leave whole.	Cut beans, 2 minutes Whole beans, 3 minutes	2 minutes 3 minutes
Beans (lima)	Shell, wash and sort according to size.	Small beans, 2 minutes Large beans, 3 minutes	
Beets	Cut off tops. Cook in salted water until tender. Cut off stems and roots, slip off skins, cool, and pack in containers whole, sliced or diced.		
Broccoli	If necessary to draw out insects, soak in salt water 20 to 30 minutes. Wash, trim off large leaves, split into 1-inch-thick pieces, and cut off the bases of longer stalks to fit container.	Small stalks, 3 minutes Large stalks, 5 minutes	3 minutes 5 minutes

PREPARING AND PROCESSING VEGETABLES FOR FREEZING AT
HIGH ALTITUDES
(CONTINUED)

Vegetable	Preparation	Processing Time to: Water-Blanch (*scald*)	Steam-Blanch
Brussels sprouts	If necessary to draw out insects, soak in salt water 20 to 30 minutes. Wash carefully, remove loose outer leaves, and sort by size.	Small, 3 minutes Medium, 4 minutes Large, 5 minutes	
Carrots	Cut off tops, wash, scrape, and cut into 1¼-inch slices.	Slices, 3 minutes Small, whole, 5 minutes	3½ minutes 5½ minutes
Cauliflower	Wash, divide into flowerets, and sort according to size.	Small flowerets, 3 minutes Large flowerets, 4 minutes	4 minutes 5 minutes
Corn (on the cob)	Use only young corn. Husk and sort according to size.	Small ears, 6 minutes Medium ears, 8 minutes Large ears, 10 minutes	
Corn (kernel)	Husk. Sort by size. Process only 6 ears at a time. Cool, then cut off kernels, scraping cob with back of knife to extract milk.	Same as corn on cob	
Greens (beet, chard, collards, mustard, spinach)	Wash under running water to remove sand and grit. Discard bruised leaves, cut off tough stems. Process small amount at a time and pack lightly in containers.	2 minutes	
Mixed vegetables	Prepare and process separately. Combine after cooling.		

**PREPARING AND PROCESSING VEGETABLES FOR FREEZING AT
HIGH ALTITUDES**
(CONTINUED)

Vegetable	Preparation	Processing Time to: Water-Blanch (*scald*)	Steam-Blanch
Mushrooms	Wash quickly. Cut off stems at base of cap. Treat for darkening (see Spiced Peaches, page 000), and sort according to size.	Small buttons or quarters, 1½ minutes Medium, whole, 2 minutes	2 minutes 3 minutes
Peas	Wash pods. Shell, and discard any shriveled or dry peas.	Small peas, 1 minute Large peas, 1½ minutes	1⅓ minutes 2 minutes
Peppers (green or red sweet)	Wash, remove seeds and halve, if desired.	2 minutes	
Squash (summer)	Freeze immediately after picking. Wash, cut in ½-inch slices.	Until tender (use salted water)	4 minutes
Squash (winter and pumpkin)	Cook until tender in salted water, or steam. Mash or press through sieve and cool.		

Cookies

HIGH ALTITUDE FACTS ABOUT MAKING AND BAKING COOKIES

Cookies baked from sea-level recipes may require a reduction in the amount of baking powder, soda, cream of tartar and sugar. Butter, high-quality emulsified and hydrogenated shortening make a better-quality cookie. Brown sugar, cream and sour cream assure moistness. Care should be taken not to overmeasure dry ingredients, or overbake the cookies. The dryness in the air will rob baked cookies of their freshness if they are not quickly and carefully stored in airtight containers.

Drop Cookies

BASIC DROP COOKIES

3½ TO 4 DOZEN

1 cup shortening or butter
1 cup granulated sugar
1 cup firmly packed brown sugar
2 eggs
2 tablespoons water
1 teaspoon vanilla extract

1 teaspoon salt
1 teaspoon baking soda
2½ cups sifted all-purpose flour
1 cup chopped pecan or
    walnut meats

1. Preheat oven to 375°F. Have ready ungreased cookie sheet.
2. In mixing bowl, cream shortening or butter with sugars until light and fluffy. Add eggs, water, vanilla extract, salt and soda. Mix well.
3. Add flour to creamed mixture a little at a time, mixing well after each addition. Stir in pecan or walnut meats.
4. Drop by teaspoonfuls onto cookie sheet.
5. Bake for 10 to 12 minutes.

CHERRY DATE COOKIES: In Step 2, reduce baking soda to ½ teaspoon. Add 1 teaspoonful double-acting baking powder. Milk or cream may be substituted for water, if desired. In Step 3, add 1 cup pitted chopped dates, ⅓ cup chopped maraschino cherries, and 2¼ cups crushed cornflakes.

CHOCOLATE OR CAROB CHIP COOKIES: In Step 3, add 1 package (12 ounces) semisweet chocolate or carob pieces with nutmeats.

COCONUT-FRUIT COOKIES: In Step 3, add 1½ cups shredded coconut, ¾ cup pitted, finely chopped dates, ½ cup raisins, and 1 cup small gumdrops with nutmeats.

GRANOLA COOKIES: In Step 3, reduce flour to 2 cups and add 4 cups granola. Omit nutmeats.

PEANUT BUTTER COOKIES: In Step 2, omit water. Add 1 cup peanut butter. In Step 3, omit nutmeats.

PEANUT BUTTER OR BUTTERSCOTCH CHIP COOKIES: In Step 3, add 2 packages (6 ounces each) peanut butter or butterscotch pieces with nutmeats.

SPICE COOKIES: In Step 3, mix and sift flour with 1 teaspoon each ground nutmeg and cinnamon, and ½ teaspoon ground cloves. Use half raisins and half nutmeats, if desired.

TOLL OATS COOKIES: In Step 3, reduce flour to 1½ cups. Add 3 cups quick-cooking rolled oats and 1 package (12 ounces) semisweet chocolate pieces with nutmeats.

CARROT COOKIES WITH CITRUS GLAZE

4 TO 5 DOZEN

¾ cup butter or margarine	2 cups sifted all-purpose flour
1 cup granulated sugar	2 teaspoons double-acting
1 cup cooked and mashed carrots	baking powder
1 egg, beaten	½ teaspoon salt
½ teaspoon vanilla extract	Grated rind of 1 orange

1. Preheat oven to 350°F. Have ready greased cookie sheet.
2. In large mixing bowl, cream butter or margarine with sugar until light and fluffy. Add carrots, beaten egg and vanilla extract. Mix well.
3. Mix and sift flour, baking powder and salt together.
4. Add dry ingredients to creamed mixture a little at a time, mixing well after each addition. Add grated orange rind. Mix well.
5. Drop by teaspoonfuls onto cookie sheet.
6. Bake for about 20 minutes, or until edges of cookies are lightly browned.
7. Glaze immediately with Citrus Glaze, below.

APPLESAUCE COOKIES: In Step 2, substitute firmly packed brown sugar for granulated sugar and ½ cup applesauce for carrots. In Step 3, add ¾ teaspoon ground cinnamon and ¼ teaspoon ground cloves. In Step 4, omit grated orange rind. Add 1 cup raisins and ½ cup chopped nutmeats.

PINEAPPLE COOKIES: In Step 2, substitute ½ cup firmly packed brown sugar for ½ cup granulated sugar and 1 cup crushed pineapple for carrots. In Step 4, omit grated orange rind and add ½ cup chopped nutmeats.

CITRUS GLAZE

Juice of ½ lemon
Juice of ½ orange

1 cup sifted powdered sugar

In small mixing bowl, blend juices with powdered sugar until smooth. Thinly spread on warm cookies.

CHINESE ALMOND COOKIES

ABOUT 3 DOZEN

1 cup butter or shortening
¾ cup granulated sugar
2 eggs, separated
1 teaspoon almond extract
½ teaspoon salt

2¾ cups sifted all-purpose flour
36 to 40 whole unblanched almonds
1 tablespoon water

1. Preheat oven to 350°F. Have ready ungreased cookie sheet.
2. In mixing bowl, cream butter or shortening with sugar until light and fluffy. Beat in egg yolks, almond extract and salt.
3. Add flour to creamed mixture a little at a time, mixing thoroughly after each addition.
4. Wrap dough in waxed paper or plastic. Chill 1 hour.
5. Roll dough into 1½-inch balls. Place on cookie sheet. Flatten each ball slightly and press an almond into its center.
6. Beat egg whites and water together. Brush egg whites over cookies.
7. Bake about 15 minutes, or until golden.

CHOCOLATE DROP COOKIES

4 DOZEN

½ cup shortening or butter
2 ounces chocolate, melted
1 cup firmly packed brown sugar
1 egg, beaten
1 teaspoon vanilla extract
½ teaspoon baking soda
½ cup milk
1¾ cups sifted all-purpose flour

½ teaspoon salt
½ teaspoon double-acting baking powder
½ cup chopped walnut or pecan meats
Creamy Chocolate Frosting, page 111

1. Preheat oven to 350°F. Grease cookie sheet.
2. Melt shortening or butter and chocolate over simmering water.

3. In large mixing bowl, combine chocolate mixture with brown sugar. Add beaten egg and vanilla.
4. Dissolve soda in milk.
5. Sift flour once before measuring. Mix and sift flour, salt and baking powder together.
6. Add dry ingredients alternately with milk, mixing thoroughly after each addition. Stir in nutmeats.
7. Drop by teaspoonfuls onto cookie sheet.
8. Bake for 12 to 15 minutes.
9. Frost with Creamy Chocolate Frosting.

CHOCOLATE CHOCOLATE-CHIP COOKIES: In Step 6, stir in 1 package (6 ounces) semisweet chocolate pieces with nutmeats.

SOFT GINGER COOKIES

ABOUT 10 DOZEN

1 cup butter or shortening	1 tablespoon ground ginger
1½ cups firmly packed brown sugar	1 tablespoon ground cinnamon
3 eggs	1 teaspoon salt
½ cup dark molasses	1½ teaspoons baking soda
5 cups sifted all-purpose flour	1½ cups hot water
4 teaspoons double-acting baking powder	Pecan meats, if desired

1. Preheat oven to 375°F. Have ready ungreased cookie sheet.
2. In mixing bowl, cream butter or shortening with sugar until light and fluffy. Beat in eggs. Add molasses.
3. Mix and sift flour, baking powder, ginger, cinnamon and salt together.
4. Dissolve baking soda in hot water.
5. Add dry ingredients alternately with water, mixing thoroughly after each addition.
6. Drop by teaspoonfuls onto cookie sheet. Decorate top with pecan meat, if desired.
7. Bake for 12 to 15 minutes.

HEALTH COOKIES

ABOUT 4 DOZEN

¾ cup cooking oil
1¼ cups honey or molasses
2 eggs
2 teaspoons vanilla extract
1 cup raisins, or ½ cup raisins
    and ½ cup chopped nutmeats

1½ cups wheat germ
2 cups quick-cooking rolled oats
¾ cup whole-wheat or soy flour,
    or rice polish
1 teaspoon salt
½ cup instant dry milk

1. Preheat oven to 350°F. Cover cookie sheet with aluminum foil or generously greased brown paper.
2. In large mixing bowl, combine oil, honey or molasses, eggs and vanilla extract.
3. In second large bowl, combine raisins, wheat germ, rolled oats, flour or rice polish, salt and instant dry milk. Gradually add to oil-and-honey mixture. Mix until thoroughly blended.
4. Drop or push with finger from teaspoon.
5. Bake about 10 minutes.

HONEY WALNUT COOKIES

7 TO 8 DOZEN

⅔ cup shortening
1 cup granulated sugar
1 cup honey
3 eggs
1 teaspoon vanilla extract
4 cups sifted all-purpose flour

1 teaspoon baking soda
1 teaspoon salt
1 cup dairy sour cream
1 cup chopped walnut meats
½ cup shredded coconut

1. Preheat oven to 375°F. Grease cookie sheet.
2. In mixing bowl, cream shortening with sugar, honey and eggs until light and fluffy. Add vanilla extract.
3. Mix and sift flour, baking soda and salt together.
4. Add dry ingredients alternately with sour cream, mixing well after each addition. Stir in nutmeats and coconut.
5. Drop by teaspoonful onto prepared cookie sheet.
6. Bake for 10 to 12 minutes.

SESAME SEED COOKIES: In Step 4, substitute ¾ cup sesame seeds for walnut meats.

MACAROONS

~~~~~~

2½ TO 3 DOZEN

1 can (8 ounces) almond paste   *1⅓ cups sifted powdered sugar*
3 egg whites

1. Preheat oven to 325°F. Line cookie sheet with aluminum foil and grease generously.
2. In mixing bowl, combine almond paste with egg whites. Mix together. Let stand about 15 minutes.
3. Stir until smooth. Add powdered sugar.
4. Drop onto prepared cookie sheet in amounts no larger than a quarter or a half-dollar.
5. Bake 15 to 20 minutes. Cool until slightly warm on cake rack. If cookies stick, loosen with very sharp knife.

OATMEAL DROP COOKIES

~~~~~~

ABOUT 5 DOZEN

1 cup raisins   *½ teaspoon salt*
½ cup water   *1 teaspoon ground cinnamon*
1 cup butter or shortening   *1 teaspoon ground cloves*
1 cup granulated sugar   *or nutmeg*
2 eggs   *1 cup quick-cooking rolled oats*
1 teaspoon baking soda   *1 cup chopped nutmeats*
2 cups sifted all-purpose flour

1. Cook raisins in water until plumped, about 5 minutes. Cool.
2. Preheat oven to 400°F. Have ready ungreased cookie sheet.
3. In mixing bowl, cream butter or shortening with sugar until light and fluffy. Beat in eggs.
4. Dissolve soda in 4 tablespoons juice from raisins. Add to creamed mixture.
5. Mix and sift flour, salt, cinnamon and cloves or nutmeg together.
6. Add dry ingredients to creamed mixture a little at a time, mixing thoroughly after each addition. Stir in rolled oats, nuts and raisins drained of juice.
7. Drop by teaspoonfuls onto cookie sheet.
8. Bake about 12 minutes.

ORANGE COOKIES

5 TO 6 DOZEN

¾ cup shortening or butter
1¼ cups granulated sugar
2 eggs, well beaten
1 teaspoon vanilla extract
3 cups sifted all-purpose flour
2½ teaspoons double-acting
    baking powder

1 teaspoon baking soda
½ teaspoon salt
1 cup milk
½ cup orange juice
  Grated rind of orange
  Citrus Glaze, page 94

1. Preheat oven to 350°F. Grease cookie sheet.
2. In mixing bowl, cream shortening or butter with sugar until light and fluffy. Beat in eggs and vanilla extract.
3. Mix and sift flour, baking powder, soda and salt together.
4. Add dry ingredients alternately with milk and orange juice, mixing thoroughly after each addition. Add grated orange rind.
5. Drop by teaspoonful onto prepared cookie sheet.
6. Bake for 10 minutes. Cool. Frost with Citrus Glaze.

PUMKPIN COOKIES: In Step 2, add 1½ cups cooked pumpkin and 1½ teaspoons grated lemon rind or 1 teaspoon lemon extract. In Step 3, add ½ teaspoon ground ginger, ½ teaspoon ground nutmeg, ½ teaspoon ground allspice and 1 teaspoon ground cinnamon. In Step 4, omit orange rind and add 1 cup chopped nutmeats and 1 cup cut-up candied fruits, if desired.

PECAN KISSES

ABOUT 9 DOZEN

6 egg whites
2¼ cups firmly packed brown sugar
3 tablespoons sifted all-purpose
    flour

½ teaspoon salt
4 cups chopped pecan meats

1. Preheat oven to 350°F. Generously grease cookie sheet.
2. In mixing bowl, beat egg whites until foamy. Gradually add brown sugar. Continue to beat until mixture stands in high, firm but moist peaks.
3. Mix flour and salt together. Slowly fold into egg-white mixture. Fold in pecan meats.
4. Drop by small teaspoonfuls onto prepared cookie sheet.
5. Bake for 10 to 12 minutes.

SHORTBREAD COOKIES

ABOUT 2 DOZEN

1 *cup softened butter*	½ *cup cornstarch*
1 *cup sifted all-purpose flour*	½ *teaspoon salt*
½ *cup powdered sugar*	½ *teaspoon vanilla extract*

1. Preheat oven to 300°F. Have ready ungreased cookie sheet.
2. Place all ingredients in mixing bowl. Mix together, but do not whip or over-blend.
3. Form dough into 1-inch balls. Place 3 inches apart on cookie sheet. Press with fork to make crisscross design.
4. Bake for about 20 minutes, or until edges of cookies are lightly browned.

LACE COOKIES

ABOUT 4 DOZEN

6 *tablespoons melted butter*	½ *teaspoon salt*
2 *cups firmly packed brown sugar*	2 *teaspoons vanilla extract*
2 *eggs*	2 *cups finely chopped pecan meats*
½ *cup plus 2 tablespoons sifted*	
all-purpose flour	

1. Preheat oven to 325°F. Generously grease and flour cookie sheet.
2. In mixing bowl, cream melted butter with sugar. Beat in eggs.
3. Mix and sift flour and salt together.
4. Add dry ingredients to creamed mixture a little at a time, mixing thoroughly after each addition. Add vanilla extract. Mix well. Stir in nutmeats.
5. Drop by teaspoonfuls 2 inches apart onto prepared cookie sheet.
6. Bake for 5 minutes. Remove from cookie sheet while still warm.

CHIFFON COOKIES

ABOUT 5 DOZEN

½ *cup shortening*	½ *teaspoon baking soda*
1 *cup minus 1 tablespoon*	½ *cup plus 2 tablespoons dairy*
granulated sugar	*sour cream*
1 *egg*	2 *cups sifted all-purpose flour*
1 *teaspoon vanilla extract*	

1. Preheat oven to 400°F. Have ready ungreased cookie sheet.
2. In mixing bowl, cream shortening with sugar until light and fluffy. Beat in egg. Add vanilla extract.
3. Dissolve soda in sour cream.
4. Add flour alternately with sour cream, mixing thoroughly after each addition.
5. Drop by teaspoonfuls onto cookie sheet.
6. Bake for 4 to 6 minutes. Cookies should be lightly brown, soft and cakelike. Store in airtight container.

FLAVORFUL ADDITIONS TO CHIFFON COOKIES:

Sprinkle warm cookies with granulated sugar, nutmeg or finely chopped nutmeats.

In Step 4, add 1 cup shredded coconut.

In Step 2, add 1 teaspoon ground cinnamon and ¼ teaspoon each ground nutmeg and cloves.

In Step 4, add 1 cup raisins or chopped dates, and 1 cup chopped walnut meats.

SWEDISH TOSCAS

3 DOZEN

CRUST

¾ cup butter	1 cup sifted all-purpose flour
½ cup granulated sugar	½ teaspoon salt

FILLING

⅔ cup very finely chopped almonds	¼ cup butter
½ cup granulated sugar	3 tablespoons half-and-half
	4 teaspoons all-purpose flour

1. Preheat oven to 350°F. Have ready muffin pan with 1¼-inch cups or cast-iron tea-cake pans.
2. In medium mixing bowl, cream butter with sugar until light and fluffy. Gradually add flour and salt.
3. Pack into bottom and halfway up sides of muffin pan cups.
4. Bake 10 to 12 minutes or just until pastry is puffy. Do not brown.
5. In small saucepan, combine almonds, sugar, butter, cream and flour. Cook over high heat, stirring constantly, until boiling. Remove from heat. Pour 1 teaspoonful filling into each baked shell. Do not overfill.
6. Bake 15 minutes. Remove from oven. Loosen from pans. Store in airtight container.

Rolled and Molded Cookies

BUTTERSCOTCH REFRIGERATOR COOKIES

ABOUT 8 DOZEN

1¼ cups butter or ¾ cup butter
    and ½ cup shortening
1¾ cups firmly packed brown sugar
  2 eggs
  1 teaspoon vanilla extract

4 cups sifted all-purpose flour
½ teaspoon salt
1 teaspoon baking soda
1 teaspoon fresh cream of tartar
1 cup chopped nutmeats

1. Preheat oven to 375°F. Have ready ungreased cookie sheet.
2. In mixing bowl, cream butter, or butter and shortening, with sugar until light and fluffy. Beat in eggs. Add vanilla extract.
3. Mix and sift flour, salt, soda and cream of tartar together.
4. Add dry ingredients to creamed mixture a little at a time, mixing thoroughly after each addition. Stir in nutmeats.
5. Form dough into rolls 2 inches in diameter. Wrap in waxed paper or plastic. Refrigerate until firm.
6. Cut into slices ¼ inch thick. Place on cookie sheet.
7. Bake 12 to 15 minutes, or until lightly browned.

DATE REFRIGERATOR COOKIES: In Step 2, add 2 tablespoons cream or milk. In Step 4, add 1 cup pitted, chopped dates with nutmeats.

BASIC BUTTER COOKIES

3 TO 4 DOZEN

¾ cup butter
1 cup granulated or sifted
   powdered sugar
2 egg yolks or 1 whole egg, beaten
1 teaspoon vanilla, lemon or
   almond extract

2 cups sifted all-purpose flour
½ teaspoon salt
½ teaspoon baking soda
½ teaspoon fresh cream of tartar
   Colored sugars or candied fruit
   or nutmeats

1. Preheat oven to 350°F. Have ready ungreased cookie sheet.
2. In mixing bowl, cream butter with sugar. Add beaten egg yolks or whole egg and vanilla, lemon or almond extract.
3. Mix and sift flour, salt, soda and cream of tartar together.
4. Add dry ingredients to creamed mixture a little at a time, mixing thoroughly after each addition. Chill dough if sticky.
5. Form dough into 1-inch balls. Place on cookie sheet. Flatten with fork, *or* on lightly floured board, roll out dough to ⅛ inch thick; cut in desired shapes with cookie cutters. *Or* put through cookie press or pastry tube. Sprinkle cookies with colored sugar, or decorate with candied fruit or nutmeats.
6. Bake for about 15 minutes, or until lightly browned around edges.

CHERRY CRUNCHIES: In Step 2, use half granulated and half brown sugar. Use 2 whole eggs. In Step 3, increase flour to 2¼ cups. Substitute 1 teaspoon double-acting baking powder for cream of tartar. In Step 4, add 1 cup chopped pecan meats, 1 cup chopped dates and ⅓ cup sliced maraschino cherries. Crush 2½ cups cornflakes. In Step 5, roll each ball in crushed cornflakes. Place on greased cookie sheet. Top with slice of maraschino cherry.

CHOCOLATE BUTTER COOKIES: In Step 2, add 2 ounces melted unsweetened chocolate and 1 tablespoon rum or brandy, if desired. Do not use lemon extract. In Step 4, add 1 cup finely chopped nutmeats, if desired.

LEMON BUTTER COOKIES: In Step 2, use lemon extract and add 2 teaspoons grated lemon rind.

FLAVORFUL ADDITIONS TO BASIC BUTTER COOKIES:

Sprinkle with colored sugars, cinnamon-sugar mix, chocolate shot or colored decorations.

Cut rolled out dough into squares, rounds, or triangles. Place 1 teaspoonful jelly, mincemeat, fruit filling, or few chocolate pieces in center of one cookie. Top with another cookie and seal edges with fingers or fork.

Divide dough into rolls 1½ inches in diameter. Roll dough in finely chopped nutmeats, colored sugars or crushed cereal flakes. Cut in slices ¼ inch thick.

Frost with Chocolate Glaze, page 113, Powdered Sugar Glaze, page 114, or brush with cream or egg white.

CRESCENTS

4 TO 5 DOZEN

½ cup butter
½ cup shortening
1½ cups sifted powdered sugar
1 tablespoon water

1 tablespoon vanilla extract
½ teaspoon salt
2 cups sifted all-purpose flour
1¼ cups ground almonds

1. Preheat oven to 350°F. Have ready ungreased cookie sheet.
2. In mixing bowl, cream butter and shortening with 1 cup sugar until light and fluffy. Add water, vanilla extract and salt.
3. Add sifted flour to creamed mixture a little at a time, mixing thoroughly after each addition. Blend in ground almonds.
4. Shape dough into 1-inch balls or crescents, using 1 level tablespoon of dough for each cookie. Place on cookie sheet.
5. Bake for about 15 minutes, or until lightly browned. Roll in remaining ½ cup powdered sugar while still warm.

GRANDMOTHER'S SUGAR COOKIES

ABOUT 4 DOZEN

½ cup plus 1 tablespoon shortening
1 cup granulated sugar
1 egg
1 teaspoon vanilla extract
1 teaspoon baking soda

½ cup buttermilk
3 cups sifted all-purpose flour
1 teaspoon double-acting
baking powder
½ teaspoon salt

1. Preheat oven to 425°F. Have ready ungreased cookie sheet.
2. In mixing bowl, cream shortening with sugar until light and fluffy. Beat in egg and vanilla extract.
3. Dissolve soda in buttermilk.
4. Mix and sift flour, baking powder and salt together.
5. Add dry ingredients alternately with buttermilk, mixing thoroughly after each addition.
6. On lightly floured surface, roll out dough ⅛ inch thick. Cut into desired size or shape. Sprinkle with additional granulated sugar (colored sugars are nice at Christmas time). Place on cookie sheet.
7. Bake for 5 to 6 minutes.

CLASSIC SUGAR COOKIES: In Step 2, increase eggs to 2. Substitute 1 teaspoon lemon juice and grated rind of 1 lemon for vanilla extract, if desired. In Step 3, omit buttermilk. Add 2 tablespoons half-and-half, and ¼ teaspoon each ground cinnamon and nutmeg, if desired.

SWEDISH SPRITZ

ABOUT 5 DOZEN

1 cup butter (do not substitute)	2¼ cups sifted all-purpose flour
¾ cup granulated sugar	½ teaspoon double-acting
1 egg	baking powder
1 teaspoon almond extract	¼ teaspoon salt

1. Preheat oven to 400°F. Have ready ungreased cookie sheet.
2. In mixing bowl, cream butter with sugar until light and fluffy. Add egg and almond extract. Beat well.
3. Mix and sift flour, baking powder and salt together.
4. Add dry ingredients to creamed mixture a little at a time, mixing thoroughly after each addition.
5. Fill cookie press or pastry tube with dough. Form cookies in desired shapes on ungreased cookie sheet.
6. Bake for 10 to 12 minutes. Decorate, if desired.

SPICED MOLASSES NUGGETS

3½ DOZEN

½ cup melted butter or shortening	1 teaspoon ground cinnamon
¼ cup granulated sugar	½ teaspoon ground ginger
⅓ cup molasses	½ cup chopped nutmeats
1½ cups sifted all-purpose flour	Powdered sugar
¼ teaspoon salt	

1. Preheat oven to 350°F. Have ready ungreased cookie sheet.
2. In mixing bowl, combine melted butter or shortening with sugar and molasses. Blend well.
3. Mix and sift flour, salt, cinnamon and ginger together.
4. Add dry ingredients to molasses mixture a little at a time, mixing thoroughly after each addition. Stir in nutmeats.
5. Roll dough into ¾-inch balls. Place 1 inch apart on cookie sheet.
6. Bake for 15 minutes. Roll in powdered sugar while still warm. Keeps well in tightly covered container.

Bars and Squares

BASIC BROWNIES

½ cup butter or margarine
2 ounces unsweetened chocolate
1 cup granulated sugar
2 eggs, beaten
1 teaspoon vanilla extract

½ cup plus 2 tablespoons sifted
  all-purpose flour
¼ teaspoon salt
½ to 1 cup chopped nutmeats

1. Preheat oven to 350°F. Grease and flour 8 × 8 × 2-inch pan.
2. In top of double boiler, melt butter or margarine with chocolate over simmering water. Remove from heat. Cool to lukewarm.
3. Gradually blend in sugar. Add beaten eggs and vanilla extract. Add sifted flour and salt to chocolate mixture a little at a time, mixing thoroughly after each addition. Stir in nutmeats. Spread batter into prepared pan.
4. Bake 25 minutes. Cool. Frost with one-half recipe Fudge Frosting, page 000, or dust with powdered sugar. Cut into bars.

CHOCOLATE-CHIP BROWNIES: In Step 3, add 1 package (6 ounces) semisweet chocolate pieces with nutmeats.

SAUCEPAN BROWNIES

ABOUT 2 DOZEN

⅓ cup shortening
⅓ cup cocoa
1 cup granulated sugar
¼ cup milk
½ cup sifted all-purpose flour
¼ teaspoon double-acting
    baking powder

½ teaspoon salt
2 eggs, well beaten
1 teaspoon vanilla extract
½ cup chopped nutmeats

1. Preheat oven to 350°F. Generously grease and flour 8 × 8 × 2-inch pan.
2. In saucepan large enough to hold all ingredients, over medium heat, melt shortening and cocoa together. Add sugar and milk. Bring to boil. Remove from heat.
3. Mix and sift flour, baking powder and salt together. Gradually add to hot mixture. Stir until smooth. Add well-beaten eggs and vanilla extract. Beat until well blended. Add nutmeats.
4. Pour into prepared pan.
5. Bake 25 to 30 minutes. Cool. Cut into bars.

NOTE: This recipe is easily doubled or tripled.

LEMON SQUARES

ABOUT 1½ DOZEN

½ cup butter or margarine
1 cup plus 2 tablespoons flour
¼ cup sifted powdered sugar
1 cup granulated sugar
½ teaspoon double-acting
    baking powder

2 teaspoons lemon juice
   Grated rind of 1 lemon
2 eggs, slightly beaten

1. Preheat oven to 350°F. Grease and flour 9 × 9 × 2-inch pan.
2. In small bowl, cut butter or margarine into 1 cup flour and powdered sugar with two table knives or pastry blender until consistency of small grain. Pat into bottom of prepared pan.
3. Bake 15 minutes.
4. Meanwhile, in same bowl, combine granulated sugar, remaining 2 table-spoons flour and baking powder. Add lemon juice, rind and eggs. Pour over baked crust.
5. Bake 20 to 25 minutes. Sprinkle with additional powdered sugar. Cool. Cut into squares.

OATMEAL RAISIN BARS

ABOUT 1½ DOZEN

½ cup butter or margarine
½ cup honey
1 egg, beaten
1 teaspoon vanilla extract
1¼ cups quick-cooking oats

½ cup whole-wheat flour
1 teaspoon baking powder
½ teaspoon salt
½ cup chopped nutmeats
½ cup raisins

1. Preheat oven to 350°F. Grease and flour 8 × 8 × 2-inch pan.
2. In medium mixing bowl, cream together butter or margarine, honey, egg and vanilla extract.
3. In medium bowl, mix together oats, flour, baking powder and salt. Add nutmeats and raisins. Combine with egg mixture. Spread evenly in prepared pan.
4. Bake 25 minutes. Cool. Cut into bars.

ROCKY MOUNTAIN TOFFEE BARS

ABOUT 3 DOZEN

1 cup shortening or butter
1 cup firmly packed brown sugar
1 egg yolk, beaten
1 teaspoon vanilla extract
2 cups sifted all-purpose flour

1 teaspoon salt
1 package (6 ounces) semisweet
  chocolate pieces, melted
½ cup finely chopped nutmeats

1. Preheat oven to 350°F. Grease 13 × 9 × 2-inch pan or cookie sheet.
2. In mixing bowl, cream shortening or butter with brown sugar until light and fluffy. Add beaten egg yolk and vanilla extract.
3. Mix and sift flour and salt together.
4. Add dry ingredients to creamed mixture a little at a time, mixing thoroughly after each addition. Press dough into prepared pan or cookie sheet.
5. Bake for 15 to 20 minutes. Remove from oven. Spread melted chocolate over top of bars. Sprinkle with nutmeats. Cool. Cut into bars.

Frostings, Fillings, Toppings and Glazes

HIGH ALTITUDE FACTS ABOUT MAKING FROSTINGS

Watch cooked frostings closely above 2,500 feet. The thinner air allows them to reach the done stage more quickly. See High Altitude Facts About Making Candies, page 65.

BASIC COOKED FROSTING

FILLING AND FROSTING FOR THREE 8- OR 9-INCH LAYERS, OR FROSTING FOR 14 × 9 × 2-INCH SHEET CAKE

3 egg whites	1 tablespoon light corn syrup
2¼ cups granulated sugar	½ cup water
¼ teaspoon salt	1 teaspoon vanilla extract

1. In top of double boiler, combine egg whites, sugar, salt, corn syrup and water.
2. Cook over boiling water, beating continually with electric mixer set at high speed, until frosting holds shape when beater is raised and is of a consistency for spreading. Do not let frosting crystallize. Add vanilla extract.

COOKED LEMON FROSTING: In Step 1, substitute ¼ cup lemon juice for ¼ cup water. In Step 2 substitute 1 teaspoon grated lemon rind for vanilla extract.

COOKED ORANGE FROSTING: In Step 1, substitute ½ cup orange juice for water. In Step 2, add ¼ teaspoon *fresh* cream of tartar and 8 marshmallows, quartered. Substitute ½ teaspoon grated orange rind for vanilla extract. Fold marshmallows into cooked mixture immediately after removing from heat, stirring until partially dissolved.

COOKED PEPPERMINT CANDY FROSTING: In Step 2, add 1 cup crushed peppermint candy.

LADY BALTIMORE FROSTING: In Step 2, add ⅓ cup chopped, dried figs, ⅔ cup pitted, chopped dates and ½ cup chopped golden raisins after removing from heat.

SEAFOAM FROSTING: In Step 1, substitute brown sugar for granulated sugar and dark corn syrup for light, if desired.

BUTTERCREAM FROSTING

FILLING AND FROSTING FOR TWO 8- OR 9-INCH LAYERS, OR FROSTING FOR ONE 14 × 9 × 2-INCH SHEET CAKE

⅓ cup softened butter	*¼ cup cream, evaporated milk*
¼ teaspoon salt	*or milk, or 2 egg yolks or*
3½ cups (1 pound) sifted	*1 egg*
powdered sugar	*1 teaspoon vanilla extract*

1. In mixing bowl, blend together butter, salt and half of powdered sugar.
2. With electric mixer or spoon, beat until smooth. Alternately add cream, evaporated milk, milk, egg yolks or egg and remaining powdered sugar. Beat until smooth, fluffy and consistency for spreading. Add vanilla extract. If too thin, add a little powdered sugar. If too thick, add a few drops of milk.

ALMOND BUTTERCREAM FROSTING: In Step 2, substitute ¾ teaspoon almond extract for vanilla extract.

AMARETTO CREAM FROSTING: In Step 2, substitute 1 tablespoon amaretto liqueur for vanilla extract.

LEMON BUTTERCREAM FROSTING: In Step 2, use egg yolks. Add 3½ tablespoons lemon juice. Substitute ½ to 1 teaspoon grated lemon rind for vanilla extract.

MAPLE BUTTERCREAM FROSTING: In Step 2, substitute ⅓ cup maple syrup for cream, milk, egg yolks or egg.

ORANGE BUTTERCREAM FROSTING: In Step 2, substitute 3½ tablespoons orange juice for cream or milk or egg yolks or egg. Substitute 1 to 2 teaspoons grated orange rind for vanilla extract.

PEACH BRANDY CREAM FROSTING: In Step 2, substitute 1 tablespoon peach brandy for vanilla extract.

CARAMEL BUTTERCREAM FROSTING: Make caramel syrup. In heavy pan, melt ¼ cup granulated sugar over low heat until dark golden brown, stirring constantly. Add ¼ cup boiling water. Remove from heat. Stir until sugar is dissolved. In Step 2, substitute ⅓ cup caramel syrup for cream, milk, egg yolks, or eggs.

CHOCOLATE BUTTERCREAM FROSTING: In Step 2, add ⅓ cup cocoa or carob powder, *or* add 2½ ounces unsweetened chocolate, melted together with ½ cup plus 1 tablespoon cream over simmering water.

CHOCOLATE MINT BUTTERCREAM FROSTING: Follow directions for Chocolate Buttercream Frosting. In Step 2, substitute ½ teaspoon peppermint extract or oil of peppermint for vanilla extract.

COFFEE BUTTERCREAM FROSTING: In Step 2, substitute ¼ cup strong coffee for cream, milk, egg yolks or eggs, *or* add 2 tablespoons instant coffee.

BLUE RIBBON BUTTER FROSTING

FILLING AND FROSTING FOR THREE 8- OR 9-INCH LAYERS
OR FROSTING FOR ONE 14 × 9 × 2-INCH SHEET CAKE

5 tablespoons cake flour	½ teaspoon salt
1 cup milk	1¾ cups sifted powdered sugar
1 cup softened butter	½ cup coarsely chopped nutmeats,
1 cup granulated sugar	if desired
1 teaspoon vanilla extract	

1. In top of double boiler, gradually blend together flour and milk. Cook over boiling water, stirring constantly, until mixture forms a thick, nearly stiff, paste. Cover with plastic wrap. Cool.
2. In mixing bowl, cream butter with sugar until very light and fluffy. Add cooled paste, vanilla extract, and salt. Beat until smooth.
3. Fill cake with one-third of mixture.
4. Add powdered sugar to remaining two-thirds. Add nutmeats if desired. Blend well. Spread on top and sides of cake.

CRÈME DE CACAO FROSTING: In Step 1, reduce milk to ¾ cup. After cooking, add ¼ cup crème de cacao.

CREAMY CHOCOLATE FROSTING

FROSTING FOR TWO 8- OR 9-INCH LAYERS
OR ONE 14 × 9 × 2-INCH SHEET CAKE

2 ounces unsweetened chocolate
4 tablespoons water
6 tablespoons butter
2 egg yolks, beaten

½ teaspoon salt
3½ cups (1 pound) sifted
powdered sugar

1. In top of double boiler, melt chocolate, water and butter together over simmering water. Cool. Add beaten egg yolks and salt.
2. Bring to boil over medium-low heat. Cook 2 minutes, stirring constantly.
3. Remove from heat. Blend in powdered sugar. Beat well until consistency for easy spreading.

ROCKY ROAD FROSTING: In Step 1, add 1 cup miniature marshmallows. In Step 3, stir in 1 additional cup miniature marshmallows and ½ cup chopped walnut meats.

COCONUT-NUT FROSTING

FILLING AND FROSTING FOR TOPS OF THREE 8- OR 9-INCH LAYERS
OR ONE 14 × 9 × 2-INCH SHEET CAKE

1½ cups butter
½ cup evaporated milk
½ cup half-and-half
1 cup granulated sugar
3 egg yolks, beaten

½ teaspoon salt
1 teaspoon vanilla extract
1 cup shredded coconut
1 cup chopped nutmeats

1. In heavy saucepan, combine butter, evaporated milk, cream, sugar, beaten egg yolks and salt. Cook over low heat, stirring constantly until mixture is thickened. Remove from heat.
2. Add vanilla extract, coconut and nutmeats. Beat until consistency for easy spreading.

CREAM CHEESE FROSTING

FILLING AND FROSTING FOR TWO 8- OR 9-INCH LAYERS
OR ONE 14 × 9 × 2-INCH SHEET CAKE

2 packages (3 ounces each)
cream cheese
4 tablespoons half-and-half
2 tablespoons softened butter

3½ cups (1 pound) sifted
powdered sugar
¼ teaspoon salt
1 teaspoon vanilla extract

In mixing bowl, beat cream cheese, half-and-half and butter together until fluffy. Gradually add powdered sugar. Add salt and vanilla extract.

CHOCOLATE CREAM CHEESE FROSTING: Add 2 ounces melted, unsweetened chocolate with cream cheese.

ORANGE CREAM CHEESE FROSTING: Substitute orange juice for half-and-half, and grated orange rind for vanilla extract.

FLAVORFUL ADDITIONS TO CREAM CHEESE FROSTING: Add ½ cup finely chopped nutmeats, shredded coconut or other well-drained fruits.

FUDGE SAUCE OR FROSTING

ABOUT 4 CUPS SAUCE OR
FILLING AND FROSTING FOR THREE 8- OR 9-INCH LAYERS

1 package (6 ounces) semisweet chocolate pieces	1½ cups evaporated milk
½ cup butter	½ teaspoon salt
3½ cups (1 pound) sifted powdered sugar	1 teaspoon vanilla extract

FUDGE SAUCE

1. In heavy saucepan, over low heat, melt chocolate pieces and butter.
2. Remove from heat. Add 2 cups powdered sugar alternately with milk, beating well after each addition. Add salt.
3. Return to heat. Bring to boil, stirring constantly. Cook, stirring constantly, 8 minutes.
4. Remove from heat. Add vanilla extract.

FUDGE FROSTING: Cool 2 cups sauce to room temperature. Blend in remaining 1½ cups powdered sugar. Beat well.

PENUCHE FROSTING

FILLING AND FROSTING FOR TWO 8- OR 9-INCH LAYERS
OR ONE 14 × 9 × 2-INCH SHEET CAKE

¾ cup granulated sugar	¼ teaspoon salt
¾ cup firmly packed brown sugar	1 tablespoon light corn syrup
½ cup butter	1 teaspoon vanilla extract
½ cup vegetable shortening	1 cup chopped nutmeats
½ cup milk	

1. In heavy saucepan combine sugars, butter, shortening, milk, salt and corn syrup. Cook over low heat to full rolling boil, stirring constantly. Boil 2 minutes.
2. Cool until lukewarm. Add vanilla extract. Beat until of consistency for spreading. Add nutmeats.

SEVEN-MINUTE FROSTING

FILLING AND FROSTING FOR TWO 8- OR 9-INCH LAYERS
OR ONE 14 × 9 × 2-INCH SHEET CAKE

2 *egg whites*	¼ *teaspoon fresh cream of tartar*
⅞ *cup granulated sugar*	2 *tablespoons light corn syrup*
3 *tablespoons cold water*	½ *teaspoon vanilla extract*

In top of double boiler, combine egg whites, sugar, water, cream of tartar and light corn syrup. Cook over boiling water, beating continually with electric mixer or rotary beater for 7 minutes, or until frosting holds shape when beater is raised and is consistency for spreading. Remove from heat. Add vanilla extract.

COCONUT SEVEN-MINUTE FROSTING: Add ½ cup shredded coconut, *or* substitute fresh coconut milk for water and add ½ cup fresh, grated coconut.

PEPPERMINT SEVEN-MINUTE FROSTING: Substitute ¼ teaspoon peppermint extract for vanilla extract, *or* add ½ cup crushed peppermint candy.

BROWN SUGAR GLAZE

GLAZE FOR ABOUT 1 DOZEN SWEET YEAST ROLLS,
1 COFFEE CAKE, OR 9-INCH SQUARE CAKE

1 *cup firmly packed brown sugar*	¼ *cup half-and-half*
2 *tablespoons butter*	⅛ *teaspoon salt*

In 1-quart heavy saucepan, combine all ingredients. Boil over medium heat for 1 minute. Remove from heat. Spread on rolls or cake while hot.

CHOCOLATE GLAZE

GLAZE FOR TOP OF AN 8- OR 9-INCH CAKE OR
1 DOZEN DOUGHNUTS, CREAM PUFFS, OR ECLAIRS

2 *tablespoons butter*	2 *tablespoons powdered sugar*
2 *ounces unsweetened chocolate*	⅛ *teaspoon salt*

In top of double boiler, blend together all ingredients. Cook over simmering water, stirring until smooth. Use while warm.

POWDERED SUGAR GLAZE

GLAZE FOR 2 DOZEN DOUGHNUTS, ECLAIRS, CREAM PUFFS, OR
SWEET ROLLS, OR 2 COFFEE CAKES

1 cup sifted powdered sugar   ½ teaspoon vanilla extract
2 tablespoons milk or half-and-half
   or 5 teaspoons water

In mixing bowl, combine all ingredients. Mix thoroughly.

CHOCOLATE POWDERED SUGAR GLAZE: Add 2 tablespoons softened butter, 1 or 2 ounces melted unsweetened chocolate, and ⅛ teaspoon salt. Use boiling water.

CITRUS POWDERED SUGAR GLAZE: Substitute juice of ½ lemon and ½ orange for milk, half-and-half or water. Add 1 tablespoon butter, if desired.

PINEAPPLE POWDERED SUGAR GLAZE: Substitute pineapple juice for water.

BAKE-ON TOPPING

TOPPING FOR 14 × 9 × 2-INCH SHEET CAKE, 1½ DOZEN
SWEET YEAST ROLLS, OR TWO 8-INCH COFFEE CAKES

6 tablespoons melted butter   1 cup chopped nutmeats, shredded
⅔ cup firmly packed brown sugar   coconut or granola
¼ cup evaporated milk

1. In mixing bowl, blend all ingredients together.
2. When cake is baked, remove from oven. Quickly spread topping over cake. Return to oven and cook under broiler as far away from flame or electric element as possible for about 5 minutes. Topping may be spread on cooled cake and placed under broiler until it bubbles.

STREUSEL TOPPING

TOPPING FOR 12 TO 15 MUFFINS OR SWEET YEAST ROLLS,
OR ONE 10-INCH COFFEE CAKE

2 tablespoons all-purpose flour
2 teaspoons ground cinnamon
½ cup firmly packed brown or
    granulated sugar

2 tablespoons melted butter
½ cup chopped pecan or
    walnut meats

1. In mixing bowl, blend flour, cinnamon and sugar together. Work in butter. (The mixture will be crumbly and dry.) Add chopped pecan or walnut meats.
2. Sprinkle over top of unbaked batter or dough.

FRENCH CUSTARD FILLING

FILLING FOR THREE 8-INCH LAYERS, 6 CREAM PUFFS OR ECLAIRS

¾ cup granulated sugar
5 tablespoons all-purpose flour, or
    3 tablespoons cornstarch
¼ teaspoon salt
2 cups scalded milk

2 eggs, beaten
1½ teaspoons vanilla extract
1 cup whipping cream whipped,
    if desired

1. In medium saucepan, mix together sugar, flour or cornstarch and salt. Over low heat, gradually stir in scalded milk. Bring slowly to boil, stirring constantly. Remove from heat. Stir a little hot mixture into beaten eggs, then gradually stir egg mixture into hot mixture. Cook over low heat, stirring constantly and vigorously for 3 minutes. (Custard will hold shape on end of spoon when lifted out of pan.)
2. Cool. Add vanilla extract. Fold in whipped cream, if desired.

ALMOND CUSTARD FILLING: In Step 2, use ¾ teaspoon each vanilla extract and almond extract. Add 1 cup chopped, toasted almonds.

BANANA CUSTARD FILLING: In Step 2, add 2 thinly sliced bananas.

BUTTERSCOTCH CUSTARD FILLING: In Step 1, substitute brown sugar for granulated sugar. Add 4 tablespoons butter and 3 tablespoons caramel syrup, if desired.

CHOCOLATE CUSTARD FILLING: In Step 1, add 2 ounces unsweetened chocolate and 2 tablespoons butter to scalded milk.

COCONUT CUSTARD FILLING: In Step 2, add ½ cup shredded or grated coconut.

COFFEE CUSTARD FILLING: In Step 1, add 2 teaspoons instant coffee to scalded milk, *or* substitute 1 cup cream and ½ cup strong coffee for milk. For stronger flavor, more coffee may be added to taste.

LEMON CUSTARD FILLING: In Step 1, use cornstarch. Increase sugar to 1 cup. Substitute 4 tablespoons lemon juice and 1¼ cups water for milk. In Step 2, omit vanilla extract. Add 1 teaspoon grated lemon rind and 1 tablespoon butter.

MACADAMIA OR HAZELNUT CUSTARD FILLING: In Step 2, add 2 cups finely chopped (in blender or food processor) hazelnuts or macadamia nuts.

SHERRY OR RUM CUSTARD FILLING: In Step 2, substitute 1 tablespoon sherry wine or rum for vanilla extract.

FRUIT FILLING FOR SWEET YEAST ROLLS, COFFEE CAKES AND COOKIES

FILLING FOR 2 DOZEN ROLLS, 2 COFFEE CAKES, OR ABOUT 5 DOZEN COOKIES

3 *cups pitted, finely chopped dates*
1 *cup water*
¼ *teaspoon salt*
½ *to 1 cup granulated or firmly packed brown sugar*

1 *tablespoon lemon or orange juice*
½ *cup finely chopped nutmeats, if desired*

In 2-quart saucepan, cook dates with water until soft. Add salt and sugar. Continue cooking over medium-low heat until thickened, stirring frequently. Add lemon or orange juice and nutmeats, if desired.

COCONUT FILLING: Substitute 1½ cups shredded coconut for dates. Reduce water and sugar to ½ cup and lemon juice to 1 teaspoon. Add ⅓ cup honey, 1 tablespoon butter, and ½ teaspoon vanilla extract. Cook until coconut absorbs most of syrup. Stir in vanilla extract and butter. Cool.

MINCEMEAT FILLINGS: Substitute prepared mincemeat for dates. Reduce sugar to ½ cup. Mix 2 tablespoons cornstarch with sugar.

PRUNE FILLING: Substitute tenderized prunes for dates. Add 1 teaspoon vanilla extract.

RAISIN OR DRIED FRUIT FILLING: Substitute raisins or other cut-up dried fruit for dates. Add 2 tablespoons butter.

QUICK LEMON FILLING

¼ cup granulated sugar	3 tablespoons lemon juice
1½ tablespoons cornstarch	½ teaspoon grated lemon rind
½ teaspoon salt	1 tablespoon butter
½ cup water	

1. In saucepan, mix together sugar, cornstarch and salt. Stir in water, lemon juice, lemon rind and butter.
2. Cook over medium heat to rolling boil. Reduce heat. Boil 1 minute, stirring constantly. Cool. Beat with rotary beater before using.

QUICK PEACH FILLING: In Step 1, substitute 1 package (10 ounces) frozen, thawed, sliced peaches and juice for water. Reduce lemon juice to 1 tablespoon. Omit lemon rind. Add a dash of nutmeg, if desired.

QUICK PINEAPPLE FILLING: In Step 1, substitute 1 can (13½ ounces) crushed pineapple and juice for water. Reduce lemon juice to 1 tablespoon. Omit lemon rind.

QUICK STRAWBERRY FILLING: In Step 1, substitute 1 package (10 ounces) frozen, thawed, sliced or halved strawberries and juice for water. Omit lemon juice and rind.

Desserts and Dessert Sauces

HIGH ALTITUDE FACTS ABOUT MAKING DESSERTS AND DESSERT SAUCES

The greatest difference in making desserts at high altitudes is in the cooking times and temperatures.

Generally, it is necessary to increase time and/or temperature when making desserts on the top of the stove or in the oven.

Direct heat and a heavy saucepan work more satisfactorily than the customary double boiler used for making custards, puddings and fillings. Not only does direct heat hasten the cooking process, but when a recipe calls for cornstarch or flour, direct heat is the most efficient means by which to obtain maximum thickening of the starch and to eliminate the raw taste that comes from undercooking. Desserts and dessert sauces cooked on top of the stove must be constantly stirred to prevent scorching.

The addition of a small amount of liquid in batters or pastries may be needed to offset the effects of drier air. Extra-large eggs benefit all desserts that call for eggs, adding moisture and stabilizing cheesecakes, mousses, soufflés and other baked dessert mixtures.

APPLE OR PEACH TURNOVERS

6 SERVINGS

6 *medium apples or peaches*
½ *cup boiling water*
¾ *cup granulated sugar*
¼ *teaspoon salt*

½ *teaspoon ground cinnamon*
½ *teaspoon ground nutmeg*
2-*crust pastry of choice, page 000*
Lemon Sauce, page 138

1. Preheat oven to 400°F. Have ungreased cookie sheet ready.
2. Peel, core and slice apples or peaches. Place in saucepan with cover.
3. Add water. Cover. Cook over medium heat 10 minutes. Stir in sugar, salt, cinnamon and nutmeg. Simmer 2 minutes to dissolve sugar. Cool.
4. On lightly floured board, roll out pastry to ⅛ inch thick. Divide pastry into 7-inch squares or circles. Fill center of each square or circle with ¼ cup fruit mixture. Dampen edges of pastry with water. Fold pastry over filling in triangle or half-moon shape. Press edges together tightly. Crimp with fork. Prick crust or cut slits to allow steam to escape during baking.
5. Bake for 30 minutes. Serve with Lemon Sauce.

BLUEBERRY SUPREME

ABOUT 6 SERVINGS

CRUST

1¼ *cups sifted all-purpose flour*
2 *tablespoons sugar*

½ *cup butter*

1. Preheat oven to 400°F. Have ready 9-inch baking dish.
2. Into small mixing bowl, sift flour and sugar together. With two table knives or pastry blender, cut butter into dry ingredients until mixture resembles small grain.
3. Press dough into bottom of baking dish with fingers. Bake for 25 minutes. Meanwhile, prepare filling:

FILLING

Follow directions for French Custard Filling, page 115. In Step 1, add 3 tablespoons flour with eggs. Cool. Pour into baked crust.

BLUEBERRY TOPPING

6 *tablespoons granulated sugar*
3 *tablespoons cornstarch*
⅛ *teaspoon salt*
4 *cups canned drained blueberries*
   (*reserve juice*)

2 *teaspoons butter*
2 *teaspoons lemon juice*
1 *cup whipping cream, whipped*

1. In saucepan, mix sugar, cornstarch and salt together. Gradually add 1 cup blueberry juice. Cook over low heat, stirring constantly, until thickened and clear; do not undercook.
2. Add butter, blueberries and lemon juice.
3. Remove from heat. Pour over custard filling. Top with whipped cream.

BREAD PUDDING

6 TO 8 SERVINGS

2 cups dry bread or cake cubes	¼ teaspoon salt
4 cups scalded milk	¼ teaspoon ground nutmeg
¼ cup melted butter	4 eggs, beaten
1 tablespoon cornstarch	1 teaspoon vanilla extract
1 cup granulated sugar	½ cup raisins

1. Preheat oven to 350°F. Butter 2-quart casserole or baking dish.
2. In mixing bowl, soak bread or cake cubes in scalded milk for 5 minutes. Add melted butter, cornstarch, sugar, salt and nutmeg. Slowly add beaten eggs. Add vanilla extract and raisins.
3. Pour into prepared baking dish. Place in pan on oven rack. Pour boiling water into pan to depth of 1 inch.
4. Bake about 1 hour and 15 minutes, or until knife inserted in center comes out clean.

APPLE BREAD PUDDING: In Step 2, separate eggs (beat whites until stiff, but not dry). Add 2 cups peeled and finely chopped apples. Add ½ teaspoon ground cinnamon, 1 tablespoon lemon juice, ½ cup chopped citron and ½ cup finely chopped almonds, if desired. At end of Step 2, fold in stiffly beaten egg whites. Omit raisins.

CARAMEL BREAD PUDDING: In Step 2, in small skillet, over low heat, melt ½ cup granulated sugar until golden brown. Dissolve in scalded milk. Use remaining ½ cup granulated sugar as directed. Add ¼ cup kirsch or rum, if desired. Omit raisins.

CHOCOLATE BREAD PUDDING: In Step 2, add 2 ounces melted unsweetened chocolate with eggs. Substitute cinnamon for nutmeg and chopped nutmeats for raisins.

LEMON BREAD PUDDING: In Step 2, add 2 tablespoons grated lemon rind, 2 tablespoons lemon juice and ½ cup nutmeats, if desired. Omit nutmeg. Reduce vanilla extract to ½ teaspoon. Omit raisins.

WHOLE-WHEAT BREAD PUDDING: In Step 2, substitute whole-wheat bread for white bread cubes. Add 1 cup pitted chopped dates. Omit raisins. Before baking, sprinkle top of pudding generously with shredded coconut.

FAMOUS CHEESECAKE WITH FILLING AND STRAWBERRY GLAZE

▼▼

ABOUT 8 TO 10 SERVINGS

CRUST

1 *cup sifted all-purpose flour*	½ *teaspoon vanilla extract*
¼ *cup granulated sugar*	1 *egg yolk*
1 *teaspoon grated lemon peel*	¼ *cup softened butter*

1. Generously butter 9-inch springform pan.
2. In small mixing bowl, mix together flour, sugar, lemon peel and vanilla extract. Add egg yolk and butter. Mix together with fingers until dry ingredients are worked into butter and egg. Press into bottom and around sides of prepared pan. Refrigerate until ready to fill.

FILLING

(Have all ingredients at room temperature.)

½ *cup granulated sugar*	1 *teaspoon vanilla extract*
2 *tablespoons all-purpose flour*	4 *eggs, separated (beat whites*
¼ *teaspoon salt*	*until stiff, but not dry)*
2 *packages (8 ounces each)*	1 *cup half-and-half*
cream cheese	

1. Preheat oven to 325°F.
2. In mixing bowl, blend sugar with flour and salt. Add cream cheese and vanilla extract. Beat until blended and fluffy, using hand or electric beater, food processor or blender. Add egg yolks. Beat well. Gradually add half-and-half. Blend thoroughly.
3. With pliable rubber scraper or whisk, fold stiffly beaten egg whites into cheese mixture. Pour mixture into crust.
4. Bake 1 hour and 30 minutes, or until set in center. Turn off heat, open oven door and leave cake in oven to cool. *Or* if sour cream topping is desired, *do not* turn off heat. Gently remove from oven and spread with topping.

SOUR CREAM TOPPING

2 *cups dairy sour cream*	1 *teaspoon vanilla extract*
½ *cup granulated sugar*	

1. *Increase* oven temperature to 350°F.
2. In small mixing bowl, combine all ingredients. Very gently spread over cheesecake.
3. Bake for 7 to 9 minutes. Remove from oven and let cool away from draft. When cool, a strawberry glaze may be added, if desired. *Or* sour cream topping may be omitted and only the glaze added.

STRAWBERRY GLAZE

4 cups fresh or whole frozen,
thawed strawberries

½ cup granulated sugar

1 tablespoon cornstarch

¼ cup water

1 tablespoon lemon juice

1 teaspoon butter

Few drops red food coloring,
if desired

1. Wash, pick over and remove stems or hulls from fresh berries. Crush enough to fill ½ cup. Leave remaining berries whole.
2. In saucepan, combine crushed berries, sugar, cornstarch, water and lemon juice. Cook over medium heat, stirring constantly, until thickened and clear, or about 3 minutes after mixture reaches rolling boil. Remove from heat.
3. Add butter and food coloring, if desired. Strain through fine sieve. Cool.
4. Do not remove pan sides from cake. Arrange whole or halved berries on top of *cooled* cheesecake. Pour *cooled* sauce over berries. Chill in refrigerator at least 4 hours. Do not freeze cheesecake after glaze has been added.

NOTE: Blueberries or cherries may be substituted for strawberries, or canned blueberry or cherry pie filling may be substituted for strawberry glaze.

CHERRY COBBLER

▼▼

6 SERVINGS

2 cups canned pitted red cherries
(reserve juice)

1 tablespoon quick-cooking tapioca

⅓ cup granulated sugar

⅛ teaspoon salt

¾ cup cherry juice

½ teaspoon almond or vanilla
extract

1 tablespoon lemon juice

Few drops red food coloring,
if desired

1. Preheat oven to 425°F. Grease 8-inch square pan.
2. Place cherries in prepared pan. Sprinkle tapioca over cherries.
3. Combine sugar, salt, cherry juice, almond or vanilla extract, lemon juice and food coloring. Pour over cherries.

TOPPING

1¼ cups sifted all-purpose flour

1½ teaspoons double-acting
baking powder

½ teaspoon salt

2 tablespoons granulated sugar

¼ cup shortening

¼ cup finely chopped almonds or
pecan meats, if desired

½ cup milk

1. In small mixing bowl, mix and sift flour, baking powder, salt and sugar together.
2. With two table knives or pastry blender, cut shortening into flour mixture until mixture has consistency of small grain. Add almonds or pecan meats if desired. Mix well. Add milk. Mix thoroughly with fork. Drop by tablespoonfuls

onto cherry mixture. A design may be formed by spacing the dough uniformly in rows.

3. Bake at 425°F. for 15 minutes. *Reduce* heat to 350°F. Bake 20 minutes more. Serve plain or topped with cream or ice cream.

BERRY OR FRUIT CRISP

4 SERVINGS

2½ cups peeled, thinly sliced
    apples, peaches or pears, or
    blueberries or cherries
  2 tablespoons lemon juice
  2 tablespoons granulated sugar
 ½ cup sifted all-purpose flour
 ½ cup firmly packed brown sugar

½ cup quick-cooking rolled oats
    or granola
¼ teaspoon salt
½ teaspoon ground cinnamon
¼ teaspoon ground nutmeg
½ teaspoon baking powder
½ cup softened butter, margarine
    or shortening

1. Preheat oven to 375°F. Grease 10 × 6 × 2-inch baking dish.
2. Place fruit or berries in bottom of prepared dish. Sprinkle with lemon juice, then with granulated sugar.
3. In mixing bowl, combine flour, brown sugar, rolled oats or granola, salt, cinnamon, nutmeg and baking powder. With fork, mix in butter, margarine or shortening. Sprinkle crumbly mixture over fruit.
4. Bake for about 25 minutes. Serve hot with cream, or cold with ice cream.

NOTE: Many of the natural grain-and-nut mixtures, such as trail mix or backpacker's nibble, can be substituted for oats or granola.

MERINGUE SHELL OR SHELLS

6 INDIVIDUAL SHELLS OR ONE 9-INCH SHELL

  3 egg whites
 ⅛ teaspoon fresh cream of tartar
 ¼ teaspoon salt
  1 teaspoon vanilla extract
  1 teaspoon vinegar
  1 teaspoon water
 ¾ cup sifted granulated sugar

¾ cup finely chopped walnut
    meats, hazelnuts or crisp rice
    cereal, if desired
Fresh fruit, French Custard
    Filling, page 115, whipped
    cream or ice cream

1. Preheat oven to 275°F. Lightly butter and flour 9-inch pie plate or spring-form pan.
2. In medium-size mixing bowl, beat egg whites until frothy. Add cream of tartar and salt. Beat egg whites until stiff but not dry. Mix vanilla extract, vinegar and water together. Gradually add sugar to egg whites a small spoon-

ful at a time, alternately with a few drops of liquid. With a pliable rubber scraper or whisk, gently fold in nutmeats or crisp rice cereal, if desired.

3. Spread meringue in prepared pie plate or pan, building up sides to shape a nest or shell. For individual shells, shape meringue batter into 6 bird's nests on buttered cookie sheet.

4. Bake large shell 1 hour. Bake individual shells 45 minutes. Fill cooled shell or shells with fresh fruit, or one of the suggested fillings.

CHOCOLATE MERINGUE SHELL: In Step 2, gradually fold in ½ cup cocoa or carob powder before folding in nutmeats or crisp rice cereal.

PECAN-DATE DELIGHT

12 SERVINGS

6 *eggs, beaten*	7 *coarsely crumbled saltine*
1¾ *cups granulated sugar*	*crackers*
1 *teaspoon vanilla extract*	2 *cups pitted, chopped dates*
2 *teaspoons double-acting*	2 *cups chopped pecan meats*
baking powder	*Whipped cream*

1. Preheat oven to 350°F. Butter 14 × 9 × 2-inch baking pan.

2. In mixing bowl, combine beaten eggs, sugar, vanilla extract, baking powder and saltine crackers. Blend thoroughly. Add dates and pecan meats. Spread in prepared pan.

3. Bake for 30 minutes. Refrigerate.

4. To serve, cut into squares. Top with whipped cream.

PLUM TART

8 SERVINGS

2 *eggs, well beaten*	2 *cups sifted all-purpose flour*
1½ *cups granulated sugar*	4 *cups sliced fresh plums*
1 *cup shortening*	½ *cup butter*
½ *teaspoon salt*	*Ground cinnamon*

1. Preheat oven to 400°F. Generously grease 14 × 9 × 2-inch baking pan.

2. In large mixing bowl, blend together eggs, 1 cup sugar, shortening and salt until fluffy. Gradually add flour.

3. Spread dough evenly over prepared pan bottom.

4. Arrange plum slices evenly over dough. Dot with butter. Sprinkle with remaining ½ cup sugar and cinnamon.

5. Bake for 35 minutes.

APPLE OR BLUEBERRY TART: In Step 4, substitute sliced apples or fresh or frozen and thawed blueberries for plums.

Custards
and Puddings

BLANCMANGE (CORNSTARCH PUDDING)

4 SERVINGS

2 cups milk
2 tablespoons cornstarch
4 tablespoons granulated sugar

¼ teaspoon salt
1 egg, beaten
¾ teaspoon vanilla extract

1. In medium-size heavy saucepan, scald 1¾ cups milk.
2. Mix together cornstarch, sugar and salt. Add remaining ¼ cup milk, stirring until dissolved. Add to scalded milk.
3. Cook over low heat, stirring constantly, until thickened or about 10 minutes. Remove from heat. Add a little hot mixture to beaten egg. Stir egg into hot mixture. Return to low heat. Cook, stirring constantly, until mixture comes to a boil. Remove from heat. Add vanilla extract. Cool.

BUTTERSCOTCH BLANCMANGE: In Step 2, substitute ⅔ cup firmly packed brown sugar for granulated sugar. Add 2 tablespoons butter to scalded milk.

CHOCOLATE BLANCMANGE: In Step 2, add 1 ounce unsweetened chocolate or ½ cup semisweet chocolate pieces. A few drops of peppermint extract may be added, if desired.

MOCHA BLANCMANGE: In Step 1, add 1 ounce unsweetened chocolate and ½ teaspoon instant coffee.

CRÈME BRÛLÉE

6 SERVINGS

3 cups whipping cream
6 tablespoons granulated sugar
6 egg yolks
1 teaspoon vanilla extract

½ cup brown sugar
Sweetened fresh strawberries,
    peaches, pineapple chunks or
    raspberries, if desired

1. In top of double boiler, over boiling water, scald cream.
2. In mixing bowl, beat sugar and egg yolks until blended. Gradually add scalded cream to beaten egg yolks.
3. Return mixture to top of double boiler. Cook over boiling water, stirring constantly, until thickened and will coat metal spoon. Cook 3 minutes more. Add vanilla extract.
4. Pour into oven-proof serving or soufflé dish. Refrigerate until set.
5. When ready to serve, sprinkle top with brown sugar.
6. Set serving dish in tray of crushed ice. Place 5 inches from preheated broiler until sugar melts and caramelizes. Serve immediately with or without fruit of choice.

CRÈME CARAMEL

8 TO 10 SERVINGS

1 cup plus 7 tablespoons
    granulated sugar
10 eggs
4 cups half-and-half

¾ teaspoon salt
1 teaspoon vanilla or lemon extract
Whipped cream
Fresh strawberries

1. Preheat oven to 300°F.
2. Over low heat, melt 1 cup sugar in 2-quart mold until golden brown. Remove from heat. Coat inside of mold by swishing caramelized sugar around sides.
3. In large mixing bowl, beat eggs slightly. Add 4 tablespoons sugar. Stir. Add remaining 3 tablespoons sugar. Stir. Add half-and-half, salt and vanilla or lemon extract. Stir gently. Pour into mold.
4. Place mold in shallow pan on oven rack. Pour boiling water into pan to depth of 1 inch.
5. Bake for 1½ to 2 hours, or until a knife inserted in center comes out clean. Cool. Refrigerate overnight.
6. Unmold. Serve with whipped cream and garnish with fresh strawberries.

NOTE: A famous French chef uses five whole eggs and ten egg yolks.

BAKED CUSTARD

6 SERVINGS

2 cups milk
3 eggs
¼ cup granulated sugar

¼ teaspoon salt
½ teaspoon vanilla extract
Ground nutmeg

1. Preheat oven to 350°F. Have ready 6 individual custard cups or 1½-quart baking dish.
2. Scald milk gently over medium heat until a film begins to form on top and tiny bubbles appear around edge of pan.
3. In mixing bowl large enough to accommodate all ingredients, beat eggs. Add sugar, salt and vanilla extract. Add milk *gradually* to egg mixture. (If added all at once the hot milk will curdle the eggs.)
4. Pour custard into cups or baking dish. Sprinkle with nutmeg.
5. Place cups or baking dish in pan on oven rack. Pour boiling water into pan to within 1 inch of rim of cup or dish.
6. Bake individual custards about 30 to 40 minutes; large custard for about 45 minutes to 1 hour, or until firm and knife comes out clean when inserted in center.

SOFT VANILLA CUSTARD

4 TO 6 SERVINGS

¼ cup granulated sugar
¼ teaspoon salt
2 eggs or 3 egg yolks, slightly
    beaten

¼ teaspoon ground nutmeg,
    if desired
1½ cups milk
1 teaspoon vanilla extract

1. In heavy 1-quart saucepan, mix together sugar, salt, eggs or egg yolks and nutmeg, if desired. Stir in milk. Mix very well.
2. Cook over simmering water or low heat, stirring frequently, until custard will coat a metal spoon. It should be slightly thicker than unbeaten egg whites.
3. Remove from heat. Add vanilla extract. Refrigerate.

INDIAN PUDDING

ABOUT 6 SERVINGS

4 cups milk
¼ cup cornmeal
½ cup molasses
1 teaspoon salt
2 tablespoons butter
½ teaspoon ground nutmeg or
    cinnamon

½ teaspoon ground ginger
3 tablespoons granulated sugar,
    if desired
1 egg, beaten

1. Preheat oven to 350°F. Butter 1½-quart baking dish.
2. In medium-sized saucepan, scald 3 cups milk. Very gradually stir in corn-meal. Cook over low heat for 15 to 20 minutes. Add molasses, salt, butter, nutmeg or cinnamon, ginger and sugar, if desired. Remove from heat. Gradually add beaten egg. Stir in remaining 1 cup milk.
3. Pour into prepared baking dish. Place in shallow pan on oven rack. Pour boiling water into pan to depth of 1-inch.
4. Bake for 1½ to 2 hours, or until set. Serve hot.

NOTE: The original recipe called for 4 "great" spoons cornmeal and un-sulfured molasses.

LEMON SPONGE

4 SERVINGS

2 eggs, separated (beat whites
    until stiff, but not dry)
1 cup granulated sugar
¼ teaspoon salt
2 tablespoons all-purpose flour

2 tablespoons melted butter
Juice of 1 lemon
Grated rind of 1 lemon
1 cup milk

1. Preheat oven to 350°F. Butter 1-quart baking dish.
2. In mixing bowl, beat egg yolks until lemon-colored. Add sugar and salt. Beat well. Add flour, melted butter, lemon juice and rind. Mix well. Gradually add milk.
3. With pliable rubber scraper or whisk, gently fold in stiffly beaten egg whites.
4. Pour into prepared baking dish. Place in shallow pan on oven rack. Pour boiling water into pan to depth of 1 inch.
5. Bake for 25 minutes, or until knife inserted in center comes out clean.

RICE PUDDING

6 TO 8 SERVINGS

½ cup uncooked rice
4 cups scalded milk
½ teaspoon salt
½ cup granulated sugar
2 eggs, beaten
1 tablespoon butter

¼ teaspoon ground or freshly
　grated nutmeg
½ cup raisins
1 teaspoon vanilla extract
1 teaspoon grated lemon rind
1 teaspoon lemon juice

1. Preheat oven to 325°F. Butter 2-quart casserole or baking dish.
2. In sieve, wash rice thoroughly under cold running water.
3. In mixing bowl, combine all remaining ingredients. Beat well. Add washed rice. Pour into prepared casserole or baking dish.
4. Place in pan on oven rack. Pour boiling water into pan to depth of 1 inch.
5. Bake for 1 hour, stirring three times to prevent rice from settling. Bake for 1½ hours longer, or until knife inserted in center comes out clean.

CARAMEL RICE PUDDING: In Step 3, substitute brown sugar for granulated sugar. Omit lemon rind and juice.

VANILLA SOUFFLÉ

4 TO 6 SERVINGS

2 tablespoons butter
¼ cup all-purpose flour
1 cup hot milk
4 eggs, separated, plus 1 egg white

½ cup granulated sugar
¼ teaspoon salt
½ teaspoon vanilla extract
1 tablespoon cognac, if desired

1. Preheat oven to 350°F. Generously butter 1½-quart soufflé dish or casserole. Sprinkle bottom and sides lightly with granulated sugar. Refrigerate dish or casserole.
2. In medium-size saucepan, melt butter over low heat. Stir in flour. Cook for few minutes, or until bubbly, without browning. Slowly add hot milk, stirring constantly. Cook until thickened. Remove from heat. Cool.
3. Beat egg yolks. Gradually add to milk mixture. Add ¼ cup sugar, salt, vanilla extract and cognac, if desired.
4. Beat egg whites until stiff but not dry. Gradually add remaining ¼ cup sugar. With pliable rubber scraper or whisk, fold egg whites into milk mixture.
5. Pour into prepared dish or casserole. Bake for about 1 hour, or until knife inserted in center comes out clean. Serve immediately.

CHOCOLATE MOUSSE

8 SERVINGS

18 *ounces semisweet chocolate*
   pieces
8 *extra-large eggs, separated (beat*
   whites until stiff but not dry)
1 *teaspoon vanilla extract*

½ *teaspoon salt*
2 *teaspoons crème de cacao*
1 *cup whipping cream, whipped*
16 *strawberries, halved*

1. In top of double boiler, melt chocolate over simmering water.
2. Slightly beat egg yolks. Add to melted chocolate, stirring constantly.
3. Fold stiffly beaten egg whites into chocolate mixture. Stir in vanilla and salt. Cool.
4. Add liqueur. Pour into eight dessert dishes. Chill at least 8 hours.
5. To serve, top with whipped cream and garnish with strawberries.

CHOCOLATE SOUFFLÉ WITH SAUCE GRAND MARNIER

6 SERVINGS

3 *tablespoon butter or margarine*
¼ *cup sifted all-purpose flour*
¼ *teaspoon salt*
1 *cup milk*
2 *ounces unsweetened chocolate*

4 *eggs (beat whites until stiff,*
   but not dry)
½ *cup granulated sugar*
¼ *teaspoon fresh cream of tartar*
   Sauce Grand Marnier, page 137

1. Have ready 1½-quart soufflé dish.
2. In heavy saucepan, melt butter or margarine. Blend in flour and salt. Add milk. Cook, stirring constantly, until thickened. Add chocolate. Stir until melted.
3. Beat egg yolks until thick and lemon-colored. Beat sugar into yolks a little at a time. Blend chocolate into egg yolks.
4. Fold cream of tartar into stiffly beaten egg whites. Gently fold stiffly beaten egg whites into chocolate mixture.
5. Pour or spoon into soufflé dish, filling dish to top or at least ½ inch of top.
6. Bake at 350°F. for 1 hour, or until a knife inserted in center comes out clean. Serve topped with Sauce Grand Marnier.

CREAM PUFFS OR ÉCLAIRS

12 TO 18 LARGE OR ABOUT 36 SMALL PUFFS OR ECLAIRS

1 *cup boiling water*
½ *cup butter*
¼ *teaspoon salt*
1 *cup sifted all-purpose flour*
4 *eggs*

French Custard Filling, page
115, or sweetened whipped
cream or ice cream
Chocolate Glaze, page 113

1. Preheat oven to 450°F. Generously grease cookie sheet.
2. In medium-size saucepan, combine boiling water, butter and salt. When butter is melted, add flour all at once. Stir vigorously. Cook, stirring constantly, over low heat until batter is quite dry and comes cleanly away from pan sides. Remove from heat. Cool slightly.
3. Add eggs, one at a time, beating constantly, until mixture is smooth.
4. Drop spoonfuls of batter onto prepared cookie sheet in mounds 2 inches wide, allowing 2 inches between puffs. Elongate the dough into ovals for éclairs.
5. Bake at 450°F. for 15 minutes. *Reduce* temperature to 325°F. Bake 25 minutes more. Puffs are done when a test puff does not fall when removed from oven. Cool.
6. Cut tops off with sharp knife. Remove soft centers. Fill with French Custard Filling, whipped or ice cream.
7. Frost with Chocolate Glaze.

DOUBLE CHOCOLATE ÉCLAIRS: In Step 6, fill with Chocolate Custard Filling, page 115.

ZABAGLIONE (SABAYON)

4 SERVINGS

6 *egg yolks*
1 *cup granulated sugar*
½ *cup Marsala or sherry*

5 *teaspoons lemon juice, if desired*
2 *teaspoons grated lemon rind,*
if desired

1. In top of double boiler, combine all ingredients. Cook over boiling water, beating constantly with rotary beater, until mixture is thickened and fluffy as whipped cream. Remove from heat.
2. Pour into sherbet, parfait or champagne glasses. Serve hot or cold, or serve over fruit or cake.

Ice Cream, Sherberts, Ices and Frozen Desserts

OLD-FASHIONED VANILLA ICE CREAM

2 QUARTS

4 cups half-and-half or whipping
    cream
2 eggs, beaten
1 cup granulated sugar

⅛ teaspoon salt
2 teaspoons vanilla extract
    (more, if desired)

1. Scald 1¼ cups half-and-half. In large heavy saucepan, combine eggs, sugar, salt and vanilla extract. Gradually add scalded half-and-half to egg mixture. Cook over low heat, stirring constantly, until mixture will coat spoon, or is like a thin custard. Cool. Add remaining 2¾ cups cream. Pour into 2-quart ice cream freezer, or three freezing trays.
2. Freeze in refrigerator until mixture resembles heavy mush, or in ice cream freezer using eight parts crushed ice and one part ice cream salt, turning crank rapidly until it becomes difficult to turn.
3. If making ice cream in refrigerator, have ready chilled 2-quart bowl. Remove heavy mush from trays. Quickly beat with rotary or electric beater until smooth. Return to trays. Freeze until firm.
4. If making ice cream in ice cream freezer, remove dasher when ice cream is almost firm. Drain off water. Allow to ripen. Repack freezer with 1 quart crushed ice and 1 cup ice cream salt, if serving within 2 hours, or 2 quarts crushed ice to 1 cup salt, if serving in 3 to 4 hours. Cover freezer with heavy burlap bag, cloth or paper.

BANANA ICE CREAM: In Step 1, add 4 mashed bananas to cooled egg mixture and 2 tablespoons rum, if desired.

BUTTER-PECAN ICE CREAM: In Step 1, in heavy skillet over low heat, melt sugar until golden. Add to scalded half-and-half. Sauté 1 cup broken pecan meats in ¼ cup butter until golden brown. Add after vanilla extract.

CHOCOLATE-CHIP ICE CREAM: In Step 1, add ¾ cup finely chopped semi-sweet chocolate before freezing.

CHOCOLATE ICE CREAM: In Step 1, add 2 or 3 ounces unsweetened chocolate to half-and-half before scalding. Mix until chocolate is melted.

CHOCOLATE-MINT ICE CREAM: In Step 1, add ¼ teaspoon peppermint extract to Chocolate Ice Cream.

COFFEE ICE CREAM: In Step 1, substitute 1 cup double-strength coffee for 1 cup half-and-half.

FRESH PEACH ICE CREAM: In Step 1, add 2 cups fresh, crushed peaches and ½ teaspoon almond extract. Reduce vanilla extract to ½ teaspoon.

MOCHA ICE CREAM: Follow directions for Coffee Ice Cream. In Step 1, add ¾ cup finely chopped semisweet chocolate before freezing.

NESSELRODE ICE CREAM: In Step 1, substitute ⅓ cup rum for vanilla extract. Add 1¼ cups finely chopped mixed candied fruit or finely crushed macaroons. Add ¼ teaspoon ground ginger, ¼ teaspoon ground mace and ¼ teaspoon ground cardamom, if desired.

PEPPERMINT-CANDY ICE CREAM: Steep ½ pound crushed peppermint candy in half-and-half overnight before proceeding with Step 1.

STRAWBERRY ICE CREAM: In Step 1, omit 1 cup half-and-half. Add 1 quart washed, hulled, mashed strawberries to cooled egg mixture.

FRUIT ICE

1½ QUARTS

1 tablespoon unflavored gelatin	2 egg whites, beaten very stiff
2 tablespoons cold water	2 cups fresh-frozen pineapple juice
½ cup granulated sugar	2 cups fresh-frozen orange juice
½ cup light corn syrup	2 tablespoons lemon juice

1. Soak gelatin in cold water.
2. In small saucepan, combine sugar and corn syrup. Cook over low heat, stirring constantly, for 5 minutes. Remove from heat.
3. Dissolve gelatin in hot syrup. Add hot syrup to beaten egg whites.
4. In 3-quart bowl, combine pineapple, orange and lemon juice. Stir syrup–egg white mixture into juices.

5. Place in freezing unit of refrigerator. Freeze until almost solid.
6. Remove from freezer. Quickly beat with electric or rotary beater until smooth, being careful not to let mixture liquefy. (Place in bowl of ice while beating, if necessary.)
7. Pour into two freezing trays. Freeze until firm, stirring several times. Pack in refrigerator container with tight-fitting cover. Freeze.

APPLE OR CHAMPAGNE ICE: In Step 4, substitute 4 cups apple juice or champagne for pineapple and orange juices.

KIWI ICE: Before beginning to make Kiwi Ice, peel 5 kiwi fruit and purée in blender with 2 cups water. In Step 3, add kiwi fruit before egg whites. In Step 4, omit orange and pineapple juice. Increase lemon juice to ¼ cup.

STEAMED PUDDINGS

A pressure cooker processes steamed puddings more quickly at high altitudes. Also, it eliminates the need for frequent additions of water during steaming (which are otherwise necessary at altitudes above 2,000 feet because of the rapid evaporation rate).

STEAMED CHOCOLATE PUDDING

6 TO 8 SERVINGS

2 *tablespoons butter*	2 *tablespoons cocoa*
½ *cup granulated sugar*	¼ *teaspoon salt*
2 *eggs, separated (beat whites until*	¼ *teaspoon ground cinnamon,*
stiff but not dry)	*if desired*
1 *cup sifted all-purpose flour*	½ *cup milk*
1 *teaspoon double-acting baking*	½ *teaspoon vanilla extract*
powder	

1. Butter 1-quart mold or 1-pound coffee can.
2. In mixing bowl, cream butter. Gradually add sugar. Add egg yolks one at a time, beating well after each addition.
3. Mix and sift together flour, baking powder, cocoa, salt and cinnamon, if desired. Add dry ingredients alternately with milk to creamed mixture. Add vanilla extract.
4. With pliable rubber scraper or whisk, gently fold in beaten egg whites.
5. Pour into prepared mold or coffee can. Cover. Set container on trivet or rack in kettle. Add enough boiling water to immerse one-half of mold. Steam

for about 1 hour. Serve with Soft Vanilla Custard, page 127, or whipped cream, if desired.

NOTE: Pudding may be cooked in electric slow cooker according to directions in user's instruction manual.

PLUM PUDDING

2-QUART PUDDING, 10-INCH TUBE OR
THREE 1-POUND PUDDINGS

2 eggs, slightly beaten
½ cup granulated sugar
1 cup light molasses
1 cup ground suet
1 cup plus 2 tablespoons dried
   bread crumbs
2 cups sifted all-purpose flour
1 teaspoon ground cloves

1 teaspoon ground cinnamon
1½ teaspoons baking soda
½ teaspoon salt
1 cup milk
1½ cups chopped walnut meats
1 package (15 ounces) raisins or
   dates, if desired

1. In large mixing bowl, combine eggs, sugar, molasses, suet and bread crumbs.
2. Mix and sift together flour, cloves, cinnamon, soda and salt.
3. Add dry ingredients alternately with milk to first mixture. Batter will be quite stiff. Add walnut meats and raisins or dates, if desired.
4. Grease three 1-pound coffee cans or 2-quart pudding mold or 10-inch tube pan. Pour batter into prepared cans, mold or pan, filling only two-thirds full. Cover tightly with lid or aluminum foil.
5. Set containers on rack or trivet in large kettle. Add enough boiling water to immerse one-half of mold. Cook pudding for 3 hours over boiling water, adding additional water whenever necessary to maintain original level. If using double boiler, cook covered over boiling water, adding additional water when necessary. If prepared ahead, reheat pudding over boiling water, or in top of double boiler for about 1 hour. Serve with Honey Rum Sauce, page 138.

NOTE: Pudding may be cooked in electric slow cooker according to user's instruction manual.

Dessert Sauces

BERRY SAUCE

1 *quart fresh raspberries, blackberries, strawberries, boysenberries or blueberries*	2 *cups granulated sugar* 2 *teaspoons lemon juice*

1. In 2-quart saucepan, slightly crush berries with wooden spoon or potato masher. Mix sugar and lemon juice with fruit. Let stand 1 hour.
2. Over medium heat, slowly bring fruit to boil. When fruit in center begins to boil, cook over high heat, stirring frequently, until mixture is thickened and becomes syrupy. Remove from heat.
3. Press through sieve, making sure to scrape remaining pulp from underside of sieve. Cool at room temperature.

CARAMEL SAUCE

ABOUT 2 CUPS

1 *cup granulated sugar* 1½ *cups milk* 1 *tablespoon all-purpose flour*	3 *egg yolks, beaten* ½ *teaspoon vanilla extract*

1. In small skillet or saucepan, melt sugar over low heat until golden brown.
2. Mix small amount of milk with flour, then add remaining milk to flour. Add to caramelized sugar. Boil over medium-low heat for 3 to 4 minutes, stirring constantly.
3. Put beaten egg yolks in top of double boiler. Add caramel mixture and vanilla extract. Cook over boiling water, stirring constantly, until thickened.

NEVER-FAIL CHOCOLATE SAUCE

ABOUT 1½ CUPS

2 ounces unsweetened chocolate
2½ tablespoons butter
1 cup granulated sugar

⅓ cup boiling water
⅛ teaspoon salt
2 tablespoons light corn syrup

In small saucepan, over low heat, melt chocolate and butter. Add sugar, water, salt and corn syrup. Bring to boil. Cook until sauce will coat spoon. Remove from heat. Sauce will get hard when refrigerated. Add few drops of water and reheat for serving.

FOAMY SAUCE

ABOUT 2 CUPS

½ cup butter
1 cup powdered sugar
⅛ teaspoon salt
2 eggs, separated (beat whites until stiff, but not dry)

2 tablespoons brandy or sherry
½ teaspoon vanilla extract
½ cup whipping cream, whipped
Ground nutmeg

1. In top of double boiler, combine butter, powdered sugar, salt and egg yolks. Cook, stirring constantly, over boiling water for 10 minutes. Remove from heat. Add brandy or sherry and vanilla extract. Cool.
2. Fold in beaten egg whites and whipped cream. Garnish with nutmeg.

SAUCE GRAND MARNIER

1 CUP

¼ cup granulated sugar
1 tablespoon cornstarch
¾ cup orange juice

¼ cup Grand Marnier
¼ cup toasted slivered almonds

In small saucepan, combine sugar and cornstarch. Add orange juice. Cook over medium-low heat until mixture comes to boil, stirring constantly. *Reduce* heat to low. Stir in liqueur and almonds. Heat through. Serve hot.

HONEY RUM SAUCE

ABOUT 4 CUPS

2⅓ cups firmly packed brown sugar
1 cup honey
¼ teaspoon salt

½ cup apple juice
1 cup butter
½ cup rum

In heavy saucepan, combine all ingredients except rum. Mix well. Simmer over low heat for about 45 minutes. Remove from heat. Cool. Add rum. Store sauce at room temperature.

VANILLA SAUCE

1⅓ CUPS

½ cup granulated sugar
1 tablespoon cornstarch
¼ teaspoon salt
1 cup boiling water

2 tablespoons butter
1 teaspoon vanilla extract
1 tablespoon rum, if desired

In small saucepan, combine sugar, cornstarch and salt. Add water gradually, stirring constantly. Cook over low heat, stirring constantly, for 5 minutes, or until mixture is clear and begins to thicken. Add butter, vanilla extract and rum, if desired.

LEMON SAUCE: Omit vanilla extract. Add 1½ tablespoons lemon juice and dash of ground nutmeg.

BUTTERSCOTCH SAUCE

ABOUT 2½ CUPS

1¼ cups firmly packed brown sugar
⅔ cup light corn syrup

4 tablespoons butter
⅔ cup half-and-half

1. In heavy saucepan, combine sugar, corn syrup and butter. Bring to boil over low heat.
2. Cook, stirring constantly, until a small quantity dropped into cold water forms a soft ball. Gradually add half-and-half. Remove from heat.

Egg and Cheese Dishes

HIGH ALTITUDE FACTS ABOUT EGG COOKERY

All egg cookery takes longer at high altitudes, but do not increase heat in cooking omelets and frying eggs. A 3-minute egg will take 4 minutes at 5,000 feet. In frying eggs, use a heavy skillet. Poaching an egg takes 4 to 6 minutes or longer. All recipes in this book call for extra-large eggs. Beat egg whites only until stiff, not dry.

SOFT-COOKED EGGS

Fill saucepan with cold water to cover 1 inch above eggs. Bring water to *furious* boil. Cover. Turn off heat. Begin timing. Let stand 4 to 6 minutes depending on size of eggs and individual taste.

HARD-COOKED EGGS

Fill saucepan with cold water to cover 1 inch above eggs. Bring water to *furious* boil. Cover. Reduce heat to low. Cook for 20 minutes. Cool immediately in cold water.

CHILIES RELLENOS CASSEROLE

5 cans (4 ounces each) whole mild
  green chilies
¾ pound coarsely grated sharp
  cheddar
¾ pound coarsely grated Monterey
  Jack
4 eggs, separated (beat whites
  until stiff but not dry)

1 can (13½ ounces) evaporated
  milk
2 tablespoons all-purpose flour
1 teaspoon salt
¼ teaspoon ground pepper or
  seasoned pepper
2 cups canned or bottled green
  chili salsa

1. Split chilies and remove seeds.
2. Preheat oven to 350°F. Butter generously 13 × 9 × 2-inch casserole.
3. Cover bottom of casserole with half of green chilies. Top with grated cheddar and cover with layer of remaining green chilies. Top with grated Monterey Jack.
4. In large mixing bowl, beat egg yolks. Add milk, flour, salt and pepper. Fold in beaten egg whites. Pour evenly over top of mixture in casserole.
5. Pour green chili salsa evenly over top.
6. Bake for 45 minutes, or until center is set.

CHILIES RELLENOS CASSEROLE WITH BEEF: In Step 1, brown 1½ pounds lean ground beef. Season to taste with salt and pepper. In Step 3, spread evenly over bottom of casserole before using green chilies.

CHEESE SOUFFLÉ

Ingredient adjustments have been made to make these soufflés successful at higher altitudes.

Flour
Grated Parmesan or fine bread
  crumbs
4 eggs, separated (beat whites
  until stiff but not dry)
¼ cup butter

1 cup milk
1 cup grated cheddar
½ teaspoon salt
½ teaspoon prepared mustard
⅛ teaspoon pepper

1. Preheat oven to 350°F. Butter 1½-quart soufflé dish. Dust lightly with flour and grated Parmesan or fine bread crumbs.
2. Beat egg yolks until thick and lemon-colored. Set aside. In saucepan, melt butter. Stir in ¼ cup flour. Gradually add milk. Cook 3 to 5 minutes, stirring

constantly, until mixture is thickened. Add cheddar, salt, mustard and pepper. Stir until cheese melts.

3. Add a little hot sauce slowly to beaten yolks, mixing thoroughly. Add remainder of sauce and mix.

4. Fold in beaten egg whites.

5. Pour or spoon mixture into prepared soufflé dish, filling dish at least to within ½ inch of top. (This assures good volume and attractive browning.)

6. Set soufflé in shallow pan on oven rack. Pour boiling water into pan to depth of 1 inch.

7. Bake for 25 to 35 minutes, or until a knife inserted into soufflé halfway between center and outside edge comes out clean. Serve immediately.

FISH, SHELLFISH OR VEGETABLE SOUFFLÉ: In Step 2, add 1 cup flaked cooked fish or shellfish; or 1 cup finely chopped raw asparagus, broccoli or mushrooms.

BAKED CHEESE SOUFFLÉ SANDWICH

6 SERVINGS

12 *slices day-old white bread, trimmed of edges*	3 *drops liquid hot pepper sauce*
6 *generous slices cheddar*	1 *teaspoon salt*
4 *eggs, slightly beaten*	½ *teaspoon ground or seasoned pepper*
3 *cups milk*	¼ *teaspoon dry mustard*
1 *teaspoon Worcestershire sauce*	*Dash garlic powder*

1. Preheat oven to 350°F. Butter 13 × 9 × 2-inch oblong pan.

2. Place 6 slices bread in buttered pan. Top each slice with cheese. Cover with remaining 6 slices bread.

3. In mixing bowl, combine remaining ingredients. Blend well. Pour over sandwiches.

4. Bake for 1½ hours, or until custard is set and top is golden brown. Allow to set for 15 minutes before serving.

TURKEY, ARTICHOKE HEARTS AND WATER CHESTNUT SOUFFLÉ SANDWICH: In Step 2, arrange 2 cups diced cooked turkey, 2 cups drained canned or thawed frozen artichoke hearts and ½ cup sliced canned water chestnuts over bread. Substitute Monterey Jack for cheddar.

ARTICHOKE AND MUSHROOM QUICHE

6 SERVINGS

10-inch unbaked pie shell,
   pages 222–224
1 small onion, finely chopped
2 tablespoons butter
1 cup cooked artichoke hearts,
   cut up
1½ cups washed, dried and
   sliced mushrooms

1 cup grated Swiss cheese
4 eggs, beaten
2 cups half-and-half
1 tablespoon melted butter
½ teaspoon ground nutmeg
¼ teaspoon salt
Dash cayenne
¼ teaspoon ground pepper

1. Preheat oven to 400°F. Have ready unbaked pie shell.
2. In skillet, sauté onion in butter until limp.
3. Arrange artichoke hearts and mushrooms in pie shell.
4. Combine remaining ingredients. Pour over vegetables.
5. Bake at 400°F. for 15 minutes, *reduce* temperature to 350°F. Bake 45 minutes more, or until knife inserted in center comes out clean. Cut in wedges and serve hot.

Fish and Shellfish

HIGH ALTITUDE FACTS ABOUT FISH AND SHELLFISH COOKERY

Because of the rapid evaporation at higher altitudes, fish and shellfish must be cooked with tender loving care to preserve natural moisture. Use of butter, wine, sauces, court bouillon, fumet and batter help to maintain moisture. Aluminum foil seals in natural juices; in fact, some believe cooking in foil is the *only* way to cook fish at high altitude. When sautéeing or pan-frying, be careful not to overcook. Fish should be barely cooked at the backbone where it is thickest, to avoid making the thin parts too dry or overcooked. Leaving the head and tail on when baking a whole fish helps to ensure retention of natural juices.

DEEP-FAT-FRIED FISH OR SHELLFISH

Coat fish or shellfish with Fish Batter, page 146, or batter used for Shrimp or Vegetable Tempura, page 156. In large cooking pan or electric deep-fat fryer, heat cooking oil or shortening to 350°F. to 360°F. Have sufficient oil or shortening to float fish or shellfish, or at least 1½ inches deep. Fry batter-coated fish or shellfish a few at a time, until evenly browned on all sides.

OVEN-FRIED FISH

Preheat oven to 425°F. Place fish fillets, steaks or pieces in shallow baking pan. Drizzle with melted butter or margarine, salt and pepper or seasoned pepper; *or* dip in milk or cream, then in seasoned bread crumbs or cornmeal, and cover with melted butter or margarine. Oven-fry for 20 to 30 minutes, or until fish flakes easily.

POACHED FISH

Tie fish fillets, steaks, chunks or whole fish in cheesecloth or place on poaching rack or trivet. Lower into shallow pan filled with simmering Court Bouillon, below. Cover. Simmer until fish is tender, about 10 minutes for fillets, steaks or pieces; longer for whole fish depending on size and variety of fish. A rule of thumb for whole fish is ½ to 1 minute per ounce. Remove fish, allow broth to drain off and remove cheesecloth. Serve with Sauce Chablis, page 164, Mustard Sauce for Fish, page 167, or Béarnaise Sauce, page 163.

COURT BOUILLON FOR FISH

6 CUPS

Poaching or boiling fish or shellfish in Court Bouillon is a recommended method for high altitude because of the moist heat.

1 *tablespoon butter or margarine*	6 *peppercorns*
1 *large onion, chopped*	2 *whole cloves*
1 *large carrot, chopped*	1 *bay leaf*
2 *stalks celery, chopped*	1 *tablespoon chopped parsley*
2 *quarts water*	2 *tablespoons vinegar or lemon*
1 *teaspoon salt*	*juice*

1. In skillet or saucepan large enough to accommodate all ingredients, melt butter or margarine. Sauté onion, carrot and celery until limp, about 10 minutes.
2. Add remaining ingredients. Cover tightly. Bring to boil. Reduce heat. Simmer 30 minutes. Strain before using. Court Bouillon keeps for several days if refrigerated, but should be disposed of after being used.

BAKED STUFFED FISH

ALLOW ¾ POUND PER SERVING

Baking a whole fish with the head on helps to seal in juices at higher elevations. Serve baked fish as soon as it's taken from the oven, so it will not become soggy.

Preheat oven to 375°F. Use fish no smaller than 3 pounds. Rub inside with salt and pepper. Stuff cavity ⅔ full with Wine Stuffing, page 261. Close cavity with skewers or toothpicks. Place fish on greased rack in roasting pan. Brush with melted butter or margarine, sprinkle with herbs and/or salt and pepper. Bake, basting with pan juices, until fish is tender and flakes easily, about 12 to

20 minutes a pound for fish over 5 pounds, and about 1 to 2 minutes per ounce for smaller fish. Serve with Mustard Sauce for Fish, page 167, Béarnaise Sauce, page 163, or Sauce Chablis, page 164.

NOTE: Fish may be wrapped in aluminum foil before baking.

FISH BAKED, BROILED OR BARBECUED IN FOIL

6 SERVINGS

The airtight foil produces flaky, tender, moist results.

6 *fillets, steaks, or whole small pan-dressed fish (about 2 pounds)*	*Dried dill seed, parsley or rosemary, if desired*
6 *sheets heavy aluminum foil*	*Butter*
Salt	6 *lemon or lime slices*
Ground black pepper or seasoned pepper	6 *to 12 tablespoons dry white wine*

1. Preheat oven to 400°F., preheat broiler or have charcoal at cooking temperature in barbecue grill.
2. Place each individual serving of fish on a sheet of foil. Sprinkle with salt, seasoned pepper or pepper, and dill, parsley or rosemary, if desired. Dot generously with butter. Top with slice of lemon or lime. Pour 1 to 2 tablespoons wine over fish. Fold foil up around fish and seal by folding, allowing a little space on top of fish.
3. Bake 20 to 30 minutes in oven, or for 15 to 20 minutes in broiler, or for 15 to 20 minutes over glowing charcoal. Fish will be tender and flake easily when done.

STEAMED FISH

Wipe fish with damp cloth. Tie fish in cheesecloth so that it may be lifted by the knot of the cheesecloth to remove it from the cooking pan. Fill deep pan with about 2 inches of water or Court Bouillon, opposite. Place metal rack or substitute in bottom of pan, so fish will not touch liquid. Bring liquid to boil. Place fish on rack. Cover pan tightly. Steam, basting occasionally with liquid from pan, until fish flakes easily. Do not overcook. The time of cooking varies with size of fish; a general rule to follow is to allow about 1 minute for each ounce of fish.

FISH BATTER

▼▼

1 cup sifted all-purpose flour	¼ teaspoon pepper
¾ teaspoon double-acting	1 egg
baking powder	¾ cup water
1 teaspoon salt	

Sift flour, baking powder and salt into mixing bowl. Add remaining ingredients. Beat until batter is smooth.

FISH AND CHEESE ENCHILADAS

▼▼

6 SERVINGS

6 thick fillets (about 2 pounds) of fresh or frozen and thawed cod or other fish	1 can (4 ounces) diced green chilies, drained
2 cups water	1 teaspoon chili powder
1 bay leaf	½ teaspoon crumbled dried oregano
½ teaspoon onion powder	¼ teaspoon celery seed
1 teaspoon salt	8 corn tortillas
1½ cups chopped onion	1 cup half-and-half
1 clove garlic, finely chopped	½ cup shredded Monterey Jack
½ cup salad oil	1 cup dairy sour cream or guacamole
1 can (8 ounces) tomato sauce	
1 can (6 ounces) tomato paste	

1. Preheat oven to 350°F. Have ready flat baking dish.
2. In heavy skillet large enough to accommodate fish in one layer, combine 1 cup water, bay leaf, onion powder and salt. Bring to boil.
3. Arrange fish in skillet. Bring just to boil. Cover. Reduce heat and simmer 8 minutes. Remove fish with spatula. Drain. Set aside.
4. In medium skillet, over moderate heat, sauté onion and garlic in 2 tablespoons oil until onion is limp. Stir in tomato sauce, tomato paste, chilies, remaining 1 cup water, chili powder, oregano and celery seed. Bring just to boil, mixing very well. Cover. Reduce heat. Simmer 15 minutes, stirring occasionally.
5. In mixing bowl, break poached fish into chunky pieces. Add 2 cups tomato sauce mixture, mixing lightly.
6. In medium-size skillet, heat 2 tablespoons oil. One by one, heat each tortilla in hot oil until it softens and begins to blister, adding more oil as needed. Drain on paper towels.
7. Pour half-and-half into shallow bowl.
8. To assemble enchiladas, dip each softened tortilla into half-and-half, spoon onto center about ½ cup fish mixture. Roll up. Place in a row, seam side down,

in baking dish. Pour remaining half-and-half over tortillas. Cover with remaining tomato sauce mixture. Top with cheese.

9. Bake for 20 minutes, or until well heated through and cheese on top is bubbly. To serve, top with dollop of sour cream or guacamole, or both.

FISH AND NOODLE CASSEROLE

6 SERVINGS

2 cups White Sauce, page 169
8 ounces pimiento cheese, cut
    into chunks
3 cups cooked noodles
1 cup canned tuna fish, salmon or
    other cooked fish, drained
    and flaked

¾ pound fresh mushrooms,
    washed, dried and sliced
½ cup chopped pimiento
½ cup chopped green pepper
2 hard-cooked eggs, chopped
⅔ cup sliced stuffed green olives

1. Preheat oven to 375°F. Grease 2-quart casserole.
2. In 2-quart saucepan, over low heat, warm white sauce with cheese until cheese is melted. Add remaining ingredients. Mix gently but thoroughly to blend mixture. Pour into prepared casserole.
3. Bake 1 hour.

RED SNAPPER OR MAHIMAHI WITH HERBS

4 SERVINGS

2 tablespoons cooking oil
2 tablespoons margarine
1½ pounds fresh or frozen and
    thawed red snapper or
    mahimahi, cut into
    serving-size pieces

¼ cup flour
¼ teaspoon each crumbled dried
    marjoram, oregano and
    sweet basil

1. In large skillet with tight-fitting cover, melt oil with margarine.
2. Lightly sprinkle fish with flour.
3. Cook over medium heat, cavity side down. Turn. Sprinkle with herbs. Cover.
4. Cook 5 minutes more, or until done and fish flakes easily and is light in color.

SEA BASS WITH WINE AND SESAME SEEDS

4 SERVINGS

4 fillets sea bass (about 1½ pounds)
Salt
6 tablespoons softened butter or margarine
2 tablespoons chopped fresh chives or young green onion tops

1 teaspoon finely grated fresh ginger, or ½ teaspoon freshly ground pepper
3 tablespoons sesame seeds
¼ cup dry white wine

1. Preheat oven to 350°F. Have ready shallow baking pan.
2. Arrange fish in pan.
3. In small saucepan, combine remaining ingredients. Bring just to boil. Remove from heat. Pour over fish.
4. Bake for 20 minutes, or until fish is tender and flakes easily, basting occasionally with pan juices.

FLORIDA-STYLE FISH FILLETS

4 SERVINGS

2 green onions, including tops, finely chopped
6 fillets (about 2 pounds) of fresh or frozen and thawed red snapper, halibut, grouper or haddock
2 tablespoons olive oil

1 teaspoon salt
¼ teaspoon ground pepper
1 cup brown gravy
½ cup dry white wine
1 tablespoon dried sweet pepper, or 2 tablespoons chopped green pepper

1. Preheat oven to 350°F.
2. Select baking dish that will accommodate fish fillets without overlapping. Line dish with aluminum foil. Sprinkle onions evenly over bottom. Arrange fish fillets over onions.
3. In small bowl, mix together oil, salt, pepper, gravy and wine. Spoon over fillets. Sprinkle sweet or green pepper over top.
4. Bake for about 30 minutes, or until fish flakes easily.

FILLET OF SOLE WITH MACADAMIA NUTS AND GREEN PEPPERCORNS

▼▼

4 SERVINGS

4 *fillets (about 1½ pounds) of*
fresh or frozen and thawed
sole
½ *cup chopped macadamia nuts*
½ *cup softened butter or margarine*

4 *teaspoons chopped fresh chives*
or young green onion tops
3 *teaspoons drained green*
peppercorns

1. Preheat oven to 400°F.
2. Arrange fish in shallow baking pan. Sprinkle with nuts.
3. In saucepan, melt butter. Add chives or green onion tops and peppercorns. Sauté over medium heat until onions are limp. Pour over fish.
4. Bake for 15 minutes, or until fish is tender and flakes easily.

STUFFED FISH ROLLS

▼▼

4 SERVINGS

1 *cup cottage cheese*
1 *teaspoon seasoned salt*
½ *teaspoon seasoned pepper*
1 *teaspoon dried parsley flakes*

4 *fillets (about 1½ pounds) of*
fresh or frozen and thawed
turbot, sole or flounder
Aluminum foil

1. Preheat oven to 350°F. Have ready flat baking dish.
2. In bowl, combine cottage cheese, salt, pepper and ½ teaspoon parsley. Mix lightly.
3. Spoon cottage cheese on each fillet. Roll up, place seam side down on baking dish. Sprinkle with remaining parsley. Cover with aluminum foil.
4. Bake for 20 minutes, or until fish flakes easily.

TROUT AMANDINE

▼▼

6 SERVINGS

¼ *cup cream*
3 *eggs, beaten*
Salt to taste
Pepper to taste
6 *pan-ready trout (8 ounces each),*
boned and butterflied

Flour
½ *cup cooking oil*
½ *cup butter*
¾ *cup slivered blanched almonds*
Juice of 1 lemon

1. In flat dish, combine cream, eggs, salt and pepper. Dip trout in flour, then in egg mixture.
2. In skillet, heat cooking oil and butter. Over medium-high heat, sauté trout on both sides until golden, or about 3 minutes per side. Remove to warm platter.
3. In same butter, sauté almonds. Squeeze lemon juice over trout. Top with almonds and remaining butter.

HIGH-COUNTRY TROUT

6 SERVINGS

6 *trout (8 ounces each)*
2 *sticks butter, cut into 18 slices*
Salt

Pepper
Lemon wedges

1. Preheat oven to 450°F. Have ready flat baking dish or pan.
2. Place each trout on top of 3 slices butter.
3. Bake on bottom shelf of oven until butter begins to brown, about 12 to 15 minutes. Salt and pepper trout to taste. Turn trout, cooked side up. Return to oven, and bake until done, about 10 minutes more. Serve with lemon wedges or Amandine Sauce, page 162.

FISH POACHED IN ROSÉ

4 SERVINGS

Butter
4 *pan-ready whole fish (¾ to 1 pound each)*
1 *bottle (25 ounces) rosé*
4 *tablespoons chopped green onion*
1 *cup thick hollandaise sauce,* **or** 1 *can (6 ounces) hollandaise sauce*

2 *tablespoons whipping cream*
½ *to 1 teaspoon crumbled dried tarragon*
Freshly ground pepper

1. Preheat oven to 350°F. Butter flat baking dish large enough to accommodate fish and wine.
2. Place fish in prepared dish. Cover with wine. Sprinkle with green onion. Cover dish with buttered waxed paper.
3. Bake for 20 to 30 minutes, or until fish is tender.
4. Carefully remove fish and place on clean tea towel. Remove skin. Arrange on heated serving platter. Keep warm.
5. In same cooking dish over medium-low heat, reduce wine until slightly thickened and measures about 1 cup liquid. Cool slightly.
6. Strain wine. Stir in hollandaise sauce, cream, tarragon and pepper to taste. Heat through, stirring until smooth, but *do not boil*. Pour over warm fish.

DEVILED CRAB

4 SERVINGS

1 cup White Sauce, page 169,
   made with half-and-half
1 tablespoon chopped parsley
¼ teaspoon dry mustard
½ teaspoon horseradish, if desired
1 teaspoon lemon juice

½ teaspoon paprika
2 cups cooked flaked crab meat
2 tablespoons Madeira or sherry
2 hard-cooked eggs, chopped
   Buttered bread crumbs

1. Preheat oven to 400°F. Butter 4 ramekins or seafood shells.
2. In saucepan, combine white sauce, parsley, mustard, horseradish if desired, lemon juice and paprika. Heat, but do not boil. Add crab meat, wine and eggs. Stir to blend.
3. Spoon crab mixture into ramekins or seafood shells. Sprinkle with buttered bread crumbs.
4. Bake until heated through or about 15 minutes.

CRAB MEAT MARYLAND: In Step 2, make white sauce, omitting mustard, horseradish, lemon juice, and paprika. Add 1 tablespoon chopped chives and 2 tablespoons Worcestershire sauce. Use sherry. Serve on buttered toast. Garnish with watercress.

DEVILED OYSTERS

8 SERVINGS

1 medium onion, finely chopped
½ cup butter
1 quart oysters, well drained and
   cut in pieces
3 eggs, beaten
4 tablespoons lemon juice
3 cups soda cracker crumbs
2 tablespoons Worcestershire
   sauce

½ teaspoon pepper
¼ teaspoon cayenne pepper
½ teaspoon paprika
   Few drops liquid hot pepper
   sauce
1 teaspoon salt

1. Preheat oven to 400°F. Butter 8 individual seafood shells or ramekins or 2-quart casserole.
2. In small skillet over medium heat, sauté onion in butter until limp. Cool.
3. In large mixing bowl, combine oysters and beaten eggs. Add onion and remaining ingredients. Mix well. Spoon into prepared shells, ramekins or casserole.
4. Bake shells or ramekins about 20 to 25 minutes, casserole about 45 minutes.

BAKED SCALLOPS AND AVOCADO

4 SERVINGS

1 tablespoon butter or margarine
1 tablespoon all-purpose flour
¾ cup milk
¼ teaspoon salt
⅛ teaspoon ground pepper
2 teaspoons finely minced onion
2 tablespoons white wine, or
    2 teaspoons lemon juice

¼ cup grated Parmesan
2 large avocados, peeled, cut in
    half and seeds removed
Aluminum foil
20 frozen fried breaded scallops

1. Preheat oven to 350°F.
2. In small saucepan, mix together butter and flour until smooth. Add milk, salt, pepper and onion. Cook over medium-low heat until thickened. Stir in wine or lemon juice and cheese. Cook until well blended. Set aside.
3. Place each avocado half on an 8-inch square piece aluminum foil. Fold foil around avocado to act as stabilizer underneath narrow end. Place one scallop in avocado center. Spoon sauce on top. Arrange 3 or 4 more scallops on top around center scallop. Do not allow sauce to run over sides.
4. Bake for 30 minutes, or until heated through and bubbly.

NOTE: Frozen fried breaded shrimp or clams may be substituted for scallops.

SCALLOPS SAUTÉED WITH NECTARINES

4 SERVINGS

¼ cup butter or margarine
½ teaspoon salt
    Dash ground pepper
1 tablespoon crumbled dried
    sweet basil

1 pound scallops
2 nectarines, washed and sliced
¼ cup chopped green onion
2 tablespoons lemon juice

1. In large skillet, melt butter or margarine. Add salt, pepper and basil. Add scallops. Cook over medium-high heat, stirring occasionally, until scallops are lightly browned, about 7 to 12 minutes.
2. Add nectarines and green onions. Cook until onions are limp.
3. Add lemon juice. Heat through.

SHERRIED SCALLOPS

▼▼

4 SERVINGS

4 tablespoons all-purpose flour
½ teaspoon seasoned salt
1 pound scallops, washed and
  drained
3 tablespoons melted butter or
  margarine

⅓ cup sherry
¼ teaspoon dried tarragon
½ teaspoon dried parsley, or
  1 teaspoon chopped parsley
Paprika
Lemon wedges

1. Mix flour and salt. Shake scallops in seasoned flour in paper bag.
2. In skillet over medium heat, sauté floured scallops in melted butter or margarine, turning to brown all sides evenly (about 7 minutes). Place sautéed scallops on heated serving dish.
3. In same skillet, simmer sherry, tarragon, and parsley, heating through. Pour over hot scallops. Sprinkle with paprika. Garnish with lemon wedges.

SHRIMP DE JONGHE

▼▼

8 SERVINGS

2 pounds shrimp, cooked, peeled
  and deveined
1 cup butter
4 cloves garlic, skewered on
  toothpicks
¼ teaspoon dried tarragon
½ teaspoon chopped parsley
½ teaspoon chopped shallots

Dash ground nutmeg
Dash ground mace
Dash ground thyme
Dash liquid hot pepper sauce
1 teaspoon salt
⅛ teaspoon pepper
½ cup dry sauterne or sherry
1 cup fine dry bread crumbs

1. Preheat oven to 400°F. Divide shrimp among 8 buttered ramekins.
2. In small heavy saucepan, melt ¾ cup butter. Over medium heat sauté garlic, tarragon, parsley and shallots just until moistened and slightly browned. Add nutmeg, mace, thyme, liquid hot pepper sauce, salt, pepper and wine. Heat, but do not boil. Remove garlic.
3. Pour sauce over shrimp. Sprinkle top with bread crumbs. Drizzle remaining ¼ cup butter over bread crumbs.
4. Bake 10 to 15 minutes, or until heated through and nicely browned.

BOILED SHRIMP OR PRAWNS

6 SERVINGS

1½ to 2 pounds raw shrimp
6 cups water
1 tablespoon salt
1 bay leaf
2 tablespoons lemon juice or
    2 lemon slices
2 tablespoons wine vinegar

4 sprigs parsley
1 stalk celery with leaves
6 peppercorns
1 small onion, sliced
12 whole allspice, if desired
12 cloves, if desired
¼ teaspoon ground thyme

1. Wash shrimp in cold water. Peel shrimp and remove dark vein by cutting down back of shrimp with sharp knife (or peel and devein after cooking, if desired).
2. Bring all ingredients, except shrimp, to boil in large pan. Add shrimp. Cover. Simmer 5 minutes. Remove from heat. Drain. Serve hot or cold.

INDIAN SHRIMP CURRY

4 TO 6 SERVINGS

¼ cup butter or margarine
2 tablespoons curry powder
¼ teaspoon ground ginger
1½ teaspoons salt
1 cup minced onion
1 large apple, cored and chopped
1 cup chopped celery
3 tablespoons all-purpose flour
1 cup chicken bouillon
1 can (14¼ ounces) evaporated
    milk

2 pounds deveined cooked shrimp
2 to 3 cups cooked rice
Curry accompaniments
    (chutney, raisins, snipped
    parsley, pineapple chunks,
    crisp bacon bits, chopped
    hard-cooked eggs, shredded
    coconut, grated orange rind
    and/or chopped salted
    peanuts)

1. In large heavy skillet over medium heat, melt butter or margarine. Stir in curry powder, ginger and salt. Cook 1 minute, stirring constantly. Add onion, apple and celery. Cook until vegetables are limp, about 8 minutes.
2. Add flour, stirring to blend. Add bouillon and evaporated milk, stirring constantly. Cook over low heat until sauce is thickened, about 10 minutes, stirring constantly. *Do not boil.* Add shrimp. Heat through, but do not boil.
3. Serve on hot cooked rice with curry accompaniments.

CRAB, FISH OR SHRIMP PARTY CASSEROLE

8 SERVINGS

10 slices bread
2 cups cooked and flaked crabmeat
 or fish, or cooked, shelled and
 deveined shrimp, cut in
 ½-inch pieces
½ cup mayonnaise
1 green pepper, seeded and
 chopped
1 cup chopped celery

1 small onion, chopped
¼ cup sunflower seeds
3 cups milk
4 eggs, beaten
 Aluminum foil or plastic wrap
1 can (10½ ounces) cream of
 mushroom soup
½ cup grated cheddar
 Paprika

1. Butter 13 × 9 × 2-inch baking dish.
2. Dice 4 slices of bread. Place in baking dish.
3. Mix fish, mayonnaise, green pepper, celery, onion and sunflower seeds. Spread over bread cubes.
4. Trim crusts from remaining slices of bread. Place trimmed slices closely together on top of shellfish.
5. Mix milk with beaten eggs. Pour over bread slices. Cover with foil or plastic wrap. Refrigerate overnight.
6. Uncover. Bake in oven preheated to 325°F. for 15 minutes. Remove from oven. Pour soup over top, then sprinkle with grated cheese and paprika. Bake 1 hour longer.

FLOUNDER OR SOLE IN CHABLIS SAUCE

6 SERVINGS

1 large slice onion, separated
 into rings
6 fresh or frozen and thawed
 flounder or sole fillets
½ cup chablis
2 tablespoons lemon juice
½ bay leaf

¼ teaspoon salt
6 peppercorns
 Buttered waxed paper
1 tablespoon butter
1 tablespoon all-purpose flour
2 egg yolks, beaten
1 tablespoon water

1. Preheat oven to 350°F.
2. In greased shallow baking dish, place onion rings. Arrange fish on onions. Add chablis, lemon juice, bay leaf, salt and peppercorns.
3. Cover with sheet of buttered waxed paper.
4. Bake for 15 minutes. Remove fillets from baking dish. Keep warm. Strain sauce, adding water if needed to make 1 cup.
5. In small saucepan, melt butter. Stir in flour. Add strained sauce a little at a time. Cook over medium-low heat, stirring constantly, until thickened.

6. Beat egg yolks with 1 tablespoon water. Add to sauce a little at a time. Cook for 1 minute, stirring vigorously.

7. Increase oven temperature to 400°F. Put fillets back in baking dish. Pour sauce over fillets. Set in pan of boiling water. Bake for 3 minutes, or until fish is heated through.

SHRIMP OR VEGETABLE TEMPURA

ABOUT 2 DOZEN

Cooking oil
1½ *pounds large shrimp, peeled and deveined, or equivalent amount of vegetable chunks (carrots, cauliflower, zucchini, green pepper, broccoli, Jerusalem artichokes, asparagus spears, turnips and sweet potatoes)*

½ *teaspoon salt*
⅛ *teaspoon ground pepper*
2 *cups ice water*
1 *teaspoon Worcestershire sauce*
Few drops liquid hot pepper sauce
1⅔ *cups all-purpose flour*

1. Preheat cooking oil to about 350° to 360°F.
2. Butterfly shrimp by splitting back to within ½ inch of tail. Press out flat. Or wash and/or peel, and dry and cut up vegetables.
3. Combine salt, pepper, water, Worcestershire sauce, liquid hot pepper sauce and flour. Mix until smooth.
4. Dip shrimp and/or vegetables in batter.
5. Drop batter-coated shrimp or vegetables into heated cooking oil. Fry until browned, or about 3 minutes. Remove with slotted spoon.

CHICKEN TEMPURA: In Step 2, substitute cooked breast of chicken, cut into 1 × 2-inch pieces.

Cooked Fruits

HIGH ALTITUDE FACTS ABOUT COOKING FRUITS

Fruits, like vegetables, must be cooked with a watchful eye. Because of the lowered boiling point of water in the fruits themselves and/or in the liquid surrounding them during cooking, it takes longer for them to become cooked and/or tender. Fruits dry out and decompose more rapidly because of the dry air, so they should be cooked while at their peak, no later, and should always be refrigerated or stored properly covered.

HIGH ALTITUDE TIMETABLE FOR COOKING DRIED FRUIT

Rinse fruit. Place in saucepan. Add enough water to cover 1½ inches above fruit. Bring to boil. Cover pan tightly. Reduce heat to simmer. Begin timing. Check package directions to shorten cooking time suggested in chart below if fruit has been processed or tenderized.

Dried Fruit	Cooking time (tightly covered) (minutes)	Amount of sugar per cup uncooked fruit
Apples	25 to 30	4 tablespoons
Apricots	25 to 30	3 tablespoons
Figs	45 to 50	0 to 1 tablespoon
Mixed Fruits	30 to 35	2 to 3 tablespoons
Peaches	35 to 40	3 to 4 tablespoons
Pears	35 to 40	3 to 4 tablespoons
Prunes	30 to 35	3 to 4 tablespoons

BAKED APPLES IN BUTTERSCOTCH SAUCE

6 SERVINGS

6 baking apples
1½ cups half-and-half
⅔ cup dark corn syrup

⅓ cup chopped nutmeats
2 tablespoons butter
1 teaspoon vanilla extract

1. Preheat oven to 350°F. Grease baking dish or casserole large enough to accommodate apples.
2. Wash and core apples.
3. In small bowl, mix together ½ cup half-and-half, ⅓ cup corn syrup and nutmeats. Fill centers of apples.
4. Bake apples 45 to 50 minutes, or until tender.
5. Meanwhile, in small saucepan, combine remaining 1 cup half-and-half, remaining ⅓ cup corn syrup and butter. Cook over medium-low heat until thickened, stirring occasionally. Add vanilla extract. Serve hot over apples.

BAKED CURRIED FRUIT

12 SERVINGS

⅓ cup butter or margarine
2 small onions, finely chopped,
   if desired
¾ cup firmly packed brown sugar
4 teaspoons curry powder
1 can (1 pound, 5 ounces) pear
   halves and juice
1 can (1 pound, 5 ounces) peach
   halves and juice

1 can (1 pound, 5 ounces) apricot
   halves and juice
1 can (1 pound, 14 ounces)
   pineapple chunks and juice
2 apples, washed, cored and
   chopped
1 cup slivered almonds, if desired

1. Preheat oven to 325°F. Butter 3-quart casserole.
2. In very large skillet, melt butter over low heat. Add onion, if desired. Sauté until limp. Add brown sugar and curry powder. Blend well. Add fruits. Add almonds, if desired. Mix gently but well. Pour into prepared casserole.
3. Bake for 1½ hours.

NOTE: May be cooked and served in an electric slow cooker.

FRUIT COMPOTE WITH KIRSCH

4 SERVINGS

¼ cup granulated sugar
¼ cup water
1 stick (1-inch) cinnamon
2 whole cloves
⅛ teaspoon salt
1 large apple

1 large pear
2 tablespoons kirsch
1 large orange
1 cup seedless grapes
    Fresh strawberries, if desired

1. In 1-quart saucepan, combine sugar, water, cinnamon, cloves and salt. Bring to boil over medium heat.
2. Wash, peel, core, and dice apple and pear. Add to syrup. Cover. Cook over low heat for 10 to 15 minutes, or until fruit is tender. Add kirsch.
3. Remove from heat. Discard cloves and cinnamon stick. Chill.
4. Shortly before serving, peel and section orange. Wash grapes. Add orange and grapes to apple-pear mixture. Spoon into sherbet glasses. Garnish with strawberries, if desired.

GRAPEFRUIT BAKED WITH HONEY AND SESAME SEEDS

4 SERVINGS

2 grapefruit
4 tablespoons honey or brown sugar
4 teaspoons butter

4 tablespoons sherry, sauterne, or
    rum, if desired
Sesame seeds

1. Preheat oven to 350°F. Have ready shallow baking dish.
2. Cut grapefruit in half. Remove center. Cut around outside edge and between sections. Remove seeds. Place fruit in baking dish.
3. Sprinkle 1 tablespoon honey or brown sugar over top of each half. Dot with 1 teaspoon butter. Spoon 1 tablespoon of sherry, sauterne, or rum, if desired, into center. Sprinkle with sesame seeds.
4. Bake 20 to 30 minutes.

BROILED GRAPEFRUIT: Follow directions for preparation of baked grapefruit. Place about 6 inches from broiler heat. Broil about 10 minutes, or until heated through.

ORANGES IN BORDEAUX

8 SERVINGS

8 *large navel oranges*
3 *tablespoons grated orange rind*
1 *cup red Bordeaux*
1 *cup water*
2 *slices lemon*

¾ *cup granulated sugar*
1 *stick (1-inch) cinnamon*
3 *whole cloves*
Dash nutmeg

1. Peel and section oranges, removing all white pith and membrane. Place in serving dish. Sprinkle with rind. Cover. Set aside.
2. In saucepan, combine remaining ingredients. Bring to boil. Cover. Simmer 5 minutes over low heat. Strain. Pour over oranges.
3. Serve chilled.

PEACHES OR PEARS IN PORT

4 SERVINGS

4 *peaches or pears*
½ *cup sugar*
½ *cup water*

1 *tablespoon lemon juice*
¼ *teaspoon ground cinnamon*
½ *cup port*

1. Peel peaches or pears, leaving them whole and, if possible, preserving stems.
2. In 1-quart saucepan with cover, combine sugar, water, lemon juice, cinnamon and wine. Bring to boil. Arrange peaches or pears in liquid so that they are as submerged as possible. Cover. Cook 5 minutes over medium-low heat. Turn peaches or pears. Re-cover and cook 15 to 20 minutes longer.
3. Refrigerate until thoroughly chilled.

Gravies, Sauces, Glazes and Marinades for Meat, Fish, Poultry, Game and Vegetables

HIGH ALTITUDE FACTS ABOUT MAKING GRAVIES

Allow extra cooking time over medium-low heat to avoid a raw taste in thickened gravies. Cook the roux before adding liquid. Direct heat and a heavy saucepan or skillet are preferable to a double boiler for gravy-making.

PAN GRAVY

1 CUP

Remove meat or poultry from cooking pan to heated platter. Skim off excess fat, leaving bits and pieces in pan. Blend flour into drippings, stirring to make a roux. Add milk, water, stock or consommé to mixture. Bring to boil, stirring constantly. Reduce heat. Simmer, stirring constantly, until thickened 3 to 5 minutes. Season with salt, pepper and herbs to taste. Add Kitchen Bouquet for color, if desired.

	Fat	Flour	Fat-free pan drippings, milk, water, stock or consommé	Salt, pepper, herbs
Thin	1 tablespoon	1 tablespoon	1 cup	to taste
Medium	1½ tablespoons	1½ tablespoons	1 cup	to taste
Thick	2 tablespoons	2 tablespoons	1 cup	to taste

AMANDINE SAUCE

1 CUP

For hot vegetables, fish and some meats.

½ cup butter
⅓ cup slivered almonds

¼ teaspoon salt
2 tablespoons lemon juice

In saucepan, melt butter. Over medium heat, sauté almonds until lightly browned. Remove from heat. Add salt and lemon juice. Serve hot.

BARBECUE SAUCE

2 CUPS

¼ cup chopped onion
½ clove garlic, minced
¼ cup catsup
2 tablespoons Worcestershire sauce
¼ cup cider vinegar
1 can (10½ ounces) tomato soup

2 teaspoons butter
1 teaspoon brown sugar
⅛ teaspoon pepper
Dash cayenne pepper
¼ teaspoon smoke salt

In medium-size saucepan with cover, combine all ingredients. Bring to boil. Cover. Reduce heat. Simmer 1 hour, stirring occasionally, adding a small amount of water if needed.

BÉARNAISE SAUCE

ABOUT ¾ CUP

For any red meat, fish, eggs or some vegetables.

¼ cup butter
2 tablespoons hot water
2 egg yolks
1 tablespoon tarragon vinegar
1 teaspoon finely chopped shallot
    or onion

¾ teaspoon finely chopped parsley
⅛ teaspoon salt
Paprika

1. In top of double boiler over boiling water, melt butter with hot water. Stir in egg yolks. Beat with wire whisk or rotary beater until frothy. Stir in remaining ingredients.
2. Cook, stirring constantly, just until thickened and smooth, about 8 minutes. Remove from heat at once.
3. Serve warm.

BROWN SAUCE

1 CUP

The base for many sauces.

1½ tablespoons butter
1½ tablespoons all-purpose flour
  2 cups Beef Stock, page 252, or
     1 can (10½ ounces) beef
     bouillon or consommé

½ cup water

In small heavy saucepan, melt butter. Blend in flour. Cook, stirring constantly, over low heat until browned. Stir in stock, bouillon or consommé and water. Cook, stirring constantly, until thickened.

SAUCE CHABLIS

ABOUT 1 CUP

For delicate fish, such as flounder, sole or turbot.

½ cup chablis	Water
2 tablespoons fresh lemon juice	1 tablespoon butter
½ bay leaf	1 tablespoon all-purpose flour
¼ teaspoon salt	2 egg yolks, beaten with
6 peppercorns	1 tablespoon water

1. In small heavy saucepan, combine wine, lemon juice, bay leaf, salt and peppercorns. Cook 5 minutes, over low heat, stirring to blend. Strain sauce, adding enough water to make 1 cup.
2. In separate saucepan, melt butter, stir in flour. Add strained sauce. Cook over medium heat, stirring constantly, until thickened. Add beaten egg yolks a little at a time. Cook for 2 minutes, stirring vigorously. Pour over cooked fish.

CHASSEUR SAUCE

2 CUPS

2 tablespoons minced shallots or onion	½ cup tomato sauce
	1 cup brown gravy
2 tablespoons butter	Salt
1 cup sliced mushrooms	Pepper
½ cup dry white wine	1 teaspoon chopped parsley
1 tablespoon brandy	

1. In small heavy saucepan, over medium heat, sauté shallots or onion in butter until limp. Add mushrooms. Brown lightly. Stir in wine and brandy. Simmer until reduced by one half.
2. Add tomato sauce and gravy. Cook 5 minutes, stirring occasionally. Add salt and pepper to taste and parsley. Serve hot.

CHERRY SAUCE

2½ CUPS

For poultry, ham or lamb.

1½ tablespoons cornstarch
1 cup canned cherry juice
2 tablespoons melted ham
   drippings or butter
½ cup water
¼ cup lemon juice

1 teaspoon grated lemon rind
⅛ teaspoon salt
¼ cup firmly packed brown sugar
1 cup drained canned
   unsweetened cherries
   (reserve juice)

1. Dissolve cornstarch in cherry juice.
2. In saucepan, combine all remaining ingredients, except cherries. Bring to boil. Stir in cherry juice. Cook over medium heat, stirring constantly, until thickened. Add cherries. Heat through, but do not boil. Serve hot.

CURRY SAUCE

ABOUT 4 CUPS

3 medium onions, chopped
3 to 4 tablespoons butter or
   olive oil
1 teaspoon ground ginger
2 teaspoons ground cumin
2 teaspoons garlic powder
1 tablespoon curry powder or
   to taste

Flour
1 can (1 pound, 14 ounces)
   tomatoes, finely chopped,
   and juice
1 cup dairy sour cream
1 cup buttermilk
¼ cup coconut milk
   Salt to taste

1. In large heavy skillet over medium heat, sauté onion in butter or olive oil until limp. Stir in ginger, cumin, garlic and curry powder. Blend completely. Stir in a little flour to make paste.
2. Add remaining ingredients. Heat through, but do not boil, stirring to blend flavors.

SAMBALS FOR CURRY: In individual small dishes, offer any or all of these accompaniments: chutney, raisins, snipped parsley, pineapple chunks, crisp bacon bits, chopped hard-cooked eggs, sliced bananas sprinkled with lemon and chili, shredded coconut, hot cucumber relish, onion and red pepper relish, toasted coconut chips, apple relish, chopped salted peanuts, grated orange rind, dried currants.

PIQUANT SAUCE

1¼ CUPS

For seafood, hamburgers and frankfurters.

1 *cup chili sauce or catsup*	2 *teaspoons sherry, if desired, or*
2 *tablespoons prepared mustard*	2 *teaspoons horseradish, if desired*

Combine all ingredients. Serve at room temperature.

SPICY SAUCE FOR POULTRY OR GAME

3 CUPS

1 *cup water*	1½ *teaspoons ground cinnamon*
1 *cup dry sherry*	¾ *teaspoon ground cloves*
½ *cup firmly packed brown sugar*	¾ *teaspoon ground ginger*
¼ *cup Japanese soy sauce*	2 *large cloves garlic, crushed*
½ *cup pear or peach nectar, pineapple, apple or orange juice*	1 *to* 1½ *tablespoons cornstarch*

1. In saucepan with cover, combine all ingredients except cornstarch. Bring to boil. Cover. Reduce heat. Simmer for 30 minutes.
2. Add cornstarch dissolved in a little water. Cook, stirring constantly, until thickened. Sauce will keep for weeks refrigerated.

GREEN PEPPER SAUCE

ABOUT 5 CUPS

For steaks, chops, roasts, ground meats or meat loaf.

3 *tablespoons melted butter*	4 *cups brown gravy*
4 *medium green peppers, seeded and coarsely chopped*	*Dash garlic powder, if desired*
	¼ *cup burgundy or sherry*

In skillet, melt butter. Over medium heat, sauté green pepper until soft. Stir in gravy. Add garlic powder, if desired. Cook, over medium-low heat, for 10 minutes. Remove from heat. Add wine. Pour over meat.

HOLLANDAISE SAUCE

1¾ CUPS

½ cup butter
¼ cup boiling water
4 egg yolks

2 tablespoons lemon juice
¼ teaspoon salt
Dash cayenne pepper

1. In top of double boiler, melt butter. Stir in boiling water. Slowly add egg yolks, beating constantly with wire whisk until mixture is almost doubled in bulk.
2. Continue beating while adding lemon juice a little at a time. Cook, stirring constantly, over simmering but not boiling water, until smooth and thick. This may take as long as 15 minutes at high altitude. Stir in salt and cayenne pepper.
3. Remove from heat. Serve immediately.

MINT SAUCE

1 CUP

3 tablespoons water
3 tablespoons powdered sugar

⅓ cup finely chopped mint leaves,
     or 2 tablespoons dried mint
¼ cup cider vinegar

In small saucepan over medium heat, bring all ingredients to boil. Simmer a few minutes. Serve hot or cold.

MUSTARD SAUCE FOR FISH

ABOUT 1½ CUPS

1 tablespoon butter
2 tablespoons all-purpose flour
½ teaspoon salt
¼ teaspoon paprika

¼ teaspoon Worcestershire sauce
1 cup half-and-half
1½ tablespoons prepared mustard
     or 2 teaspoons dry mustard

In small heavy saucepan, melt butter. Add flour, stirring until smooth. Add salt, paprika and Worcestershire sauce. Add half-and-half and mustard, blending well. Cook over medium-low heat, stirring constantly, until smooth and thickened, about 5 minutes or more. Serve hot.

HOT MUSTARD SAUCE

3 CUPS

For ham, pork, cold cuts, tempura and sandwiches.

1 cup dry mustard
1 cup white vinegar

1 cup granulated sugar
3 eggs, well beaten

In heavy saucepan, blend together mustard and vinegar until smooth. Add sugar and eggs. Over medium-low heat, cook, stirring constantly, until thickened, or about 15 minutes.

ITALIAN MEAT SAUCE

8 CUPS

1 large onion, finely chopped
2 cloves garlic, minced
2 tablespoons olive or cooking oil
1½ pounds lean ground beef
2 cans (1 pound 12 ounces each) tomatoes
2 cans (6 ounces each) tomato paste
½ cup water

¼ cup chopped celery
¼ cup chopped parsley
1 can (3 ounces) sliced mushrooms
1 tablespoon salt
2 teaspoons granulated sugar
1 teaspoon dried sweet basil
¼ teaspoon pepper
2 bay leaves

1. In large skillet with cover, over medium heat, sauté onion and garlic in hot oil. Add beef, chopping into fine granules as it browns. Stir in remaining ingredients.
2. Bring mixture to boil. Cover. Reduce heat. Simmer, stirring occasionally, 2½ to 3 hours, or until sauce is thick. Or, bake at 300°F. for 4 hours. Remove bay leaves and skim off fat before serving.

ORANGE SAUCE FOR DUCK (SAUCE BIGARADE)

2 CUPS

½ cup red currant jelly
1 peppercorn
1½ cups brown gravy
Juice of 2 oranges

Grated rind of 1 orange
Grated rind of ½ lemon
1 tablespoon Madeira

1. In saucepan, melt jelly. Add peppercorn, ½ cup gravy, orange juice and rind, and lemon rind. Bring to boil. Reduce heat. Simmer 20 minutes, or just until thickened.
2. Add remaining 1 cup brown gravy. Heat, but do not boil.
3. Strain sauce and stir in wine. Serve hot.

WHITE SAUCE (BÉCHAMEL SAUCE)

For creaming vegetables, meats and fish, and as a base for other sauces. Margarine may be substituted for butter, but the flavor will not be as good. A heavy saucepan instead of a double boiler is recommended to avoid a raw taste and to hasten cooking time.

	Butter	All-Purpose Flour	Milk	Salt	White Pepper
Thin	1 tablespoon	1 tablespoon	1 cup	½ teaspoon	⅛ teaspoon
Medium	2 tablespoons	2 tablespoons	1 cup	½ teaspoon	⅛ teaspoon
Thick	3 tablespoons	3 tablespoons	1 cup	½ teaspoon	⅛ teaspoon

1. In small heavy saucepan, melt butter over medium-low heat. Add flour, blending with wooden spoon until smooth. Cook for 2 minutes, stirring constantly.
2. Slowly stir in milk. Cook, stirring constantly with wire whisk or wooden spoon, until thickened, smooth and thoroughly cooked.
3. Add salt and pepper.

EGG CREAM SAUCE: In Step 3, add 2 chopped hard-cooked eggs and 1 tablespoon finely chopped pickles to 1 cup Medium White Sauce.

HORSERADISH SAUCE (SAUCE ALBERT): In Step 2, add 3 tablespoons prepared horseradish, 2 tablespoons whipping cream, 1 teaspoon granulated sugar, 1 teaspoon dry mustard and 1 tablespoon wine vinegar to 1 cup Thin White Sauce.

CHEDDAR SAUCE: In Step 3, add ¾ cup grated sharp cheddar, ½ teaspoon prepared mustard, ½ teaspoon Worcestershire sauce and dash of cayenne pepper to 1 cup Medium White Sauce. Cook, stirring constantly, until cheese is melted.

MUSHROOM SAUCE: In Step 3, add 1 cup chopped cooked mushrooms to 1 cup Thin White Sauce.

OYSTER SAUCE (FOR FISH): In Step 3, after cooking, add 1 teaspoon Worcestershire sauce, ¼ teaspoon salt, 2 tablespoons chopped parsley and 1 cup chopped poached oysters and juice to 1 cup Medium White Sauce. Reheat.

ROMANO SAUCE: In Step 3, add 1 cup grated Romano and ½ teaspoon dry mustard and a dash of cayenne pepper to 1 cup Thin White Sauce. Cook, stirring constantly, until cheese is melted.

MARINADE FOR BEEF

ABOUT 1½ CUPS

This versatile marinade tenderizes less expensive meats and enhances the flavor of choice pieces of beef to be cooked indoors or outdoors.

½ cup olive oil
½ cup red wine
4 shallots or green onions, finely chopped
¾ teaspoon freshly ground pepper
½ teaspoon dried oregano

1 bay leaf
½ teaspoon dried sweet basil
¼ cup lemon juice
2 cloves garlic, sliced in half
¼ teaspoon dried rosemary

In glass or enamel bowl, combine all ingredients. Pour over meat.

TERIYAKI SAUCE OR MARINADE

1½ CUPS

Marinate meat, fish or shellfish in sauce, or baste with sauce during cooking.

⅔ cup finely chopped onion
2 tablespoons granulated sugar
1 tablespoon minced fresh ginger root or 2 teaspoons ground ginger

2 cloves garlic, minced
½ cup cider vinegar or dry white wine
⅓ cup Japanese soy sauce

In small enamel or glass bowl, combine all ingredients.

High Altitude Facts About Meat, Poultry and Game Cookery

Two problems confront the cook when preparing meat, poultry and game at high altitudes: first, retaining enough moisture to prevent toughening, and second, getting them cooked *through*.

In bread and cake baking at high altitudes, ingredient balances are responsible for success or failure. But in meat, poultry and game cookery, careful time and temperature adjustments are the basis for successful results. Read Why High Altitude Baking and Cooking Are Different, pages xiii through xv.

Because meat, poultry and game have so much liquid (natural juices) in their composition, the ever-present accelerated rate of evaporation during cooking and lowered boiling point of the liquids themselves affect the cooking results. To compensate, the cook who is accustomed to cooking at high altitude automatically adds moisturizers and cooking time; but the newcomer often finds food that he or she prepares dry and undercooked.

A good example of the variation in cooking time is that for a standing rib roast. Roasting time at sea level would be about 2½ hours at 325°F. At 5,000 feet it would take 3 hours or more at the same temperature because the meat would actually be roasting more slowly at a lower temperature. This is because the juices in the meat can only reach the boiling point of water at a given altitude—in this case, lower than at sea level.

SUGGESTIONS FOR SUCCESSFUL MEAT, POULTRY AND GAME COOKERY AT HIGH ALTITUDES:

Generous use of moistening agents, such as wine, sour cream, consommé, broth, sauces

Use of heavy-gauge stainless-steel, porcelain-coated cast-iron and ceramic saucepans, skillets and Dutch ovens with tight-fitting covers in cooking soups, stews and combination dishes

Use of aluminum foil to seal in and prevent evaporation of natural juices

Use of a meat thermometer

Use of lowered temperatures and extra cooking time to ensure doneness

Frequent basting during roasting of poultry and game birds

Careful observance to avoid scorching, adding additional liquids, if necessary

Use of high altitude timetables for meats, poultry and game

Use of a pressure cooker

Ʞeef

HIGH ALTITUDE TIMETABLE FOR ROASTING BEEF

Refrigerate beef up to time of roasting. Preheat oven. Place roast on rack in shallow pan. Do not cover, baste or add water. Place meat thermometer in center of thickest part of meat, not touching bone or fat. (Because roasts of the same weight usually vary in shape and in fat and bone content, a meat thermometer is the most accurate means of judging when a roast is done.) Roasting times per pound given in this chart are also sound guidelines for determining when meat has reached desired doneness.

Allow roasts to stand 15 to 20 minutes out of oven before carving.

Serving allowances: For boneless meat, allow ¼ pound per serving. For meat with average amount of bone, allow ½ pound per serving. For bony meat, allow 1 pound per serving.

Beef Cut	Weight (*pounds*)	Oven temperature (*preheated*)	Roasting time in minutes per pound	Meat thermometer reading
Standing Rib; Sirloin	5½ to 8	325°F.	20 to 25	140°F.—Rare
			25 to 30	160°F.—Medium
			30 to 35	170°F.—Well done
Rolled Rib	4	325°F.	30 to 35	140°F.—Rare
			35 to 40	160°F.—Medium
			40 to 45	170°F.—Well done

HIGH ALTITUDE TIMETABLE FOR ROASTING BEEF
(CONTINUED)

Tenderloin (Fillet)	4	450°F.	10 to 12	130°F.—Rare
			13 to 15	150°F.—Medium
			16 to 18	160°F.—Well done
New York Strip Roast	8	325°F.	10 to 12	Medium rare
			12 to 13	Medium

BRACIOLE

6 SERVINGS

6 *pieces top or bottom beef round*
steaks (4 to 6 ounces each),
trimmed of fat and bones
removed
Flour
2 *tablespoons cooking or olive oil*
Salt
Pepper
½ *cup dry white wine*

1 *can (8 ounces) tomato sauce*
2 *tablespoons apple cider vinegar*
1 *medium clove garlic*
3 *anchovies with capers*
1 *teaspoon instant beef bouillon*
1 *can (4 ounces) green olives*
stuffed with pimiento, drained
Water
Cooked spaghetti or other pasta

1. Dredge meat in flour.
2. In Dutch oven or large heavy skillet with tight-fitting cover, brown floured meat in oil over medium-high heat on both sides. Sprinkle each side generously with salt and pepper. Add wine. Cover. Cook until wine is evaporated, being careful not to burn meat.
3. In blender or food processor, blend remaining ingredients except water and spaghetti until almost smooth. Pour over meat.
4. Cover. Cook over low heat for about 2 hours, or until meat is tender, adding a little water if necessary. Serve over cooked pasta.

NOTE: Lamb steaks or shoulder chops may be substituted for beef.

BRISKET OF BEEF

ABOUT 6 SERVINGS

3 *pounds beef brisket*
Salt
Freshly ground pepper
1 *to 2 cloves garlic, crushed*

Paprika
2 *cups hot water*
3 *large onions, sliced*

1. Preheat oven to 350°F.
2. Place brisket in roasting pan with cover. Season with salt, pepper, garlic and paprika.

3. Brown in oven, uncovered, for 45 minutes. Add water and onions. Cover. Bake for 3½ hours. Cool. Slice very thinly.

4. Purée pan juices with onions in blender or food processor. Return strained gravy to roasting pan, arrange sliced meat in gravy. Heat through.

EAST INDIAN BEEF CURRY

6 SERVINGS

1 medium onion, finely chopped	½ teaspoon salt
2 tablespoons melted butter	1 can (4 ounces) mushrooms,
2 tablespoons curry powder	drained
2 cups boiling water	1 can (6 ounces) evaporated milk
1½ to 2 pounds beef round steak,	2 tablespoons all-purpose flour
cut into ½-inch cubes	Juice of ½ lemon
1½ cups canned tomatoes	Cooked rice
1 medium potato, peeled and	
diced	

1. In large skillet or heavy saucepan with tight-fitting cover, over medium heat, sauté onion in melted butter until limp. Add curry powder. Stir to blend. Add boiling water, cubed meat, tomatoes, potato and salt. Cover. Cook over medium-low heat 3½ hours.

2. Just before serving, add mushrooms and evaporated milk. Stir in flour, blending until smooth. Cook until thickened. Turn off heat. When sauce stops boiling, stir in lemon juice. Serve over rice.

BEEF POT ROAST

6 SERVINGS

Flour	2 bay leaves
4 pounds beef chuck, rump or	1½ cups boiling water or beef
brisket	stock
2 tablespoons cooking oil	1 teaspoon salt
1 to 2 onions, sliced	½ teaspoon seasoned pepper

1. Dredge meat in flour.

2. In heavy skillet or Dutch oven with cover, brown meat in hot cooking oil over high heat. Add onions, bay leaves, boiling water or stock, salt and pepper. Cover.

3. Bake at 325°F. for 3 hours. Remove bay leaves before serving.

POT ROAST WITH BEER: In Step 2, substitute beer for boiling water or stock, *or* pour beer over unbrowned roast, add onion, bay leaves, salt and pepper. Cover. Cook as directed.

POT ROAST WITH SOUR CREAM AND WINE: In Step 2, substitute ½ cup water and 1 cup dry red or white wine for boiling water or stock. In Step 3, stir ⅔ cup warm dairy sour cream into gravy when meat is done. Reheat, but do not boil.

PRESSURE-COOKER POT ROAST: In Step 2, brown meat in oil in pressure cooker. Place rack under meat. Add onions, bay leaves, boiling water or stock, salt and pepper. Cook 1 hour at 15 pounds' pressure at 5,000 feet, letting pressure drop of its own accord, or cook 1 hour at 15 pounds pressure and cool cooker quickly in cold water. (See High Altitude Facts About the Pressure Cooker, page xx, for additional information, altitude and time adjustments.) Add vegetables. Re-cover. Cook 8 minutes at 15 pounds pressure. Cool cooker quickly in cold water.

BEEF STEW

6 SERVINGS

¼ cup all-purpose flour	½ bay leaf
¼ teaspoon ground pepper	12 peeled carrots, cut into
½ teaspoon paprika	2-inch pieces
½ teaspoon celery seed	6 medium potatoes, peeled and
2 pounds boneless beef chuck,	quartered
shank or round, cut into	12 small white onions, peeled
1-inch cubes	1 cup frozen peas, or 1½ cups
3 tablespoons cooking oil	sliced zucchini or yellow
3½ cups boiling water	summer squash
1 clove garlic, minced, if desired	Alfalfa sprouts or chopped
1 medium onion, finely chopped	parsley

1. Combine flour, pepper, paprika and celery seed.
2. Dredge beef cubes in seasoned flour, or shake in paper or plastic bag.
3. In large, heavy skillet with tight-fitting cover or Dutch oven, over medium-high heat, sauté floured meat in cooking oil, turning to brown all sides evenly. Drain on paper toweling. Pour off excess fat.
4. Return meat to pan. Add boiling water, garlic, onion and bay leaf. Cover.
5. Bring to boil. Reduce heat. Simmer until meat is tender, about 1½ to 2 hours. Add carrots, potatoes and onions. Cook 30 minutes longer, or until vegetables are tender. Add peas or squash. Cook 8 minutes longer. Serve sprinkled with alfalfa sprouts or chopped parsley.

BEEF STEW WITH BURGUNDY: In Step 3, substitute bacon drippings for cooking oil. In Step 4, add ¼ teaspoon dried crumbled marjoram, ¼ teaspoon powdered thyme, and increase chopped onions to 3 onions. Substitute 2 cups beef bouillon and 1 cup burgundy, claret or other dry red dinner wine for boiling water. In Step 5, substitute 1 pound fresh sliced mushrooms for vegetables. Serve with cooked rice or noodles.

HARVEST BEEF STEW: In Step 5, substitute 1 cup frozen lima beans, 1 cup whole-kernel corn, 1 cup sliced mushrooms, 1 cup diced carrots, 1 cup chopped tomatoes and 1 cup uncooked macaroni for vegetables. Add ½ teaspoon powdered thyme.

OVEN BEEF STEW: In Step 4, substitute hot tomato juice for boiling water. Add 2 teaspoons prepared mustard. In Step 5, place stew in oven preheated to 325°F. Bake 1½ hours. Add carrots, potatoes and onions. Bake 1 hour longer. Add peas. Cook 30 minutes longer.

BEEF-RONI CASSEROLE

6 SERVINGS

2 pounds lean ground beef	1½ teaspoons salt
1 cup chopped onion	¼ teaspoon ground pepper
1 cup chopped green pepper	⅔ cup water
1 cup chopped celery	1 cup elbow macaroni
1 large clove garlic, minced	1 cup grated cheddar
2 cups tomato and herb sauce	1½ cups frozen mixed vegetables

1. Preheat oven to 350°F. Have ready 2-quart casserole.
2. In large skillet, over medium-high heat, sauté meat, stirring and chopping with wooden spoon into small granules as it browns. Add onion, green pepper, celery and garlic. Cook until onion is limp. Add tomato and herb sauce, salt, pepper, water, elbowroni, grated cheddar and mixed vegetables. Mix well. Pour into casserole.
3. Bake for 1 hour.

HUNGARIAN GOULASH

6 SERVINGS

3 pounds boneless beef chuck,
   cut into 2-inch cubes
Salt
Pepper
Cooking oil
1 cup finely chopped onion
1 cup tomato paste
2 tablespoons all-purpose flour
4 cups water, beef broth or
   bouillon

3 bay leaves
1/8 teaspoon powdered thyme
1/2 teaspoon dried rosemary
1 cup canned mushrooms and
   broth
1 to 2 teaspoons cornstarch
1 teaspoon caraway seeds
   (preferably ground)
1 1/2 cups dairy sour cream
Cooked noodles

1. Season meat with salt and pepper.
2. In large heavy skillet or Dutch oven with cover, over medium-high heat, sauté seasoned meat in cooking oil. Add chopped onion, tomato paste and flour. Stir until smooth. Add water, broth or bouillon, and bay leaves, thyme and rosemary. Stir. Cover. Simmer for 2 to 2½ hours, or bake at 325°F. for about 3 hours.
3. Add mushrooms and broth.
4. Mix cornstarch and caraway seeds into sour cream. Stir into pan juices. Heat, but do not boil. Serve over noodles.

BAVARIAN BEEF ROLLS

4 SERVINGS

2 pounds round steak, cut
   1/4 -inch thick
Salt
Pepper
Prepared mustard
1/2 pound sliced bacon
2 dill pickles, cut into julienne
   strips

1 large onion, finely chopped
Flour
2 tablespoons tomato paste
2 cups beef stock, consommé,
   bouillon or water
Cooked noodles, rice or mashed
   potatoes

1. Preheat oven to 450°F. Lightly grease flat baking dish.
2. Cut meat into 10 × 5-inch pieces. Sprinkle with salt and pepper. Spread with mustard. Place half a slice of bacon, a strip of pickle and a heaping tea-spoonful of chopped onion on each piece. Roll up. Fasten with toothpick.
3. Place beef rolls in baking dish. Bake until browned. Remove from oven. Dust with flour. Spread with tomato paste. Brown in oven again.
4. Add beef stock, consommé, bouillon or water. Reduce temperature to 350°F. Bake 2 hours more, or until tender. Serve with noodles, mashed potatoes or rice.

FAVORITE MEAT LOAF

▼▼▼▼▼▼▼▼▼▼▼▼▼▼▼▼▼▼▼▼▼▼▼▼▼▼▼▼▼▼▼▼▼▼▼▼▼

4 SERVINGS

1 *egg, beaten*
1 *can (8 ounces) tomato sauce*
1 *teaspoon salt*
¼ *teaspoon ground pepper*
¼ *teaspoon garlic powder*
½ *teaspoon dried fines herbes*
¼ *teaspoon dried mustard*

2 *tablespoons Worcestershire*
   sauce
1½ *pounds lean ground beef*
⅓ *cup crushed saltine crackers*
   Catsup
   Bean sprouts

1. Preheat oven to 350°F. Have ready shallow baking or loaf pan.
2. In large mixing bowl, mix together egg, tomato sauce, salt, pepper, garlic powder, herbs, mustard and Worcestershire sauce. Add beef and crackers. Mix very well. Form meat mixture into loaf. Place in pan.
3. Bake at 350°F. for 1¼ to 1½ hours. Serve garnished with bean sprouts.

SAUERBRATEN

▼▼▼▼▼▼▼▼▼▼▼▼▼▼▼▼▼▼▼▼▼▼▼▼▼▼▼▼▼▼▼▼▼▼▼▼▼

6 TO 8 SERVINGS

¾ *cup beer, ale or dry wine*
1½ *cups cider vinegar*
¾ *cup water*
3 *medium onions, sliced*
2 *tablespoons mixed pickling*
   spices
3 *bay leaves*
4 *pounds beef: boneless rump,*
   chuck or round

2 *tablespoons all-purpose flour*
1½ *teaspoons salt*
⅛ *teaspoon ground pepper*
2 *tablespoons cooking oil*
⅓ *cup gingersnap crumbs*
½ *cup dairy sour cream*

1. In deep bowl or crock, combine beer, ale or wine with vinegar, water, onions, pickling spices and bay leaves. Place meat in marinade. Allow to marinate in refrigerator 2 to 4 days, turning occasionally.
2. Remove meat from marinade and pat dry. Reserve marinade.
3. Blend flour, salt and pepper together. Dredge meat in seasoned flour.
4. In large heavy skillet with tight-fitting cover or Dutch oven, heat cooking oil. Brown meat over medium-high heat, turning to brown all sides, about 15 to 20 minutes. Add ¾ cup reserved marinade. Cover. Reduce heat. Simmer over low heat for 3½ to 4 hours, or until meat is very tender. Add small amount of marinade, if necessary to prevent cooking dry. Remove meat to heated platter.
5. Make gravy: Drain drippings. Measure and return ⅓ cup to skillet. Add gingersnap crumbs. Stir in 2 cups strained marinade. Cook over medium heat, stirring constantly, until thickened. Blend in sour cream. Heat, but *do not boil.*
6. Slice meat and pour sauce over it before serving.

PRESSURE-COOKER SAUERBRATEN: In Step 4, brown meat in pressure cooker. Place rack under meat. Add marinade and ½ cup water. Cover and cook at 15 pounds pressure for 1 hour at 5,000 feet, letting pressure drop of its own accord. (See High Altitude Facts About the Pressure Cooker, page xx, for additional information, altitude and time adjustments.) Prepare gravy as directed above.

SIRLOIN TIPS WITH WALNUTS

6 SERVINGS

2 *pounds sirloin tips, cut into 1-inch cubes*	6 *tablespoons chopped walnut meats*
¼ *cup all-purpose flour*	1 *tablespoon sherry*
4 *tablespoons butter*	1 *tablespoon dry mustard*
1½ *cups boiling water*	¾ *teaspoon powdered cardamom*
½ *cup chopped onion*	3 *tablespoons claret or other dry red wine*

1. Dredge meat in flour.
2. In large heavy skillet or Dutch oven with cover, brown floured meat in 2 tablespoons butter over medium heat. Add boiling water and chopped onion. Cover. Bring to boil. Reduce heat. Simmer 45 minutes to 1 hour, or until tender. Place meat on heated platter. Pour juices from pan; reserve ½ cup.
3. Make sauce: Melt remaining 2 tablespoons butter in same cooking pan. Add walnuts and sherry. Bring to boil. Add mustard and cardamom, stirring well. Add reserved ½ cup meat juices. Bring to boil. Cook 3 to 4 minutes, covered. Remove cover and simmer to reduce and thicken liquid. Add wine, stir quickly and pour over meat.

TOURNEDOS

6 SERVINGS

6 *beef tenderloin steaks, cut 2 inches thick*	2 *tablespoons chopped tarragon*
¾ *cup butter*	½ *cup Madeira*
2 *shallots or green onions, finely chopped*	1 *cup beef stock or consommé*
	Freshly ground pepper
	Salt
½ *cup brandy*	2 *large mushrooms, thinly sliced*

1. In heavy skillet, over medium-high heat, sauté meat in ½ cup butter to rare or medium doneness.
2. Add shallots or onions. Brown slightly. Add brandy. Ignite. Place meat on heated platter. Keep warm.

3. To sauce in skillet, add tarragon and ¼ cup wine. Cook until sauce is reduced to one-third. Add beef stock. Boil 5 minutes. Season with pepper and salt. Remove from heat. Blend in remaining ¼ cup wine and ¼ cup butter. Add mushrooms and cook slightly. Place mushrooms on tournedos. Pour sauce over meat.

ASIATIC STEW

6 SERVINGS

2 tablespoons cooking oil	10 green onions
2½ pounds beef chuck, cut into 1-inch cubes and trimmed of fat	1 teaspoon salt
	½ teaspoon freshly ground pepper
	¼ cup red wine vinegar
2½ cups boiling water	½ cup honey
¾ teaspoon ground coriander	½ teaspoon garlic powder
¾ teaspoon ground cinnamon	1 cup sliced almonds
1½ cups sliced onion	1 can (17 ounces) figs, drained
1 carrot, peeled and sliced	

1. In large heavy skillet with tight-fitting cover, heat oil. Add meat. Sauté over medium-high heat until browned. Add water, coriander, cinnamon, onion, carrot and green onions. Cover. Cook over low heat for 1½ hours.
2. Add salt, pepper, vinegar, honey, garlic powder, almonds and figs. Re-cover. Simmer 1 hour more. Do not boil.

HIGH-TEMPERATURE ROAST BEEF

8 SERVINGS

1 standing rib roast (6 pounds) at room temperature	1 large head cabbage, cut in eight wedges
2 cloves garlic, cut in slivers, if desired	1 large head cauliflower, cut in eight wedges
2 large onions, quartered	
8 carrots, peeled	

1. Preheat oven to 550°F.
2. With sharp knife, cut slits in beef. Insert garlic slivers into slits.
3. Place beef in shallow roasting pan. Arrange vegetables around beef. Add water.
4. Bake at 550°F. for 20 minutes. *Reduce* heat to 300°F. Bake 1½ hours more. Turn off oven. Open oven door. Let roast stand on opened door 20 minutes before carving.

STEAK AU POIVRE VERT

1 to 1½-inch sirloin steak (about
   3 pounds)
1 tablespoon cognac
1 tablespoon drained green
   peppercorns, mashed with fork

¼ cup whipping cream
½ teaspoon Dijon mustard
¼ teaspoon dried dill weed

1. Have ready large heavy skillet. Place platter in oven to warm.
2. Cut fat off steak. Over high heat, heat skillet, rub fat on inside bottom. Discard fat.
3. Pan-fry steak to desired doneness, turning only once. Transfer cooked steak to warm platter. Keep warm.
4. In same skillet, combine cognac, peppercorns, cream, mustard and dill weed, stirring to blend ingredients and loosen bits from pan bottom. Spoon sauce over steak.
5. To serve, cut steak across grain in thin slices.

LIVER IN SOUR CREAM

1½ pounds calves or beef liver, cut
   ⅜ to ½ inch thick
2 teaspoons softened butter or
   margarine
Juice of 1 lemon

Salt
Ground pepper
½ cup dairy sour cream
2 teaspoons prepared mustard

1. Arrange liver in shallow baking pan lined with aluminum foil.
2. Spread butter evenly over surface of liver. Sprinkle with lemon juice. Let stand for 30 minutes.
3. Broil liver just until lightly browned on one side only. Remove from heat. Sprinkle with salt and pepper. Reduce oven temperature to 350°F.
4. In small bowl, mix together sour cream and mustard. Spread evenly over liver.
5. Bake at 350°F. for 10 to 15 minutes, depending on thickness of liver.

BRAISED OXTAILS

2 *pounds oxtails, cut into pieces*
    at joints
Salt
Pepper
Flour
3 *tablespoons shortening or*
    cooking oil

1 *medium onion, sliced*
1 *cup boiling water*
1 *can (8 ounces) tomato sauce*
1 *bay leaf*
2 *tablespoons vinegar*

1. Wash oxtails in cold running water. Pat dry. Season with salt and pepper. Dredge in flour.
2. Over medium-high heat, quickly sauté meat in hot shortening or cooking oil, turning to brown all sides. Pour off excess fat. Add remaining ingredients. Bring to boil. Reduce temperature. Cover.
3. Simmer 2½ to 3 hours, or until meat is tender, or bake at 325°F. for 2½ to 3 hours, adding more boiling water if needed.

BOILED BEEF TONGUE AND SAUCE

1 *beef tongue (2 to 5 pounds)*
1 *cup coarsely chopped onion*
2 *cups water*
2 *bay leaves*

6 *whole cloves*
2 *tablespoons cream-style*
    horseradish
1 *cup dairy sour cream*

1. Scrub tongue under cold running water. Place in large, deep kettle with tight-fitting cover. Add onion, water, bay leaves and cloves. Cover.
2. Bring to boil. Reduce heat. Simmer 3½ to 4½ hours, depending on size of tongue, or until fork will penetrate readily to center of meat. Allow tongue to remain in cooking water until cool enough to handle.
3. Peel off outer skin, cut out membranous portions. Reheat in liquid.
4. In small bowl, mix together horseradish and sour cream.
5. Slice tongue and serve hot or cold with sauce.

Ham and Fresh Pork

HIGH ALTITUDE TIMETABLE FOR ROASTING HAM AND FRESH PORK

Refrigerate meat up to time of roasting. Preheat oven. Place in shallow pan or on meat rack. Do not cover, baste or add water. Place meat thermometer in thickest part of meat, not touching bone or fat. (Because roasts of the same weight usually vary in shape and in fat and bone content, a meat thermometer is the most accurate means of judging when a roast is done.) Roasting times per pound given below also provide sound guidelines for determining when meat has reached a desired doneness.

Allow either ham or pork roasts to stand 15 to 20 minutes out of oven before carving.

Serving allowances: For boneless meat, allow ¼ pound per serving. For meat with average amount of bone, allow ½ pound per serving. For bony meat, allow ¾ to 1 pound per serving.

Ham	Weight (*pounds*)	Oven temperature (*preheated*)	Approximate roasting time (*hours*)	Meat thermometer reading	Additional
Uncooked whole	10 to 15	325°F.	4 to 5¾	170°F.	Add 10 minutes per pound if boned and rolled

HIGH ALTITUDE TIMETABLE FOR ROASTING HAM AND FRESH PORK
(CONTINUED)

Ham	Weight (*pounds*)	Oven temperature (*preheated*)	Approximate roasting time (*hours*)	Meat thermometer reading	Additional
Uncooked half	4 to 8	325°F.	2¼ to 3½	170°F.	Add 10 minutes per pound if boned and rolled
Precooked whole	10 to 12	325°F.	2½ to 3	140°F.	
	12 to 15	325°F.	3 to 3½	140°F.	
	15 to 18	325°F.	3½ to 4	140°F.	
Precooked half	5 to 8	325°F.	1½ to 2⅓	140°F.	
	8 to 10	325°F.	2⅓ to 3	140°F.	
Uncooked whole picnic	5 to 8	325°F.	3 to 4	170°F.	
	8 to 10	325°F.	4 to 5	170°F.	
Canned *or* precooked rolled	3 to 5	325°F.	1 to 1⅔	140°F.	
	5 to 8	325°F.	1⅔ to 2¼	140°F.	

Fresh Pork					
Loin	2 to 3	325°F.	1⅔ to 2½	185°F. to 190°F.	Add 10 minutes per pound if loin is boned and rolled
	5 to 7	325°F.	3½ to 4½	185°F. to 190°F.	
Shoulder (Picnic or Boston butt)	4 to 6	325°F.	3½ to 4½	185°F. to 190°F.	Add 10 minutes per pound if shoulder is boned and rolled
Crown (unstuffed)	4 to 6	325°F.	3½ to 4½	185°F. to 190°F.	

Ham

HAM LOAF

1½ pounds lean ham ground with
    1½ pounds lean pork
2 eggs, beaten
⅔ cup milk
⅔ cup cracker crumbs
2 teaspoons grated onion

½ teaspoon salt
⅛ teaspoon ground pepper
⅔ cup firmly packed brown sugar
2 tablespoons prepared mustard
¼ teaspoon ground cloves
2 tablespoons cider vinegar

1. Preheat oven to 350°F. Have ready a 9 × 5 × 3-inch loaf pan or shallow baking pan.
2. In mixing bowl, combine ham, pork, eggs, milk, cracker crumbs, onion, salt and pepper. Mix thoroughly.
3. Mix together brown sugar, mustard, cloves and vinegar. Add to meat mixture. Blend well. Press into loaf pan or form in loaf and place in baking pan.
4. Bake for 1½ hours.
5. Serve hot or cold.

HAM, NOODLE AND GREEN PEPPER CASSEROLE

6 SERVINGS

3 cups cooked noodles, rice
 or macaroni
1 cup cooked diced or
 ground ham
¾ cup grated sharp cheddar
½ cup finely chopped green
 pepper
½ cup finely chopped celery

1½ cups milk or tomato juice
2 eggs
¼ teaspoon salt
¼ teaspoon paprika or ground
 pepper
Bread crumbs
Butter

1. Preheat oven to 350°F. Grease 2½-quart casserole.
2. Combine cooked noodles, rice or macaroni with ham, cheese, green pepper and celery.
3. In separate bowl, beat together milk or tomato juice, eggs, salt and paprika or pepper. Combine with noodle mixture. Spoon into prepared casserole. Sprinkle with bread crumbs. Dot with butter.
4. Bake for 40 minutes, or until golden brown and bubbly.

QUICK HAM ROLLS

6 SERVINGS

1¼ pounds ham ground with
 ½ pound pork
1 teaspoon onion salt
1 egg, beaten

1 cup milk
¼ cup crisp rice cereal
6 slices bacon

1. Preheat oven to 350°F. Have ready flat baking dish.
2. Mix together all ingredients except bacon. Toss lightly with fork to mix. Shape into 6 rolls. Wrap each roll with slice of bacon, securing with toothpick. Place in baking dish.
3. Bake for 40 minutes.

Fresh Pork

STUFFED PORK CHOPS

6 SERVINGS

6 lean center-cut pork chops,
    1 inch thick
1 cup bread crumbs
¼ cup chopped celery
¼ cup finely chopped onion
2 tablespoons chopped parsley

½ to ¾ cup consommé or bouillon
¼ teaspoon salt
¼ teaspoon powdered thyme
⅛ teaspoon paprika
2 tablespoons cooking oil
½ cup half-and-half

1. Preheat oven to 350°F. Have ready flat baking dish with cover.
2. Trim off excess fat from chops. Cut large slit, or pocket, into side of each chop.
3. Combine bread crumbs, celery, onions, parsley and enough consommé or bouillon to moisten. Add salt, thyme and paprika.
4. Fill pockets of chops. Close with toothpicks or skewers.
5. In skillet, quickly brown stuffed chops in cooking oil. Place browned chops in baking dish. Add half-and-half. Tuck any remaining stuffing in between. Cover.
6. Bake 1 hour, or until tender.

PORK CHOPS BAKED IN FOIL

4 SERVINGS

4 *pork chops, cut ¾ inch thick*
  and trimmed of fat
1 *cup condensed cream of*
  celery soup
Salt
Pepper

Garlic salt
Dried fines herbes or mixed
  fresh herbs
4 *small potatoes*
4 *carrots, quartered*
4 *zucchini, quartered*

1. Preheat oven to 350°F. Have ready cookie sheet.
2. Arrange each pork chop in center of 12-inch square of aluminum foil. Spread ¼ cup soup over each chop. Sprinkle salt, pepper, garlic salt and herbs over soup. Arrange potato, carrot and zucchini on top. Fold ends of foil to middle and seal. Tightly seal ends. Place on cookie sheet.
3. Bake for 1 hour.

PORK ROAST IN FOIL: In Step 2, substitute 4-pound pork roast for chops. Increase celery soup to 10½-ounce can. In Step 3, bake 2½ hours.

PORK ENCHILADAS

6 SERVINGS

1½ *pounds lean pork, cut into*
  ¼-inch cubes
  Cooking oil
2 *cloves garlic, minced*
2 *tablespoons all-purpose flour*
1 *cup canned or bottled*
  enchilada sauce

1 *pound longhorn cheese, grated*
2 *cups finely chopped onion*
1 *dozen corn tortillas*
6 *eggs*

1. In large heavy skillet, brown meat in 2 tablespoons cooking oil over medium heat until done. Add garlic. Cook a few minutes more.
2. Mix flour with enchilada sauce. Add to meat. Cook about 15 minutes, stirring occasionally.
3. In bowl, mix together cheese and onion.
4. In another large skillet, pour cooking oil to cover pan bottom. Heat oil. When hot, quickly cook one tortilla a few seconds on each side. Dip tortilla in meat sauce. Place on preheated serving plate. Put generous spoonful meat sauce on tortilla. Sprinkle with layer of cheese-and-onion mixture. Continue to cook and fill tortillas until all filling and tortillas are used. Place in oven to keep warm.
5. Quickly fry eggs and place on top of each enchilada. Serve immediately.

NOTE: Chicken or beef may be substituted for pork.

BARBECUED PORK RIBS

4 SERVINGS

4 pounds pork ribs
⅔ cup dry white wine
1 large clove garlic, minced
1 tablespoon brown sugar

1 teaspoon salt
¼ teaspoon ground pepper
1 cup finely chopped onion
⅔ cup chili sauce

1. In glass baking dish large enough to accommodate all ribs, arrange ribs in bottom.
2. In small mixing bowl, combine wine, garlic, sugar, salt and pepper. Pour over ribs. Cover with aluminum foil. Refrigerate overnight, or at least 4 hours.
3. Remove ribs from marinade. Reserve marinade. Cut ribs into serving-size pieces. Place in shallow pan lined with aluminum foil.
4. Broil ribs 5 inches from heat until well browned.
5. Add onion and chili sauce to reserved marinade. Mix well.
6. Place ribs in large casserole with tight-fitting cover. Pour marinade over ribs. Cover.
7. Bake in 350°F. oven for about 2 hours.

NOTE: Beef short ribs or lamb breast may be substituted for pork.

PORK PIE

6 SERVINGS

1 cup water
1½ pounds ground lean pork
1 teaspoon salt
¼ teaspoon ground pepper
¼ teaspoon dried summer
  savory or sage

⅛ teaspoon ground cloves
⅛ teaspoon ground allspice
1 cup finely chopped onion
½ cup dry bread crumbs, or
  1 tablespoon flour
Pastry for 2-crust 9-inch pie

1. In large heavy saucepan with cover, mix together water, meat, salt, pepper, savory or sage, cloves, allspice and onion. Cover. Simmer for 30 minutes, stirring occasionally to prevent sticking. Stir in bread crumbs or flour. Cook 10 minutes. Cool.
2. Preheat oven to 450°F. Line 9-inch pie plate with pastry.
3. Pour meat mixture into pastry shell. Cover with top crust. Seal edges. Prick crust, or cut slits to allow steam to escape.
4. Bake at 450°F. for 15 minutes. *Reduce* heat to 350°F. Bake 25 minutes longer, or until browned.

Lamb

HIGH ALTITUDE TIMETABLE FOR ROASTING LAMB

Refrigerate meat up to time of roasting. Preheat oven. Place meat in shallow pan on meat rack. Do not cover, baste or add water. Place meat thermometer in thickest part of meat, not touching bone or fat. Because roasts of the same weight usually vary in shape and in fat and bone content, a meat thermometer is the most accurate means of judging when a roast is done. Roasting time per pound also provides sound guidelines for determining when meat has reached a desired doneness. Cooking lamb to well-done is *not* recommended.

Allow roast to stand 15 to 20 minutes out of oven before carving, except for Rack, which should be served after resting 5 minutes.

Serving allowances: For boneless meat, allow ¼ pound per serving. For meat with bone, allow ½ pound per serving.

Lamb Cut	Weight (*pounds*)	Oven temperature (*pre-heated*)	Approximate minutes roasting time (*per pound*)	Meat thermometer reading
Leg (bone-in)	5–9	325°F.	20–25 25–30 30–35	140–Rare 160–Medium 170–Well
Leg (boneless)	4–7	325°F.	25–30 30–35 35–40	140–Rare 160–Medium 170–Well

HIGH ALTITUDE TIMETABLE FOR ROASTING LAMB
(CONTINUED)

Rack or crown	2½–4	325°F.	25–30	140–Rare
			30–35	160–Medium
			35–40	170–Well
Square-cut shoulder	4–6	325°F.	25–30	160–Medium
			30–35	170–Well
Boneless shoulder	3½–5	325°F.	35–40	160–Medium
			40–45	170–Well
Cushion shoulder	3½–5	325°F.	30–35	170–Well

NOTE: A rack of lamb may be roasted at 375°F. instead of 325°F., or may be broiled satisfactorily. Or broil to brown, then insert thermometer and finish in oven to desired degree of doneness.

TERIYAKI LAMB CHOPS OR STEAKS

4 SERVINGS

1½ to 2 pounds lamb chops or
    steaks, trimmed of fat
¼ cup lemon or lime juice
¼ cup Japanese soy sauce
¼ teaspoon ground pepper
¼ teaspoon garlic powder, or
    1 clove garlic, mashed

2 tablespoon brown sugar, honey
    or apple-mint jelly
¼ teaspoon dry mustard
¼ teaspoon ground ginger

1. Arrange lamb in shallow baking dish.
2. In small mixing bowl, combine remaining ingredients. Pour over meat. Cover with aluminum foil. Refrigerate 4 hours or overnight.
3. Remove meat from marinade. Reserve marinade.
4. Preheat broiler. Broil meat 3 inches from heat for 6 to 8 minutes basting frequently with marinade. Turn and broil 6 to 8 minutes more, or to desired degree of doneness, basting frequently with marinade.

HIGH ALTITUDE ROAST LEG OF LAMB

8 SERVINGS

Leg of lamb (6 pounds), at room
    temperature, partially trimmed
    of fat
2 cloves garlic, cut into slivers
  Salt
  Freshly ground pepper

½ teaspoon dried summer savory
½ teaspoon crumbled dried
    sweet basil
½ teaspoon dried rosemary
3 tablespoons dry vermouth
3 tablespoons olive oil

1. Preheat oven to 550°F.
2. Place lamb fat side up in shallow roasting pan.
3. With sharp knife, cut slits in lamb. Insert garlic slivers in slits.
4. In small bowl, combine remaining ingredients. Rub over lamb.
5. Bake at 550°F. for 15 minutes (rare), 20 minutes (medium) or 25 minutes (well). Turn off oven. Do *not* open oven door or peek for 3½ hours.
6. Pour off pan liquid. Strain. Reheat strained juices. Serve over lamb slices.

SWEET AND SOUR LAMB CHOPS

4 SERVINGS

4 *lamb shoulder chops* or 8 *rib chops, 1 inch thick*	⅛ *teaspoon ground pepper*
¼ *cup vinegar*	¼ *teaspoon ground ginger*
¼ *cup firmly packed brown sugar*	1 *medium orange, sliced*
1 *teaspoon salt*	1 *medium lemon, sliced*

1. Preheat oven to 325°F. Butter 1½-quart casserole with cover.
2. Broil chops, turning to brown both sides. Place in casserole.
3. Combine vinegar, sugar, salt, pepper and ginger. Pour over chops. Cover chops with orange and lemon slices. Cover.
4. Bake at 325°F. for 30 minutes, or until meat is tender.

SETTLER'S LEG OF LAMB

8 SERVINGS

After their farm flocks were established, high-country settlers translated recipes used for wild game to use in cookery of other meats.

Leg of lamb (6 to 9 pounds)	¼ *teaspoon ground allspice*
½ *cup tarragon vinegar*	¼ *teaspoon ground mace*
8 *cups buttermilk*	¼ *teaspoon dried marjoram*
2 *cloves garlic, minced*	1 *teaspoon salt*
2 *large onions, thinly sliced*	½ *teaspoon freshly ground*
1 *large carrot, sliced*	*black pepper*
10 *whole peppercorns, crushed*	¾ *cup dry white wine*
12 *whole cloves*	¼ *cup bacon drippings*
2 *bay leaves*	½ *cup currant or other tart red jelly*
3 *juniper berries, crushed, if desired*	1 *teaspoon grated lemon rind*
4 *large sprigs celery leaves*	*Flour*
½ *cup finely chopped parsley*	*Buttered noodles*

1. Wipe lamb with damp cloth. Place in crock or other vessel large enough to accommodate all ingredients. Rub well with tarragon vinegar.

2. Cover with buttermilk. Add garlic, onions, carrot, peppercorns, 5 cloves, bay leaves, juniper berries (if desired), celery leaves, parsley, allspice, mace and marjoram. Marinate 4 days in refrigerator, turning twice daily and being sure to keep meat covered with marinade.

3. When ready to roast, preheat oven to 450°F. Remove lamb. Strain and reserve marinade. Wipe meat dry and rub with salt and pepper. Place in roasting pan. Stud with remaining 7 cloves. Pour wine and bacon drippings over roast.

4. Roast at 450°F. for 25 minutes, then *reduce* temperature to 325°F. Continue to bake according to timetable for roasting lamb (page 191), or to desired doneness. Baste frequently with strained marinade and pan drippings.

5. Remove roast to warm platter. Skim fat from drippings and bring to boil. Stir in jelly and lemon rind. Thicken gravy to taste with a little flour mixed to a paste with water, boiling a few moments until thoroughly cooked. Serve with hot buttered noodles.

MALAYAN LAMB OR SHRIMP CURRY

4 SERVINGS

1 tablespoon butter	4 cups cubed cooked lamb or
2 tablespoons chopped onion	shrimp
2 tablespoons curry powder	1 cup coconut milk
1 ounce preserved ginger, chopped,	1 cucumber, chopped and peeled
or ½ teaspoon ground ginger	1 tablespoon lemon juice
1 green chili, chopped	Pinch cayenne
½ cup meat stock or bouillon	Cooked rice

1. In large skillet, melt butter. Over medium-high heat sauté onion until limp. Stir in curry, ginger and chili. Pour in meat stock or bouillon. Cover. Simmer 15 minutes.

2. Add lamb or shrimp, coconut milk, cucumber, lemon juice and cayenne. Cover. Simmer 10 minutes, or until heated through. Serve over cooked rice.

LAMB KABOBS

4 SERVINGS

¼ cup olive oil	2 pounds lamb shoulder, cut into
¾ cup dry red or white wine	1- to 1½-inch cubes
1 small onion, chopped	8 small onions, parboiled
1 clove garlic, minced	8 cherry tomatoes
¼ teaspoon dried sweet basil	8 large fresh mushrooms
¼ teaspoon dried marjoram	8 one-inch chunks green pepper
¼ teaspoon dried rosemary	1 package (6 ounces) long-grain
¾ teaspoon salt	and wild rice, cooked
⅛ teaspoon ground pepper	

1. In 2-quart mixing bowl, combine oil, wine, onion, garlic, sweet basil, marjoram, rosemary, salt and pepper. Mix very well. Add meat. Cover. Refrigerate at least 4 hours or overnight.
2. Remove meat from marinade. Reserve marinade. Thread on skewers.
3. Broil 4 inches from heat about 20 minutes, turning occasionally and basting with marinade.
4. Alternate vegetables on 4 separate skewers and cook with meat for the last 10 minutes, turning occasionally and basting with marinade. Or, after meat has cooked 10 minutes, it may be rethreaded on skewers alternating with vegetables for the remainder of cooking time. Serve kabobs over bed of cooked rice.

PARTY LAMB MEATBALLS

4 TO 6 SERVINGS

1 egg, beaten	1 tablespoon grated onion
1½ cups milk	1½ pounds lean ground lamb
¼ teaspoon ground mace	3 tablespoons all-purpose flour
¼ teaspoon ground allspice	1 can (10½ ounces) consommé
1 teaspoon salt	1 cup dry white wine
1 cup fresh bread crumbs	¼ teaspoon ground pepper
1 can (5 ounces) water chestnuts, drained and finely chopped	Cooked rice
2 tablespoons chopped fresh or 1 tablespoon dried parsley	

1. In large mixing bowl, combine beaten egg, 1 cup milk, mace, allspice, salt, bread crumbs, water chestnuts, parsley, onion and meat. Mix very well. Shape meat mixture into 1-inch balls.
2. In skillet, brown meatballs on all sides. Remove meatballs from skillet with slotted spoon or spatula to casserole with tight-fitting cover. Drain off all fat except for 3 tablespoonfuls. Add flour, stirring until smooth. Gradually add consommé, wine and remaining ½ cup milk. Cook over medium-low heat until thickened, stirring constantly. Add pepper and additional salt, if necessary. Pour gravy over meatballs. Cover.
3. Cook in 350°F. oven for 45 minutes. Serve over cooked rice.

NOTE: Beef or veal may be substituted for lamb.

LAMB SHANKS BAKED IN TOMATO SAUCE

4 TO 6 SERVINGS

4 to 6 lamb shanks, about ¾
    pounds each, trimmed of fat
Olive oil
2 medium onions, cut into
    ¼-inch slices
1 teaspoon ground allspice

½ teaspoon ground nutmeg
1 teaspoon salt
½ teaspoon pepper
3 cups chopped canned tomatoes
    with juice

1. Preheat oven to 450°F. Have ready 13 × 2 × 9-inch baking dish.
2. Lightly coat lamb shanks with oil. Arrange in baking dish.
3. Bake for 30 minutes, turning once. *Reduce* heat to 350°F. Remove meat from oven. Arrange onions slices evenly over meat. Sprinkle with allspice, nutmeg, salt and pepper. Pour tomatoes evenly over all. Return lamb to oven.
4. Cook for 2 hours, or until lamb is tender, basting frequently.

IRISH LAMB STEW

6 SERVINGS

3 pounds lamb shoulder chops,
    trimmed of fat
8 medium potatoes
4 large onions, cut into ¼-inch
    slices
2 teaspoons dried summer savory
Salt

Pepper
1 cup water
4 cups sliced carrots, cooked
    tender-crisp
4 cups peas, cooked tender-crisp
½ teaspoon dried mint

1. Cut meat into 2-inch pieces. Set aside.
2. Peel potatoes and cut two potatoes into ¼-inch slices.
3. In bottom of Dutch oven or heavy casserole with tight-fitting cover, arrange a layer of potato slices and a layer using half of onion slices. Sprinkle with ½ teaspoon summer savory and generously with salt and pepper. Add lamb. Sprinkle with ½ teaspoon summer savory and generously with salt and pepper. Cover with remaining onion slices. Sprinkle with ½ teaspoon summer savory, salt and pepper. Place 6 whole potatoes on top and sprinkle with remaining ½ teaspoon summer savory, salt and pepper. Add water. Cover.
4. Bake at 300°F. for 3 hours. Serve lamb stew with cooked carrots and peas seasoned with dried mint.

SALMI OF LAMB

Follow directions for Salmi of Duck or Pheasant, page 207. Substitute cold sliced lamb for duck.

Veal

HIGH ALTITUDE TIMETABLE FOR ROASTING VEAL

Refrigerate up to time of roasting. Preheat oven. Cover veal roast with thin slices of salt pork, suet or fat bacon if it lacks a fatty coating. Place in shallow pan on meat rack. Do not cover, baste or add water. Place meat thermometer in thickest part of meat, not touching bone or fat. Because roasts of the same weight usually vary in shape and in fat and bone content, a meat thermometer is the most accurate means of judging when a roast is done. Roasting time per pound also provides sound guidelines for determining when meat has reached a desired doneness.

Allow roasts to stand 15 to 20 minutes out of oven before carving.

Serving allowances: For boneless meat, allow ¼ pound per serving. For meat with average amount of bone, allow ½ pound per serving. For bony meat, allow 1 pound per serving.

Veal Cut	Weight (*pounds*)	Oven temperature (*preheated*)	Approximate roasting time (*hours*)	Meat thermometer reading
Leg	5 to 7	325°F.	3 to 4	160°F.
Loin	5	325°F.	3 to 3½	160°F.
Shoulder	3 to 5	325°F.	2 to 3¼	160°F.
Boned and rolled leg, loin or shoulder	4	325°F.	3⅓	160°F.

VEAU AU CITRON

1 pound veal, thinly sliced or
    pounded and cut into 2-inch
    strips
4 shallots, chopped
6 large fresh mushrooms, washed,
    dried and sliced, or 1 can
    (4 ounces) sliced mushrooms,
    drained

3 tablespoons butter
½ cup dry white wine
½ teaspoon paprika
Juice of ½ lemon

In skillet, sauté veal, shallots and mushrooms in butter over medium heat until lightly browned. Add wine and paprika. Bring to boil. Reduce heat to medium-low. Cook 6 minutes. Add lemon juice.

FRENCH VEAL STEW

2 pounds boned veal shoulder, cut
    into ¾-inch cubes
    Flour
1 teaspoon salt
¼ teaspoon ground pepper
2 to 3 tablespoons olive or
    cooking oil
1 large onion, studded with
    4 whole cloves
4 cups boiling water
3 carrots, cut into 1-inch pieces

1 bay leaf
⅛ teaspoon dried thyme
2 sprigs parsley
½ cup diced celery
2 cloves garlic, crushed
12 small cooked or canned
    white onions
1 cup canned mushrooms
3 egg yolks, beaten
2 tablespoons lemon juice
1 tablespoon cream

1. Dredge veal cubes in flour mixed with salt and pepper.
2. In Dutch oven or large heavy saucepan with tight-fitting cover, over medium-heat heat, quickly brown meat in oil. Add onion studded with cloves, boiling water, carrots, bay leaf, thyme, parsley, celery and garlic. Cover. Simmer 1 hour.
3. Remove onion and bay leaf. Add white onions and mushrooms.
4. Combine egg yolks, lemon juice and cream. Add a little hot broth to egg mixture. Blend, and add to stew. Heat through, stirring constantly, but do not boil.

VEAL PAPRIKA

6 SERVINGS

2 pounds veal steak, ¼ inch
   thick, cut into serving-size
   pieces
½ cup all-purpose flour
½ teaspoon salt
⅛ teaspoon pepper

3 tablespoons butter
1 clove garlic
1½ cups hot chicken broth or stock
1 cup dairy sour cream
2 teaspoons paprika
   Buttered noodles

1. Dredge veal in flour mixed with salt and pepper.
2. In Dutch oven or heavy skillet with tight-fitting cover, over medium heat, melt butter. Add garlic. Sauté 3 minutes. Remove garlic. Add meat. Brown quickly over medium-high heat. Add hot broth or stock. Cover.
3. Bring to boil. Reduce temperature. Simmer 1 hour, or until tender.
4. Stir in sour cream and paprika. Heat through, but *do not boil*. Correct seasoning. Serve over buttered noodles.

ITALIAN VEAL ROAST OR SHANKS

4 SERVINGS

1 veal rump, round or loin roast
   (4 pounds), or 4 veal shanks
2 tablespoons olive or cooking oil
1 cup chopped carrots
1 cup chopped celery
½ cup chopped onion
½ cup dry white wine
1 piece (1 inch) lemon peel

1 teaspoon dried sweet basil
1 teaspoon dried parsley
½ teaspoon dried thyme
1 teaspoon salt
¼ teaspoon pepper
1 tablespoon all-purpose flour
1 cup water

1. Preheat oven to 325°F.
2. Place meat in Dutch oven or large casserole with tight-fitting cover.
3. In 1-quart mixing bowl, combine oil, carrots, celery, onions, wine, lemon peel, basil, parsley, thyme, salt and pepper.
4. In small bowl, mix together flour and water. Add to vegetable mixture. Pour over meat. Cover.
5. Bake for 2½ hours, or until meat is tender. Serve meat with pan sauces.

NOTE: May be cooked in electric slow cooker.

VEAL SCALLOPS

12 *slices veal steak, about*
    4 × 4 × ¼ inches each
¼ *cup all-purpose flour*
  Salt
  Pepper
3 *tablespoons butter*
4 *tablespoons olive oil*

8 *mushrooms, sliced*
1 *cucumber, peeled and diced*
1 *tomato, diced*
4 *tablespoons chopped chives*
  Dash garlic powder
¼ *cup Marsala or sherry*
2 *teaspoons fresh lemon juice*

1. Flatten veal slices between two pieces of waxed paper with side of butcher knife. Dredge lightly in flour. Sprinkle with salt and pepper.
2. In large skillet, melt butter and olive oil together. Over medium-high heat, sauté meat quickly in melted butter and oil, browning both sides. Remove meat to heated platter.
3. Sauté mushrooms in pan drippings. Add cucumbers, tomato, chives and garlic powder. Cook 2 minutes. Add wine. Stir well, and heat through.
4. Sprinkle lemon juice over hot meat. Pour sauce over meat. Serve immediately.

Game and Game Birds

HIGH ALTITUDE FACTS ABOUT GAME COOKERY

Abundant wild life is a bonus of living in regions with higher elevations. Improper care of game meat or birds at the time they are killed has contributed to some of the lack of success in their cookery by homemakers, but unpalatable dryness or an excessively gamy flavor after cooking is more often the villain. The following high-country recipes are designed to overcome the problems that sometimes prevent the full enjoyment of one of nature's greatest delicacies. Also, see High Altitude Facts About Meat, Poultry and Game Cookery, page 171, which offers general recommendations for successful meat and fowl cookery above sea level. Cook calf elk as for veal; adult elk as for beef; and the choice cuts of venison and antelope can be roasted or broiled as for beef. Other cuts of elk and venison are delicious if prepared in stews, marinades, or as for pot roasts. Ground game meat has as many effective preparations as ground beef, pork, lamb or veal. A practical and succulent approach to wild game and bird cookery is to generously ply them with sauces, gravies and wines.

Venison, Elk, Antelope and Rabbit

BROILED VENISON, ELK OR ANTELOPE STEAKS OR CHOPS

ALLOW 1 STEAK OR CHOP PER SERVING

Preheat broiler. Rub steaks or chops with garlic, if desired. Brush meat with mixture of butter or olive oil, salt, pepper, paprika and ½ teaspoon Worcestershire sauce. Broil at least 3 inches away from heat for 8 to 10 minutes on each side, or to desired doneness. Serve with currant jelly or Spicy Sauce for Poultry or Game, page 166.

PAN-FRIED VENISON, ELK OR ANTELOPE STEAKS OR CHOPS

2 SERVINGS

2 tablespoons butter or olive oil
1 clove garlic, cut in half
2 venison, elk or antelope steaks
    or chops
Salt
Pepper

Paprika
¼ cup dry sherry
¼ cup cream
2 tablespoons butter
1 ½ tablespoons currant jelly

1. In skillet large enough to accommodate meat in one layer, heat butter or olive oil. Add garlic. Over medium-high heat, brown meat on both sides. Reduce heat. Season with salt, pepper and paprika. Cook just until well done on outside and juicy red or pink on inside. Remove garlic.

2. Add sherry, cream, butter and jelly. Stir well until jelly is melted and all ingredients are blended. Baste steaks or chops with sauce until they are well coated. Serve on heated platter. Spoon sauce over meat.

VENISON, ELK OR ANTELOPE POT ROAST

6 SERVINGS

Pot-roasting is a method that combats the dryness of game.

4 to 5 pounds venison, elk or antelope pot roast	*2 teaspoons salt*
4 slices bacon or salt pork	*¼ teaspoon ground pepper*
3 medium onions, chopped	*¼ cup all-purpose flour*
1 stalk celery, chopped	*4 cups beef stock, bouillon, consommé or water*
1 bay leaf	*1 cup cream*
1 carrot, chopped	*2 cups button mushrooms*

1. Preheat oven to 450°F.

2. Remove all fat, cartilage and outer membranes from meat. Wrap meat with bacon or salt pork slices. Place meat in roasting pan with cover. Add onions, celery, bay leaf, carrot, salt and pepper. Cover.

3. Bake at 450°F. for 20 minutes. *Reduce* temperature to 300°F. Cook about 3 hours longer, or until tender. Remove meat to a warmed serving dish and keep hot.

4. In same pan, sprinkle vegetables and drippings with flour; stir well. Add beef stock, bouillon, consommé or water. Cook over medium heat until liquid is reduced to 2 cups. Strain. Add cream. Cook until golden brown. Add mushrooms to sauce. Pour over meat.

VENISON, ELK OR ANTELOPE STEW

6 SERVINGS

2 pounds venison, elk or antelope,
  cut into 1½-inch cubes
½ cup vinegar
1½ cups dry white wine
  Flour
2 tablespoons bacon drippings
  or shortening
  Salt
  Pepper
1 medium onion, finely chopped

2 stalks celery, finely chopped
3 tablespoons finely chopped
  parsley
1 carrot, finely chopped
⅛ teaspoon crumbled dried thyme
1½ cups beef consommé or broth
½ pound fresh mushrooms,
  washed, dried and halved
1 can (7½ ounces) pitted black
  olives, drained and sliced

1. In dish with cover, marinate meat in vinegar and ½ cup dry white wine overnight in refrigerator. Drain thoroughly. Dry with paper toweling.
2. Dredge meat in flour.
3. In heavy skillet with tight-fitting cover, melt bacon drippings or shortening over medium-high heat. Brown meat quickly on all sides. Sprinkle with salt and pepper to taste. Add onion. Sauté until limp. Stir in celery, parsley, carrot, thyme, ½ cup wine and ¾ cup beef consommé or broth. Cover. Simmer over low heat for 1¾ hours, or until meat is almost tender. Add remaining ¾ cup consommé or broth during cooking.
4. Add mushrooms, olives and remaining ½ cup wine. Simmer 35 minutes more. Thicken liquid with about 1 tablespoon flour mixed with a little water, if desired.

FRICASSEED RABBIT

ABOUT 6 SERVINGS

2 rabbits (2 pounds each)
¼ cup butter
¼ cup shortening
2 eggs, beaten
  Water

½ cup finely ground soda
  cracker crumbs
2 medium onions, halved
  Dumplings, page 21

1. Preheat oven to 350°F.
2. Wash rabbits thoroughly. Pat dry. Cut into pieces, discarding bony rib section.
3. In Dutch oven, melt butter and shortening over medium-high heat.
4. Mix beaten eggs with 1 tablespoon water. Dip rabbit in egg. Roll in cracker crumbs.
5. Brown rabbit, turning until all sides are evenly browned. Add water to cover, and onions. Cover.
6. Bake about 2 hours, or until tender. Remove onions. Add dumplings. Cook for 20 minutes.

Game Birds

DOVES IN WINE

10 *doves*
3 *tablespoons all-purpose flour*
½ *teaspoon salt*
¼ *teaspoon ground pepper*
½ *teaspoon paprika*
¼ *teaspoon dried sweet basil*
¼ *cup melted butter*

1 *clove garlic*
1 *cup chicken consommé or bouillon*
1 *cup burgundy, Marsala, or claret*
1 *cup fresh or drained canned mushrooms*
⅔ *cup orange juice*

1. Wash doves thoroughly in cold water. Drain well. Pat dry. Reserve livers and gizzards, if desired. Split doves in half.
2. Mix together flour, salt, pepper, paprika and basil. Dredge doves in seasoned flour.
3. Put melted butter and garlic in heavy Dutch oven or skillet with cover. Brown doves quickly over medium-high heat. Remove garlic. Add livers and gizzards to bottom of pan, if desired. Pour consommé or bouillon and wine over doves. Cover.
4. Simmer, stirring frequently, for about 1 hour. Add mushrooms and orange juice. Simmer 5 minutes longer. Thicken pan juices with a little of the remaining seasoned flour.

Facts About Wild Duck

Devotees of wild duck are divided into two camps, or more, if you count the in-between possibilities. Predominantly (vocally, at least) there are those who like their duck cooked fast in a hot (450°F. to 500°F.) oven with a red-rare result. The others prefer duck roasted in a moderate oven, basted with flavorful wine, and cooked until all of the pinkness has disappeared. The in-betweens may like their duck more thoroughly done but cooked in a hot oven, or quite pink and cooked in a moderate oven. Individual good judgment is always a factor, as the bird's age and weight are necessary considerations. Wild game birds, if properly prepared and wrapped, will keep up to six months in a freezer.

ROAST WILD DUCK I

ALLOW ONE-HALF DUCK PER PERSON

Wild ducks
Seasoned salt
Seasoned pepper
Celery, coarsely chopped
Green onions, chopped

Apple, chopped
Bacon drippings or shortening
Melted butter
Madeira or dry sauterne, if desired

1. Preheat oven to 450°F.
2. Wash ducks thoroughly in cold water. Drain well. Pat dry inside and out. Remove fat gland at base of tail. Sprinkle cavity with seasoned salt and pepper. Stuff each duck with equal amounts of celery, green onions (tops included) and apple. If duck is not young, soak a small piece of cheesecloth in vinegar and place in lower cavity at base of tail. Rub skin well with bacon drippings or shortening.
3. Place on rack in roasting pan with breast side up or down, as preferred.
4. For rare duck, roast 18 minutes per pound; for medium duck, roast 22 minutes per pound. If desired, baste with butter and Madeira or sauterne.
5. Let stand 10 minutes on warmed platter before carving. (The stuffing is for flavoring only, and is not to be served.) Remove cheesecloth.

ROAST WILD DUCK II: This method is for rare to medium-rare duck. Have duck at room temperature for 4 hours. If desired, stuff as directed for Roast Wild Duck I. Add small amount of water to pan. Preheat oven to 500° to 550°F. and roast for 20 to 30 minutes, depending on size of duck and degree of doneness desired. Allow duck to stand 7 to 10 minutes on warmed serving dish before carving. Serve with ½ cup melted butter mixed and heated with 3 tablespoons lemon juice.

ROAST TEAL I: Follow directions for preparing Roast Wild Duck I for the oven. Roast teal with breast down for 30 to 34 minutes, depending on size of bird and degree of doneness desired.

ROAST TEAL II: This method is for rare to medium-rare teal. Follow directions for Roast Wild Duck II. Roast for 12 to 14 minutes, depending on size of bird and degree of rareness desired.

ROAST SPICED DUCK IN SAUCE

6 SERVINGS

3 *wild ducks* or 2 *domestic ducks*	*Lemon slices*
Salt	*Bacon slices*
Pepper	1 *cup Tokay wine*
Garlic cloves	1 *cup chicken stock or bouillon*
Whole cloves	½ *cup chopped onion*
Chopped parsley	4 *tablespoons currant jelly or*
Chopped celery	*other tart red jelly*
Chopped apple	

1. Preheat oven to 375°F.
2. Wash ducks thoroughly in cold water. Drain well. Pat dry.
3. Sprinkle each cavity with salt and pepper. Stuff each with 1 clove garlic, 1 whole clove, 1 teaspoon parsley, 1 tablespoon chopped celery, 1 tablespoon chopped apple and 1 slice lemon.
4. Arrange ducks in roasting pan. Place 2 slices bacon over each breast. Add wine, chicken stock or bouillon, and onions.
5. Roast for 1 to 1½ hours, basting frequently. Remove to heated serving dish.
6. Strain pan juices. Add jelly to juices. Heat. Serve with duck. Carry covered to the table. The wonderful fruit, herb and game perfume is too good not to be shared.

SALMI OF DUCK OR PHEASANT

4 SERVINGS

1 *roasted and cooled mallard duck* or *pheasant*, or 2 *roasted and cooled teal ducks, boned*	1 *can (4 ounces) mushrooms, drained*
	¼ *teaspoon salt*
	⅛ *teaspoon pepper*
3 *tablespoons chopped onion*	½ *teaspoon Kitchen Bouquet*
½ *clove garlic, minced*	9 *green olives, pitted*
1 *tablespoon butter*	2 *tablespoons sherry*
1½ *tablespoons flour*	4 *slices dry toast*
2 *cups chicken stock*	

1. Cut cooked duck into bite-size pieces.
2. In large heavy saucepan with cover, over medium heat, sauté onion and garlic in butter until limp. Stir in flour. Gradually add chicken stock, stirring constantly. Add mushrooms, salt, pepper, Kitchen Bouquet and olives. Cover. Simmer until pieces of duck or pheasant are warmed through and sauce is thickened. Add sherry. Serve over toast.

ROAST WILD GOOSE I

4 TO 6 SERVINGS

1 *wild goose (4 to 6 pounds)*	*Bacon or sausage drippings*
Salt	2 *cups chicken stock or bouillon*
Pepper	1 *tablespoon all-purpose flour*
½ *cup coarsely chopped celery*	1¾ *cups currant jelly or other*
⅓ *cup coarsely chopped green*	*tart red jelly*
onions	2 *to 3 tablespoons sherry*
1 *cup chopped apple*	*Sauerkraut with Gin, page 275*

1. Preheat oven to 500°F.
2. Wash goose thoroughly in cold water. Drain well and pat dry inside and out. Remove fat gland at base of tail. Sprinkle cavity with salt and pepper. Stuff with equal amounts of celery, green onions (tops included) and apple. If goose is not young, soak a small piece of cheesecloth in vinegar and place in cavity at base of tail before stuffing.
3. Rub skin well with bacon or sausage drippings.
4. Place goose on rack breast side up, or on V-shaped rack with breast side down, if preferred.
5. Roast at 500°F. for 15 minutes. *Reduce* temperature to 350°F. Roast 2½ to 3 hours more, basting frequently. If breast side is down, turn breast side up when three-fourths cooked.
6. Remove goose from oven. Let stand 10 minutes before carving. Remove cheesecloth.
7. In small saucepan, make gravy: Thicken chicken bouillon with a little flour, stirred to a paste with cold water. Skim excess fat from pan drippings. Add 2 tablespoons fat-free drippings. Cook over low heat until well blended. Add currant jelly and sherry; reheat, but do not boil. Serve with Sauerkraut with Gin.

ROAST WILD GOOSE II: Have goose at room temperature for 4 hours. Stuff as directed for Roast Wild Goose I, or use Chestnut Stuffing, page 261. Place breast side up on rack in roasting pan. Add a little water. Bake at 500°F. for about 50 minutes.

COLD ROAST WILD GOOSE: Because people are so accustomed to eating hot roast goose, this completely pleasing way is often overlooked. Follow directions for Roast Wild Goose II. After roasting, let cool, then refrigerate. Serve cold, sliced, with well-buttered bread, salt and pepper.

PHEASANT IN BRANDY GRAVY

2 SERVINGS

1 *pheasant, cut in half*	¼ *cup butter or margarine*
Salt	¼ *cup brandy*
Pepper	¼ *cup chopped onion*
1 *clove garlic*	2 *tablespoons all-purpose flour*
2 *cups milk*	2 *cups half-and-half*

1. Wash pheasant thoroughly in cold water. Drain well. Pat dry. Sprinkle generously with salt and pepper.
2. Mash garlic in bowl or glass baking dish large enough to accommodate pheasant. Add milk. Arrange pheasant, cavity side up. Spoon milk into cavities. Marinate 2 hours at room temperature.
3. In large skillet, brown pheasant in butter or margarine over medium-high heat. Remove pheasant to Dutch oven or baking dish with tight-fitting cover.
4. Pour brandy over pan drippings. Add onion and flour. Mix thoroughly. Add cream. Stir, scraping pan bottom with wooden spoon. Cook over medium heat, stirring constantly, until gravy is thickened. Pour gravy over pheasant. Cover.
5. Bake in 275°F. oven for 5 hours.

PHEASANT WITH APPLES

2 SERVINGS

1 *pheasant, skinned*	3 *large tart apples, peeled and*
½ *pound fresh salt pork slices*	*sliced*
2 *tablespoons butter or margarine*	1 *cup whipping cream*
Salt	2 *teaspoons cornstarch*
Pepper	¼ *cup Calvados*

1. Wrap pheasant in pork slices, securing them with toothpicks.
2. In medium skillet with tight-fitting cover, melt butter or margarine over medium heat. Brown pheasant on all sides. Season to taste with salt and pepper. Reduce heat. Cover. Simmer 20 minutes.
3. Add apple slices, basting apples with pan juices. Re-cover. Cook until apples are just golden, about 15 minutes.
4. Pour cream over pheasant and apples. Re-cover. Simmer 25 minutes more.
5. Remove pork slices. Discard. Stir in Calvados. Serve in cooking pan.

Poultry

HIGH ALTITUDE TIMETABLE FOR ROASTING POULTRY

Refrigerate poultry up to time of roasting. Preheat oven. Stuff just before roasting, if stuffing is used. For unstuffed poultry, a general rule is to reduce roasting time slightly, or about 2 to 5 minutes per pound depending on size of bird. Allow small birds to stand 10 minutes and large birds to stand 15 to 20 minutes out of oven before carving.

Poultry	Ready-to-cook weight (*before stuffing*)	Oven temperature (*preheated*)	Roasting time* (*stuffed*)
Chicken	2 to 3½ pounds	325°F.	1½ to 2½ hours
	4 to 5 pounds	325°F.	2½ to 3½ hours
Duckling	3½ to 5 pounds	325°F.	2 to 3 hours
Goose	4 to 8 pounds	325°F.	3¼ to 4¼ hours
Turkey (in uncovered pan)	6 to 8 pounds	325°F.	3½ to 4 hours
	8 to 12 pounds	325°F.	4 to 5 hours
	12 to 16 pounds	325°F.	5 to 5½ hours
	16 to 20 pounds	325°F.	5½ to 6½ hours
	20 to 24 pounds	325°F.	6½ to 7½ hours
Turkey (wrapped in foil)	6 to 8 pounds	450°F.	2 to 2½ hours
	8 to 12 pounds	450°F.	2½ to 3 hours
	12 to 16 pounds	450°F.	3 to 3½ hours
	16 to 20 pounds	450°F.	3½ to 4 hours
	20 to 24 pounds	450°F.	4 to 5 hours
Squab	¾ to 1 pound	350°F.	1 hour

Capon	5 to 8 pounds	325°F.	3 to 4½ hours
Rock Cornish hen	¾ to 1 pound	325°F.	1 to 1¼ hours

* Times vary according to individual birds and ovens.

OUTDOOR BARBECUED CHICKEN

8 SERVINGS

4 broiler-fryer chickens (2 to 2¼
    pounds each), cut in half
¾ cup cooking oil

¾ cup Japanese soy sauce
1 clove garlic, crushed

1. Wash and pat dry chicken halves. Place in bowl large enough to accommodate chicken.
2. In small mixing bowl, combine oil, soy sauce and garlic. Pour marinade over chicken, completely coating all sides. Marinate at least 1 hour.
3. Arrange charcoal in one layer, 1 briquette deep, over bottom of barbecue at least 22 inches in diameter. Light charcoal briquettes.
4. Raise grill 7 to 8 inches above burning coals. When coals are gray, arrange chicken halves on grill, cavity side down. Brush with marinade. Grill over low fire for 45 minutes, brushing chicken frequently with marinade.
5. Turn chicken. Fill cavity with marinade. Grill 30 minutes, brushing chicken frequently with marinade.

CHICKEN A LA BOURSIN

6 SERVINGS

3 whole chicken breasts, split,
    skinned and boned
    Garlic powder
    Powdered tarragon
2 packages (5 ounces each)
    Boursin cheese with garlic
    and herb, cut into 6 wedges
    and frozen

2 eggs beaten with ½ cup milk
    Cornstarch
½ cup butter
½ cup olive oil
1 can (14 ounces) brown gravy
½ cup burgundy

1. Flatten chicken breasts with cleaver. Sprinkle to taste with garlic and tarragon powders. Split to make 6 pieces.
2. Place cheese wedge on each chicken piece. Roll up; secure closed with toothpicks.
3. Dip stuffed breasts into egg-milk mixture, then dredge in cornstarch. Place on flat pan. Cover. Refrigerate 1 hour or longer.

4. In heavy skillet, heat butter with oil. Over medium-high heat, cook chilled, stuffed breasts in hot oil until cooked through and cheese is melted, about 20 to 30 minutes, turning only once.

5. Meanwhile, in medium pan, heat gravy. Stir in wine.

6. Serve breasts covered with gravy, removing toothpicks before serving.

CHICKEN AND ARTICHOKE CASSEROLE

4 SERVINGS

4 whole chicken breasts, washed
2½ cups water
¼ cup butter
¼ cup all-purpose flour
1½ cups chicken broth or bouillon
½ cup half-and-half
½ teaspoon salt

2 tablespoons sherry
1 package (9 ounces) frozen
artichokes, thawed and
cooked according to package
directions
½ cup finely chopped nutmeats
½ cup buttered bread crumbs

1. In 2-quart saucepan with tight-fitting cover, place chicken in water. Cover and cook over medium-low heat 1 hour. Remove meat. Reserve broth.

2. Remove chicken from bones. Discard skin. Cut chicken into bite-size pieces.

3. In heavy saucepan, melt butter over medium-low heat. Gradually add flour. Slowly add chicken broth or bouillon, and half-and-half. Cook, stirring constantly, until thickened. Add salt and sherry.

4. In 2-quart casserole, arrange alternate layers of sauce, chicken, artichokes and nutmeats. Repeat using all ingredients. Top with buttered bread crumbs.

5. Bake at 350°F. for 45 minutes.

NOTE: Can be made ahead and frozen.

CHICKEN DIJON

6 SERVINGS

3 chicken breasts, split, skinned
and boned
¼ cup Dijon mustard
⅛ teaspoon ground white pepper
1 cup chicken broth, bouillon
or consommé

1 cup dairy sour cream
Cooked barley or orzo (Italian
pasta that looks like barley)
or rice

1. Place chicken pieces in flat dish. Coat with mustard. Sprinkle with pepper. Cover. Let stand at room temperature for 2 hours, or refrigerate overnight.

2. Put in heavy casserole with tight-fitting cover. Pour over ½ cup broth, bouillon or consommé. Cover.

3. Bake at 350°F. for 45 minutes, or until tender, basting three times with juice on bottom of pan to dissolve any bits of mustard clinging to chicken.

4. Stir in sour cream and remaining ½ cup broth, bouillon or consommé. Cover. Bake 20 minutes more, or until bubbly and well heated through.

5. Serve with cooked barley, orzo or rice. Spoon pan sauces over chicken pieces.

GARLIC CHICKEN

8 SERVINGS

2 broiler-fryer chickens (about
    2½ to 3 pounds each),
    quartered, or 4 chicken
    breasts, halved
2 teaspoons salt
½ teaspoon freshly ground pepper
1 teaspoon ground tarragon
⅛ teaspoon ground nutmeg

⅔ cup olive oil
1½ cups sliced celery
¼ cup chopped parsley
32 cloves garlic, peeled
    Flour
    Water
    Heavy-duty aluminum foil
8 slices toast

1. Preheat oven to 375°F. Have ready large flat casserole with cover.
2. Wash and pat dry chicken quarters.
3. In small bowl, combine and mix salt, pepper, tarragon and nutmeg.
4. Pour oil into casserole. Arrange chicken in casserole, turning each piece to coat all sides with oil. Sprinkle with salt mixture.
5. Add celery, parsley and garlic, tucking vegetables in and around chicken. Cover casserole.
6. In bowl, make a thick paste of flour and water to be used to seal casserole bottom and cover together. Using fingers, generously spread paste around casserole edges.
7. Cover top and sides of casserole with foil.
8. Bake for 1½ hours. Do not peek, or seal will be damaged.
9. To serve, remove foil. Break seal with sharp knife. Serve chicken on toast spread with soft garlic and celery.

MEXICAN CHICKEN WITH PINE NUTS

6 SERVINGS

6 whole chicken breasts, washed
1 cup water
½ cup chicken broth or bouillon
1 can (10½ ounces) cream of
    mushroom soup
1 can (10½ ounces) cream of
    chicken soup
½ cup milk

1 onion, grated
12 corn tortillas, cut into 1 inch
    strips
1 can (4 ounces) diced green
    chilies
1 pound Monterey Jack, grated
    Pine nuts

1. The day before serving, in saucepan with cover, place chicken in water. Cover. Cook over medium-low heat 1 hour. Remove meat. Reserve broth.
2. Remove chicken from bones. Discard skin. Cut chicken into bite-size pieces

3. In medium mixing bowl, combine ½ cup chicken broth or bouillon, mushroom and chicken soups, milk and onion.

4. Butter 3-quart casserole. Alternate layers of soup mixture, tortillas, chicken, chilies and cheese, using all ingredients. Sprinkle with pine nuts. Refrigerate 24 hours.

5. Bake in 325°F. oven for 1 hour.

CHICKEN MOLE

6 SERVINGS

Mole sauce was first made in Mexico by nuns at a convent in Pueblo de los Angelos at the time that Mexico was the New Spain of the old Spanish empire.

2 *broiler-fryer chickens (about*
  2½ pounds each) cut up
4 *tablespoons cooking oil*
1 *green pepper, seeded and*
  chopped
1 *red pepper, seeded and chopped*
2 *medium onions, chopped*
2 *cloves garlic, minced*

2 *cans (15 ounces each) tomato*
  sauce
3 *to 4 tablespoons chili powder*
½ *teaspoon salt*
4 *whole cloves*
3 *tablespoons cocoa dissolved in*
  3 tablespoons boiling water

1. In large heavy saucepan with tight-fitting cover or Dutch oven, heat oil. Sauté chicken over medium-high heat until brown. Remove chicken. Keep warm in oven.

2. In same cooking pan, over medium heat, sauté peppers, onion, garlic until limp. Stir in remaining ingredients.

3. Replace chicken in pan with sauce. Cover. Cook over low heat for 1 hour.

4. Spoon sauce over chicken when serving.

EASY PARTY CHICKEN

4 SERVINGS

1 *large broiler-fryer chicken*
  (about 3 pounds), cut into
  serving pieces
  Salt
  Pepper

½ *cup apricot preserves*
½ *cup Russian salad dressing*
1 *teaspoon ground coriander*
¼ *cup white wine*

1. Preheat oven to 350°F.

2. Wash and pat dry chicken pieces. Line shallow baking pan with aluminum foil. Arrange chicken pieces in bottom.

3. In small bowl, mix together remaining ingredients. Pour over chicken.
4. Bake for 1¼ to 1½ hours, basting occasionally.

CHICKEN SCALLAPIO

▼▼

8 SERVINGS

1 *pound Italian link sausage*
5 *egg yolks*
1 *tablespoon dried oregano*
¼ *to ½ cup all-purpose flour*
½ *cup bread crumbs*
¼ *cup olive oil or sesame seed oil*
4 *chicken breasts, skinned, boned*
   and pounded ½ inch thick

4 *cups Italian Meat Sauce, page*
   000, or canned or bottled
   spaghetti sauce with meat
8 *slices provolone*
8 *slices mozzarella*
½ *pound mushrooms, washed,*
   dried and sliced
3 *tablespoons butter*
2 *tablespoons white wine*

1. Have 9 × 14 × 2-inch baking dish ready.
2. In medium saucepan, cover sausage with water. Bring to boil. Reduce heat. Simmer 30 minutes, pricking several times during cooking to allow fat to escape.
3. In medium bowl, combine egg yolks with oregano.
4. In another bowl, mix flour with bread crumbs.
5. Dip chicken pieces in egg mixture, then in crumb mixture.
6. In large skillet, heat oil. Over medium heat, brown chicken, about 15 minutes, turning once. Set aside.
7. Drain, skin and cut cooked sausage into ¼-inch slices.
8. Spoon 2 cups Italian Meat Sauce or spaghetti sauce with meat into baking dish. Place chicken breasts on sauce. Top each breast with slices of provolone, sausage slices and mozzarella.
9. In medium skillet over medium-high heat, quickly sauté mushrooms in melted butter until lightly browned. Stir in wine. Spread mushrooms with pan juices over mozzarella. Cover with remaining 2 cups sauce.
10. Bake at 350°F. for 30 to 40 minutes, or until heated through and bubbly. Allow to stand a few minutes before serving.

CHICKEN WITH WALNUTS

▼▼

4 SERVINGS

2 *broiler-fryer chickens (2½ to*
   3 pounds each) or 4 whole
   chicken breasts, cut in half
  Salt
  Pepper
¼ *cup butter*

  Juice of ½ lemon
2 *shallots or green onions,*
   finely chopped
½ *cup dry white wine*
½ *cup coarsely chopped walnuts*

1. Sprinkle chicken pieces with salt and pepper.
2. In large skillet with tight-fitting cover, melt butter. Add lemon juice. When butter bubbles, over medium-high heat, brown chicken pieces quickly on both sides, about 10 to 12 minutes. Add shallots or green onions. Cook 2 to 3 minutes. Add wine. Cover. Cook over low heat until chicken is tender.
3. Meanwhile roast walnuts in 350°F. oven for 10 minutes. Sprinkle with salt.
4. Add walnuts 5 minutes before the chicken is done.

ROCK CORNISH GAME HENS

4 SERVINGS

4 *oven-ready Rock Cornish game*	*Dried rosemary*
hens (1 pound each)	*Salt*
Stuffing of choice	*Pepper*
⅓ *cup melted butter*	

1. Preheat oven to 350°F. Stuff hens, if desired. Place stuffed hens in roasting pan breast side up (or down, if preferred). Brush with melted butter. Sprinkle with rosemary. Roast uncovered for 40 to 45 minutes.
2. Remove from oven. Salt and pepper lightly. Return to bake for 30 to 35 minutes more, basting frequently.

ROCK CORNISH HENS WITH SPICY SAUCE: In Step 1, baste hens frequently with Spicy Sauce for Poultry or Game, page 166. Hens should become rich brown. To serve, pour basting sauce over hens.

ROCK CORNISH HENS WITH HONEY-ORANGE GLAZE: In Step 1, baste hens frequently with ¼ cup honey combined with ¼ cup orange juice.

CHICKEN LIVERS AND MUSHROOMS IN MADEIRA

6 SERVINGS

Salt	1 *tablespoon finely chopped chives*
Pepper	1 *cup sliced mushrooms*
1 *pound fresh or frozen chicken*	1 *cup Madeira*
livers, thawed	1 *cup beef stock or bouillon*
¼ *cup all-purpose flour*	*Rice or buttered toast*
¼ *cup butter*	

1. Salt and pepper livers. Dredge lightly in flour.
2. In skillet, melt butter. Sauté livers over medium heat for about 5 minutes, turning once. Add chives and mushrooms. Cook 5 minutes more. Add Madeira and beef stock. Allow to simmer until slightly thickened.
3. Serve over rice or buttered toast.

RAGOUT OF DUCK WITH GREEN PEPPERCORNS IN VERMOUTH AND PORT

▼▼▼

6 TO 8 SERVINGS

2 *ducks (about 5 pounds each)*
¼ *cup olive or peanut oil*
1 *cup water*
2 *cups chicken broth or bouillon*
¼ *pound salt pork, cut into ½
    inch squares and simmered
    5 minutes in 1 quart water*
Salt
Pepper
2 *medium onions, peeled and
    sliced*
1½ *cups dry vermouth*

10 *cloves garlic, unpeeled*
2 *medium tomatoes, peeled,
    seeded and chopped*
1 *bay leaf*
½ *teaspoon ground thyme*
5 *whole allspice*
1½ *tablespoons cornstarch*
¼ *cup port*
2 *teaspoons canned green
    peppercorns, mashed*
6 *to 8 slices buttered toast*

1. Remove skin from ducks. Discard.
2. Cut ducks into serving-size pieces, removing and reserving back bones. Cut breasts in half crosswise. Cut off lower part of wings. Reserve.
3. Chop back bones, lower part of wings and necks into 2-inch pieces. Cut gizzards into several pieces.
4. In large skillet over medium-high heat, heat 3 tablespoons oil. Add pieces of bone, wings, necks and gizzards, and whole hearts. Brown quickly on all sides. Remove to medium-size saucepan.
5. To same skillet, add water. Bring to boil, scraping bottom of pan with wooden spoon or rubber scraper, and pour over browned duck giblets and parts. Reserve skillet for Step 7.
6. Pour chicken broth over duck giblets and parts. Over medium-high heat, bring to boil, reduce heat. Cover. Simmer for 1½ hours. Strain and skim off fat. Set aside.
7. In same skillet, brown salt pork in remaining tablespoon of oil. Remove pork. Set aside. Leave fat in skillet.
8. Preheat oven to 350°F. Have ready large casserole with tight-fitting cover.
9. In same skillet, over moderately high heat, brown pieces of duck. Put in casserole, season lightly with salt and pepper.
10. In same skillet, sauté onions until not quite limp. Arrange onions on top of duck in casserole.
11. Pour fat from skillet. Add vermouth. Bring just to boil, scraping sides and bottom of pan. Pour vermouth and browned bits over duck in casserole.
12. Arrange garlic cloves between and around duck pieces. Add browned salt pork, tomatoes, bay leaf, thyme and allspice. Pour reserved stock over duck (bone and giblet pieces can be discarded or used for soup). Liquid should almost cover duck. If there is not enough liquid, add a little more chicken broth. Cover.
13. Bake at 350°F. for 1 to 1½ hours, or until legs and thighs are tender when pierced with a fork.

14. In small dish, blend cornstarch and port to a smooth consistency. Stir in green peppercorns. Blend wine mixture into casserole liquid, stirring with spoon to distribute cornstarch evenly. Re-cover casserole. Bake 30 minutes more.
15. Serve duck pieces on buttered toast. Spoon casserole liquid, onion slices, pork bits and garlic over each portion.

DUCKLING WITH PEACHES

4 SERVINGS

1 duck (5 to 6 pounds)	*3 tablespoons granulated sugar*
2 tablespoons butter	*2 teaspoons cornstarch*
1 can (29 ounces) peach halves,	*¼ cup Grand Marnier or curaçao*
drained (reserve juice)	

1. Roast duck, following directions for High Altitude Timetable for Roasting Poultry, page 210, basting with butter and one-half the juice from peaches.
2. Remove duck to warmed platter. Skim off excess fat, reserving drippings.
3. In saucepan, place 2 tablespoons sugar. Moisten with part of reserved drippings. Thicken with 1 teaspoon cornstarch. Bring to boil. Reduce heat. Cook until sauce becomes golden. Slowly add remaining drippings, remaining 1 teaspoon cornstarch and Grand Marnier or curaçao.
4. Strain sauce. Sprinkle remaining tablespoon sugar over peach halves. Broil until heated through and glazed.
5. Arrange glazed peaches around duckling. Pour sauce over duck and peaches.

ROAST GOOSE WITH BURGUNDY STUFFING

See High Altitude Timetable for Roasting Poultry, p. 210.

1 goose (10 to 12 pounds)	*Burgundy Stuffing, page 260 (use*
Salt	*½ cup stuffing for each*
Pepper	*pound goose)*

1. Wash and pat dry goose.
2. Preheat oven to 325°F. Sprinkle goose with salt and pepper.
3. Fill cavities three-fourths full with stuffing. Truss the goose as for Roast Stuffed Turkey, opposite. Prick through skin into the fat layer around legs and wings. Place on rack in open roasting pan, breast side up, or breast side down if preferred.
4. Roast until meaty part of leg will move easily, about 30 minutes per pound, skimming off fat several times.

ROAST STUFFED TURKEY WITH CHESTNUT STUFFING

See High Altitude Timetable for Roasting Poultry, p. 210.

1 *turkey*	*Melted butter, margarine or*
Salt	*cooking oil*
Pepper	*Pan Gravy, page 161*
Chestnut Stuffing, page 261, or	
stuffing of choice (use ½ to	
¾ cup stuffing for each pound	
of turkey)	

1. Preheat oven to 325°F.
2. Wash and pat dry turkey. Sprinkle turkey cavities with salt and pepper.
3. Fill turkey cavities three-quarters full with stuffing of choice or stuff body loosely with one choice of stuffing, and neck cavity with another. Stuffing will expand during baking. Truss opening with wooden pick or skewers and criss-crossed string, or sew closed. Twist wing tips until they lie flat against back. Tie legs together, close to body of bird.
4. Place turkey, breast side up, on greased rack, uncovered, in roasting pan, or place on V-shaped or flat rack breast side down and turn breast side up when three-fourths cooked. Brush well with melted butter, shortening or cooking oil and baste frequently with pan drippings or additional fat.
5. Roast until meaty part of drumstick is tender when pierced with fork tines, or drumstick moves up and down readily from hip joint, or when meat thermometer inserted into center of stuffing registers 185°F.
6. Remove roasted turkey to heated platter. Allow to stand 20 minutes before carving to allow juices to be absorbed. Meanwhile, remove skewers and trussing strings. Serve with gravy.

TURKEY OR CHICKEN A LA KING

4 SERVINGS

3 *tablespoons butter*	2 *tablespoons chopped pimiento*
3 *tablespoons all-purpose flour*	¼ *teaspoon onion powder*
1 *cup half-and-half*	1 *tablespoon lemon juice*
1 *cup chicken stock or bouillon*	2 *tablespoons Madeira or sherry,*
2 *cups diced cooked turkey or*	*if desired*
chicken	2 *egg yolks, beaten*
2 *tablespoons chopped mushrooms*	*Toast slices, cooked rice or*
2 *tablespoons chopped green*	*patty shells*
pepper	

1. In saucepan, over medium heat, melt butter. Stir in flour, blending until smooth. Add half-and-half and chicken stock or bouillon. Cook, stirring constantly, until thickened.

2. Add turkey or chicken, mushrooms, green pepper, pimiento, onion powder and lemon juice. Simmer 5 minutes.

3. Add wine, if desired. Remove from heat. Add a little chicken mixture to egg yolks, then gradually stir egg yolks into chicken mixture. Cook over low heat until hot but not boiling.

4. Serve over toast slices or hot rice or in patty shells.

Pies and Pie Crusts

HIGH ALTITUDE FACTS ABOUT
MAKING AND BAKING PIES

Evaporation of liquid and drying out of flour in pie dough may be remedied by a little additional liquid. Bake fruit, berry and custard pies longer. Increase baking temperature 10 to 15 degrees. Use as small an amount of flour as possible when rolling out dough.

HIGH ALTITUDE PASTRY

Type of Pastry	Flour	Salt	Shortening	Liquid	Other
Basic 1-crust, 8-inch	1 cup sifted all-purpose	½ teaspoon	⅓ cup hydrogenated, emulsified, or lard	2½ tablespoons water	
Basic 2-crust, 8-inch	1½ cups sifted all-purpose	1 teaspoon	½ cup hydrogenated, emulsified, or lard	4 tablespoons water	
Basic 2-crust, 9-inch	2 cups sifted all-purpose	1½ teaspoons	⅔ cup hydrogenated, emulsified, or lard	5 tablespoons water	
Basic 2-crust, 10-inch	3 cups sifted all-purpose	1½ teaspoons	1 cup hydrogenated, emulsified, or lard	7½ tablespoons water	
French pastry 1-crust, 8- or 9-inch	2 cups sifted all-purpose	½ teaspoon	1 cup hydrogenated, emulsified, or butter	1 teaspoon vinegar, or 2 tablespoons lemon juice	In Step 1, add 2 tablespoons sugar, 1⅓ teaspoons double-acting baking powder, 1 egg, beaten, or 2 egg yolks beaten
Quick 2-crust, 8- or 9-inch	2¼ cups sifted all-purpose	1 teaspoon	½ cup plus 1 tablespoon cooking oil	⅓ cup cold milk	

Type of Pastry	Flour	Salt	Shortening	Liquid	Other
Cream cheese, 1-crust, 8- or 9-inch (Refrigerate overnight)	1½ cups sifted all-purpose		½ cup butter	5 tablespoons water	In Step 1, add 3 ounces cream cheese
Cream cheese, 2-crust, 8- or 9-inch (Refrigerate overnight)	2 cups sifted all-purpose		1 cup butter		In Step 1, add 8 ounces cream cheese
Cheese, 1-crust, 9-inch	1¼ cups sifted all-purpose	½ teaspoon	6 tablespoons hydrogenated, emulsified, or lard	3½ tablespoons water	In Step 1, add ½ cup grated cheddar or American cheese
Cheese, 2-crust, 9-inch	2 cups sifted all-purpose	1 teaspoon	⅔ cup hydrogenated, emulsified, or lard	5 tablespoons water	In Step 1, add 1 cup grated cheddar or American cheese
Almond Pecan Walnut Hazelnut Brazil Macadamia } 2-crust	Same as basic 2-crust pastry				In Step 1, add ⅔ cup ground almonds, pecans, walnuts, hazelnuts, Brazil or macadamia nuts
Sesame seed, 1-crust, 8- or 9-inch	1 cup sifted all-purpose	½ teaspoon	⅓ cup	3 to 4 tablespoons cold water	2 to 4 tablespoons toasted sesame seeds
Whole wheat, 1-crust, 8- or 9-inch	1½ cups whole wheat	½ teaspoon	½ cup butter or margarine	¼ cup ice water	
Whole wheat, 2-crust, 8- or 9-inch	3 cups whole wheat	1 teaspoon	½ cup cooking oil	6 tablespoons ice water	1 egg

METHOD FOR MAKING PASTRY

1. Sift flour and salt into medium mixing bowl. Add shortening.
2. With two table knives or pastry blender, cut shortening into flour until consistency of small grain. Sprinkle few drops of water or liquid over flour mixture. Quickly blend by tossing pastry dough with few light strokes of fork. Add remaining water or liquid a little at a time and repeat blending with fork.
3. With loosely cupped hands, gently form pastry into two balls, making one a little larger than the other. This is one of the secrets of flaky pastry, as the more you handle the pastry dough, the tougher it gets. *Do not roll or pack dough in palms of hands.*
4. On lightly floured surface, or between two 12-inch squares of waxed paper, or on pastry canvas, place the larger ball of dough to be rolled out. Sprinkle top with a *very* little bit of flour.
5. Roll from center toward outer edge, lifting rolling pin just before edge is reached to prevent splitting and cracking of pastry. Repeat several times, following the pattern of spokes in a wheel, forming pastry into circle 11 to 12 inches in diameter and ⅛ inch thick.
6. Fold pastry circle in half, placing in ungreased pie plate with fold along center line. Unfold by flipping pastry from center to side. Repair small breaks or holes by gently pressing edges together or using extra pastry for patches. Trim edges, if uneven, leaving as much edge as possible.
7. *For Unbaked Pie Shell:* Do not prick bottom of crust. Make filling of choice and fill pie shell. Roll out top crust, using same method used for bottom crust. Fold pastry in half along center line over filling, or gently roll pastry around rolling pin and unroll over filled pie. Even edges of top crust by trimming with scissors or sharp knife. Fold edge of bottom crust over top crust. Pinch or press two together with fingers or fork tines. Prick top crust with toothpick, or cut small slit or designs with sharp knife to allow steam to escape. Brush with lightly beaten egg white, if desired. Bake as directed for individual pie.
8. *For Baked Pie Shell:* Preheat oven to 450°F. Roll out pastry and place it on pie plate as directed for unbaked pie shell. Trim ragged edges of pastry to about ½ inch beyond outer rim of pie plate. Turn edge under and press against the under side of the rim. Flute, or design the top edge as desired. Prick bottom of crust with fork tines deeply and closely. Prick sides once every inch all the way around. Chill about ½ hour. Bake 12 to 15 minutes. Cool before filling.

HIGH ALTITUDE CRUMB CRUSTS

Pie Crust	Crumbs	Butter or Margarine	Sugar	Other Ingredients	Instructions
Graham cracker crust	about 16 crackers or 1⅓ cups crumbs	¼ cup, melted	⅓ cup granulated		Line pan: chill or bake at 375°F. for 15 minutes
Chocolate crumb crust (graham cracker, vanilla or chocolate wafers, corn or wheat flakes)	1¼ cups	¼ cup, melted	¼ cup	1 ounce grated chocolate	Line pan: bake at 375°F. for 15 minutes
Cookie crust (vanilla wafer, chocolate wafer or gingersnap)	about 20 to 24 wafers, or 1⅓ cups crumbs	6 tablespoons, soft			Line pan: chill or bake at 375°F. for 15 minutes
Zweiback crust	1¼ cups zweiback crumbs	½ cup, melted	⅓ cup, powdered	(optional) ⅓ cup unblanched almonds, ground	Line pan. Bake at 375°F. for 10 minutes (it is best baked)
Cereal crust (corn flakes, wheat flakes or crisp rice cereal)	about 3 cups cereal or 1⅓ cups crushed	¼ cup, melted	¼ cup, granulated	(optional) 1 ounce grated chocolate	Line pan: chill or bake at 375°F. for 15 minutes
Nut-crumb crust	1 cup crumbs plus ½ cup nutmeats, ground	⅓ cup, soft	¼ cup, granulated		Line pan: chill or bake at 375°F. for 5 minutes
Nut crust (pecans, peanuts, walnuts, Brazil nuts, hazelnuts or blanched almonds)	1 cup nutmeats	¼ cup, melted	2 tablespoons, granulated	(optional) 2 ounces chocolate, grated	Line pan. Do not form rim on crust: bake at 400°F. for 8 minutes

METHOD FOR MAKING CRUMB CRUST

1. Make crumbs by mashing crackers or cookies with potato masher; or by breaking into blender and blending on medium speed, inverting container occasionally to reverse crumbs and unblended pieces; or roll with rolling pin on bread board or between sheets of waxed paper; or use food processor.
2. In medium mixing bowl, mix crumbs with sugar and melted butter, or melt butter in pie plate and add crumbs and sugar.
3. Reserve 2 tablespoons crumbs to sprinkle on top of pie, if desired. Press crumbs with back of spoon or fork tines into bottom and sides of 8- or 9-inch pie plate, forming slight rim.
4. Refrigerate before filling, or bake in oven preheated to 375°F. for 10 to 15 minutes. Cool before filling.

TART SHELLS

8 SHELLS

Every pie crust and filling recipe may be made into tarts. They are particularly glamorous filled with combinations of custards with fruit glaze or filled with a froth of chiffon and topped with a swirl of whipped cream, meringue or sour cream.

French, Cream Cheese or Basic Pastry for 2-crust, 9-inch pie, pages 222–223

1. Preheat oven to 450°F.
2. Prepare and roll out pastry. Cut into eight 5-inch circles.
3. Line eight shallow, 3-inch muffin pan cups or individual pie plates with pastry circles. Press out air bubbles. Double edges under, making them stand up. Flute or press edges into design. Prick bottom and sides with fork tines.
4. Bake about 15 minutes. Cool.
5. Fill with filling, or combination of fillings. Top with meringue, whipped cream or sour cream topping.

HIGH ALTITUDE MERINGUE TOPPING

Type of Meringue	Egg Whites	Salt	Baking Powder or *Fresh* Cream of Tartar	Sugar	Flavoring
2-egg white meringue for 8-inch pie	2	⅛ tea-spoon	¼ teas-spoon	4 table-spoons	¼ teaspoon va-nilla extract

3-egg white meringue for 9-inch pie	3	⅛ tea-spoon	¼ teas-spoon	6 table-spoons	½ teaspoon vanilla extract or 1 teaspoon lemon juice
Deluxe 3-egg white meringue for 9-inch pie	3	¼ tea-spoon	¼ to ½ teaspoon	½ cup	½ teaspoon vanilla extract

METHOD FOR MAKING MERINGUE TOPPING

1. Preheat oven to 350°F. Have egg whites at room temperature.
2. In mixing bowl, combine egg whites, salt and baking powder or *fresh* cream of tartar.
3. With rotary or electric beater, beat egg whites until stiff, but not dry. Very gradually add sugar a little at a time. Continue beating until sugar is well blended. Add vanilla extract or lemon juice.
4. Spread meringue over cooled pie filling. Seal to the outer edges of the pie crust to prevent shrinking.
5. Bake for about 15 minutes, or until golden brown. Cool away from drafts to prevent falling.

MERINGUE SHELL OR SHELLS: See page 123.

GRANDMOTHER'S APPLE PIE

▼▼

6 SERVINGS

The altitude and the type of apples used may indicate additional baking time.

Pastry for 2-crust, 9-inch pie,
page 222, or Cheese Pastry,
page 223
6 *medium apples, peeled, cored*
and thinly sliced
1½ *tablespoons lemon juice*
⅓ *cup firmly packed brown sugar*
⅓ *cup granulated sugar*

1½ *tablespoons cornstarch or*
3 tablespoons all-purpose
flour
⅛ *teaspoon salt*
¾ *teaspoon ground cinnamon*
¼ *teaspoon ground nutmeg*
1½ *tablespoons butter*

1. Preheat oven to 450°F. Line 9-inch pie plate with half of rolled-out pastry.
2. Arrange apple slices in pie shell. Sprinkle lemon juice over apples.
3. In small mixing bowl combine sugars, cornstarch or flour, salt, cinnamon and nutmeg. Sprinkle over apples. Dot with butter. Cover with top crust. Seal edges. Prick crust, or cut slits or design to allow steam to escape during cooking.
4. Bake at 450°F. for 10 minutes. *Reduce* temperature to 350°F. Bake 35 to 40 minutes more, or until apples are tender.

FLAVORFUL ADDITIONS TO APPLE PIE:
Brush crust with milk or cream
Sprinkle crust with mixture of cinnamon and sugar
Sprinkle baked pie with grated cheese, then place under broiler until
cheese is melted and lightly browned
Substitute brandy for lemon juice
Substitute ground cloves for nutmeg
Substitute cooked stewed prunes for 1 cup apples
Use half apples and half green tomatoes

COOKED OR CANNED BERRY OR CHERRY PIE

6 TO 8 SERVINGS

Pastry for 2-crust, 9-inch pie,
  page 222
3½ cups canned or cooked water
  pack berries or cherries,
  drained (reserve juice)
¾ cup juice

1½ cups granulated sugar
4 tablespoons cornstarch
½ teaspoon salt
¼ teaspoon ground cinnamon
1½ teaspoons grated lemon rind
2 tablespoons butter

1. Preheat oven to 425°F. Line 9-inch pie plate with rolled-out pastry.
2. Put drained berries or cherries and juice in medium mixing bowl.
3. Combine sugar, cornstarch, salt, cinnamon and lemon rind. Gently mix with
berries.
4. Pour into pie shell. Dot with butter. Cover with top crust. Seal edges. Prick
crust, or cut slits or designs to allow steam to escape during cooking.
5. Bake for about 45 minutes. Serve with whipped cream or ice cream.

FRESH BERRY PIE

6 TO 8 SERVINGS

Fresh berry pies require a little longer baking above 3,000 feet.

Pastry for 2-crust, 9-inch pie,
  page 222
4 cups blackberries, black or red
  raspberries, loganberries,
  gooseberries, strawberries,
  blueberries, currants or
  huckleberries
1 cup granulated sugar

⅛ teaspoon salt
2 tablespoons cornstarch or 4
  tablespoons all-purpose flour
  or 2½ tablespoons
  quick-cooking tapioca
½ teaspoon ground cinnamon
1 tablespoon lemon juice
2 tablespoons butter

1. Preheat oven to 450°F. Line 9-inch pie plate with rolled-out pastry.
2. Wash and remove stems or hulls from berries. Drain in colander or sieve until quite dry.
3. In small bowl, combine sugar, salt, cornstarch or flour or tapioca, and cinnamon.
4. In large bowl, place drained berries. Sprinkle with lemon juice. Gently combine sugar mixture with berries, being careful not to bruise fruit. Let stand 15 minutes.
5. Spread berries in pie shell. Dot with butter. Cover with top or lattice crust. Seal edges. Prick crust, or cut slits or designs to allow steam to escape during cooking.
6. Bake at 450°F. for 10 minutes. *Reduce* temperature to 350°F. Bake about 45 minutes more, or until fruit is done.

CRUMBLE PEACH PIE: In Step 1, use 9-inch, unbaked pie shell. In Step 2, substitute peaches for berries. In Step 5, before baking make topping: mix together ½ cup granulated sugar, ½ cup butter and ¾ cup flour until crumbly. Sprinkle over peach filling. Bake as directed in Step 6.

FRESH APRICOT PIE: In Step 2, substitute sliced apricots for berries. In Step 3, reduce sugar to ¾ cup.

FRESH CHERRY PIE: In Step 2, substitute pitted sour pie cherries for berries. In Step 3, omit cinnamon. Add ¼ teaspoon almond extract and few drops of red food coloring. Use flour or cornstarch mixed with ¼ cup cherry juice, if desired.

FRESH PEACH PIE: In Step 2, substitute peeled, sliced peaches for berries. In Step 3, reduce sugar to ¾ cup. Substitute ¼ teaspoon ground nutmeg for cinnamon. Add 2 tablespoons peach brandy, if desired.

FRESH RHUBARB PIE: In Step 2, substitute diced rhubarb for berries.

GLAZED BERRY TART

6 TO 8 SERVINGS

9-inch baked French pastry shell,
page 222 or Crumb Crust,
page 225 or Meringue Shell,
page 123
4 cups fresh berries (strawberries,
blueberries or raspberries),
washed and hulled

3 tablespoons cornstarch
1 cup granulated sugar
2 tablespoons lemon juice
1 cup whipping cream, whipped

1. Have ready baked pie shell, crumb crust or meringue shell.
2. In saucepan, crush one half of berries with fork or pastry blender.

3. Mix together cornstarch and sugar. Stir into berries. Add lemon juice.

4. Cook over medium heat, stirring constantly, until mixture is thickened and clear. Cool.

5. Add remaining berries to cooled mixture. Pour into shell or crust. Refrigerate at least 4 hours. Serve topped with whipped cream.

GLAZED APRICOT, PEACH OR KIWI TART: In Steps 2, 3 and 5, substitute peeled, sliced apricots, peaches or kiwi fruit for berries.

HOMEMADE MINCEMEAT

▼▼▼

1 GALLON

1½ pounds ground lean beef	Juice and rind of ½ lemon
¾ pound ground beef suet	1 pound nutmeats, finely chopped
4 pounds tart apples, peeled, cored and thinly sliced	1 teaspoon ground allspice
2½ cups granulated sugar	½ teaspoon ground ginger
4 cups apple cider	1 teaspoon ground cloves
1½ pounds raisins	1½ teaspoons ground cinnamon
1¼ pounds currants	½ teaspoon pepper
¾ pound citron, chopped	1 teaspoon ground nutmeg
2 ounces candied orange peel, chopped	1 teaspoon salt
2 ounces candied lemon peel, chopped	1 cup brandy or rum, if desired

1. In large kettle with cover, combine all ingredients except brandy or rum. Cover.

2. Cook over low heat, stirring occasionally, for about 3 hours. Cool. Add brandy or rum, if desired.

3. Seal in sterilized jars (See Sterilizing Jars and Glasses, page 72) to ripen for 3 to 4 weeks, or store in stone crock in refrigerator. Use about 2 cups for an 8- or 9-inch pie.

CREAM PIE

▼▼

6 TO 8 SERVINGS

Although a double boiler is conventionally used to make cream fillings, a heavy saucepan works more efficiently at high altitude.

9-inch baked pie shell, page 000
⅔ cup granulated sugar
⅓ cup all-purpose flour or 2½
    tablespoons cornstarch
½ teaspoon salt
2 cups milk

3 egg yolks, beaten
1 tablespoon butter
1 teaspoon vanilla extract, rum
    or sherry
Meringue Topping, page 226, if
    desired

1. Have ready baked and cooled pie shell.
2. In heavy saucepan, combine sugar, flour or cornstarch, and salt. Gradually add milk. Over medium-low heat, cook, stirring constantly, until thickened. Remove from heat.
3. Add a little hot mixture to beaten egg yolks. Stir egg yolks into hot mixture. Return to low heat. Cook, stirring constantly, until thickened. Remove from heat. Add butter. Cool to room temperature. Add vanilla extract, rum or sherry.
4. Pour into pie shell. Cover with Meringue Topping, using remaining 3 egg whites, if desired.

BANANA CREAM PIE: In Step 4, add 2 to 3 sliced bananas in alternate layers with cream filling.

BUTTERSCOTCH CREAM PIE: In Step 2, substitute brown sugar for granulated sugar. In Step 3, increase butter to 3 tablespoons.

COCONUT CREAM PIE: In Step 3, add ½ cup shredded coconut to cooked filling. In Step 4, sprinkle coconut over meringue before baking.

CHOCOLATE CREAM PIE: In Step 2, add 3 ounces unsweetened chocolate or ⅓ cup cocoa. In Step 3, increase butter to 3 tablespoons.

LEMON CREAM PIE: In Step 2, increase sugar to 1 cup. In Step 3, increase butter to 3 tablespoons. Add ⅓ cup lemon juice and grated rind of 1 lemon.

PINEAPPLE CREAM PIE: In Step 3, add 1 cup well-drained, crushed pineapple and 1 tablespoon lemon juice to cooled filling.

SOUR CREAM RAISIN PIE

6 SERVINGS

Pastry for 2-crust, 9-inch pie,
page 222
1 cup seedless raisins
Water
1 cup dairy sour cream
¾ cup granulated sugar
1 egg, slightly beaten

1 teaspoon ground cinnamon
½ teaspoon ground cloves
½ teaspoon ground allspice
½ teaspoon salt
3 tablespoons vinegar
Butter
Milk or cream

1. Preheat oven to 425°F. Line 9-inch pie plate with half of rolled-out pastry.
2. In small saucepan, bring raisins to boil in a little water. Drain.
3. In mixing bowl, combine raisins with all remaining ingredients except butter and milk or cream.
4. Pour into pie shell. Dot with butter. Cover with top crust. Seal edges. Prick crust, or cut slits or designs to allow steam to escape. Brush top crusts with milk or cream. Sprinkle with sugar.
5. Bake for 30 to 40 minutes, or until done.

CUSTARD PIE

6 TO 8 SERVINGS

9-inch unbaked pie shell,
page 222
4 eggs, beaten
½ cup granulated sugar
¼ teaspoon salt

¼ teaspoon ground nutmeg or
cinnamon
1 teaspoon vanilla extract
2 cups warm milk

1. Preheat oven to 450°F. Partially bake pie shell 8 minutes.
2. In mixing bowl, combine beaten eggs, sugar, salt, nutmeg or cinnamon, and vanilla extract. Gradually add warm (not scalded) milk.
3. Pour into partially baked pie shell.
4. Bake at 450°F. for 10 minutes. *Reduce* temperature to 350°F. Bake 25 to 30 minutes more, or until knife inserted in center comes out clean.

IRISH COFFEE PIE

6 TO 8 SERVINGS

9-inch crumb crust, page 225
3 eggs, separated
½ cup double strength coffee
1 tablespoon unflavored gelatin

1 cup granulated sugar
¼ teaspoon salt
½ cup Irish whiskey
1 cup whipping cream, whipped

1. Bake and cool crumb crust.
2. Beat egg yolks lightly.
3. Into small heavy saucepan, pour coffee. Sprinkle gelatin over coffee. Add ¾ cup sugar, salt and beaten egg yolks. Mix well. Over low heat, cook, stirring constantly, until mixture thickens. Remove from heat. Add Irish whiskey. Cool.
4. In large bowl, beat egg whites until stiff, but not dry. Gradually add remaining ¼ cup sugar. Fold coffee mixture into egg whites.
5. Fold whipped cream into coffee mixture, reserving small amount to decorate top of pie.
6. Pour into crumb crust. Chill at least 4 hours, or overnight.

NOTE: Freezes well. Should be completely thawed in refrigerator before serving.

BRANDY ALEXANDER PIE: In Step 3, substitute water for coffee and substitute 3 tablespoons each crème de cacao and brandy for Irish whiskey.

CHOCOLATE MINT LIQUEUR PIE: In Step 1, use chocolate wafer crumb crust. In Step 3, substitute water for coffee and substitute ¼ cup white crème de menthe and ¼ cup chocolate mint liqueur for Irish whiskey.

DAIQUIRI PIE: In Step 3, substitute ¼ cup water for coffee and ⅓ cup lime juice mixed with ¼ cup rum for Irish whiskey. Add more sugar, if desired.

GRASSHOPPER PIE: In Step 1, use chocolate wafer crumb crust. In Step 3, substitute water for coffee and substitute ¼ cup white crème de menthe and ¼ cup crème de cacao for Irish whiskey.

HARVEY WALLBANGER PIE: In Step 3, substitute orange juice for coffee and ¼ cup Galliano mixed with 2 tablespoons vodka for Irish whiskey.

LEMON CHIFFON PIE

4 TO 8 SERVINGS

9-inch baked pie shell,
page 222, or crumb crust,
page 225
1 tablespoon unflavored gelatin
¼ cup cold water
4 eggs, separated (beat whites
until stiff, but not dry)

1 cup granulated sugar
⅓ cup lemon juice
½ teaspoon salt
1½ teaspoons grated lemon rind
Whipped cream

1. Have ready baked and cooled pie shell or crumb crust.
2. Soften gelatin in cold water.
3. Beat egg yolks lightly.

4. In heavy saucepan, combine egg yolks with sugar, lemon juice and salt. Cook over medium-low heat, stirring constantly, until thickened. Add gelatin and lemon rind, stirring until gelatin is dissolved. Remove from heat. Cool.

5. With pliable rubber scraper or whisk, gently fold in stiffly beaten egg whites.

6. Pour into pie shell or crumb crust. Chill. Top with whipped cream, if desired.

MOCHA CHIFFON PIE: In Step 2, substitute strong coffee for water. In Step 4, substitute strong coffee for lemon juice and add 6 tablespoons cocoa or 2 ounces unsweetened chocolate. Substitute 1 teaspoon vanilla extract for lemon rind. Add 1 tablespoon brandy, if desired.

PUMPKIN CHIFFON PIE: In Step 4, substitute ¾ cup brown sugar for granulated sugar, and ½ cup milk for lemon juice and omit lemon rind. Add ¼ teaspoon each ground ginger, cardamom, nutmeg or mace, and ½ teaspoon ground cinnamon, before cooking, and 1½ cups cooked pumpkin before cooling. In Step 6, serve with whipped cream flavored with rum.

STRAWBERRY CHIFFON PIE: In Step 4, add 1⅓ cups fresh or fresh-frozen mashed strawberries. Reduce lemon juice to 2 tablespoons and sugar to ⅔ cup. Omit lemon rind.

PECAN PIE

6 SERVINGS

8-inch unbaked pie shell,
  page 222
3 eggs, slightly beaten
½ cup granulated sugar
1 cup dark corn syrup

½ teaspoon salt
1 teaspoon vanilla extract
3 tablespoons melted butter
1 cup chopped pecan meats

1. Preheat oven to 350°F.

2. In mixing bowl, combine all ingredients except pecan meats. Blend well. Stir in pecan meats. Pour into unbaked pie shell.

3. Bake for 45 to 50 minutes.

PUMPKIN PIE

2 PIES OR 12 TO 14 SERVINGS

Two 9-inch unbaked pie shells,
  page 222
3½ cups canned pumpkin
1 cup firmly packed brown sugar
1 cup granulated sugar
¼ teaspoon ground cloves
2½ teaspoons ground cinnamon

2½ teaspoons ground ginger
1 teaspoon salt
4 eggs, beaten
1 cup scalded evaporated milk
1 cup scalded whipping cream
Sweetened whipped cream

1. Preheat oven to 325°F.
2. In large mixing bowl, combine pumpkin, sugars, cloves, cinnamon, ginger, salt and beaten eggs. Stir well. Add scalded milk and cream. Mix thoroughly. Pour into pie shells, dividing evenly.
3. Bake for about 1 hour, or until knife inserted in center comes out clean. Serve with sweetened whipped cream to which a little rum has been added, if desired.

NOTE: This recipe may be divided in half for one pie.

PUMPKIN PIE WITH CHEESECAKE TOPPING: Divide recipe for Pumpkin Pie in half. In Step 2, in bowl, beat together 1 package (8 ounces) cream cheese, ½ cup sugar, 1 teaspoon vanilla extract and 2 eggs. Pour over pie filling before baking. Decorate with pecan halves. Bake as directed.

PRIZE LEMON MERINGUE PIE

6 TO 8 SERVINGS

9-inch baked pie shell, page 222	⅓ cup lemon juice
6 tablespoons cornstarch	2 teaspoons grated lemon rind
1¼ cups granulated sugar	1 teaspoon lemon extract
¼ teaspoon salt	3 tablespoons butter
2½ cups water	2 teaspoons vinegar
3 egg yolks, slightly beaten	Meringue Topping, page 226

1. Preheat oven to 350°F. Have ready baked and cooled pie shell.
2. In heavy medium saucepan, combine cornstarch, sugar and salt. Slowly stir in water.
3. Cook over medium-low heat, stirring constantly, until mixture thickens and is clear. Remove from heat.
4. Combine beaten egg yolks with lemon juice. Beat well. Stir small amount of hot mixture into egg yolk mixture. Return to hot mixture. Cook over low heat, stirring constantly, until thickened.
5. Remove from heat. Stir in lemon rind and extract, butter and vinegar. Cool to lukewarm. Pour into baked pie shell.
6. Cover with Meringue Topping.
7. Bake for about 15 minutes, or until golden brown. Cool before cutting.

TRIPLE CHOCOLATE PIE

8 SERVINGS

9-inch graham cracker crust,
    page 225
3 tablespoons cocoa
1½ packages (8 ounces each)
    cream cheese at room
    temperature
1¼ cups granulated sugar
2 eggs
1 tablespoon vanilla extract
1 tablespoon crème de cacao
    or Kahlúa
1 cup dairy sour cream

2 ounces unsweetened chocolate,
    finely grated
1½ teaspoons instant coffee
2 tablespoons boiling water
4 ounces semisweet chocolate
4 eggs, separated (beat whites
    until stiff, but not dry)
½ teaspoon vanilla extract
2 tablespoons dark rum
1 cup whipping cream, whipped
Cocoa

1. Preheat oven to 375°F.
2. Follow directions for crumb crust. Add 3 tablespoons cocoa to ingredients. Bake for 10 minutes. Cool.
3. In large mixing bowl, beat cream cheese and ¾ cup sugar until light and fluffy. Add 2 eggs, one at a time. Continue beating until well mixed. Stir in 1 tablespoon vanilla extract and crème de cacao or Kahlúa.
4. Pour into baked pie crust.
5. Bake for 30 minutes. Remove from oven. Cool 10 minutes.
6. Spread sour cream over baked pie. Sprinkle with grated unsweetened chocolate. Refrigerate.
7. Meanwhile, in top of double boiler, dissolve coffee in boiling water. Add semisweet chocolate. Cook over simmering water, stirring occasionally until smooth.
8. In small bowl, beat egg yolks until thick and lemon-colored. Gradually add remaining ½ cup sugar. Beat until light yellow. Stir in chocolate mixture, ½ teaspoon vanilla extract and 1 tablespoon rum.
9. Stir ¼ of beaten egg whites into chocolate mixture. Gently fold chocolate mixture into remaining egg whites. Refrigerate.
10. Spread chocolate mixture over sour cream layer. Chill.
11. Add remaining 1 tablespoon rum to whipped cream. Spread over chocolate layer of pie. Sprinkle with cocoa. Refrigerate.

NOTE: This pie freezes well.

Rice, Cereal, Pasta and Combination Dishes

HIGH ALTITUDE FACTS ABOUT RICE, CEREAL AND PASTA COOKERY

Package directions for cooking rices, cereals and pastas offer good guidelines, but need amending for high altitudes by adding a few minutes' cooking time, a little additional liquid to offset evaporation, and *furiously* boiling water at the beginning of cooking. When cooking cereals, a heavy saucepan is preferable to the use of a double boiler.

FEATHERED RICE

3 CUPS

1 cup uncooked white or brown rice
3 cups furiously boiling water

1 teaspoon salt

1. Rinse rice in sieve under strong spray of cold water.
2. In heavy saucepan with tight-fitting cover, add rice and salt to boiling water.

Cover. Cook over low heat about 25 minutes for white rice, about 50 minutes for brown rice, stirring occasionally.

3. Pour into colander. Rinse under strong spray of cold water. Gently fluff up with fork.

4. Put small amount of water in bottom of pan. Add rice and steam it over simmering water.

CONNOISSEUR'S RICE

6 SERVINGS

1 cup uncooked rice	4 tablespoons butter
1 cup water	1 teaspoon salt
2 cans (10½ ounces each) consommé	¼ teaspoon pepper

In casserole with cover, combine all ingredients. Stir to mix. Cover. Bake at 350°F. for 1½ hours.

BAKED RICE WITH HERBS: Add ⅛ teaspoon dried thyme, oregano, sage, rosemary, basil or savory, or ½ teaspoon celery seed, or 2 teaspoons poppy seeds, or any combination of herbs and spices.

BAKED RICE WITH HONEY, SUNFLOWER SEEDS AND RAISINS: Add ¼ cup honey and 2 tablespoons each raisins and sunflower seeds.

RICE RING WITH PINE NUTS

ABOUT 6 SERVINGS

2½ cups cooked rice	⅛ teaspoon pepper
2 tablespoons butter or margarine, melted	3 eggs, separated
6 tablespoons cream	½ cup pine nuts or 3 tablespoons sesame seeds
½ teaspoon salt	2 tablespoons sliced pimiento

1. Preheat oven to 325°F. Butter 1½-quart ring mold.

2. In mixing bowl, combine rice, butter or margarine, cream, salt and pepper.

3. Beat egg yolks until thick and lemon-colored. Add to rice mixture. Stir in pine nuts or sesame seeds, and pimiento.

4. Beat egg whites until stiff, but not dry. With pliable rubber scraper or whisk, gently fold into rice mixture.

5. Pour into prepared ring mold. Place in shallow pan on oven rack. Pour boiling water into pan to depth of 1 inch.

6. Bake for about 35 minutes.

WILD RICE AND SAUSAGE CASSEROLE

1 *pound ground sausage*
1 *cup chopped onion*
1 *pound mushrooms, washed, dried and sliced*
1 *cup uncooked wild rice, well washed*
6 *cups boiling water*
1 *tablespoon salt*
¼ *cup all-purpose flour*

¼ *cup whipping cream*
2½ *cups condensed chicken broth*
  Salt
  Pepper
  Dash liquid hot pepper sauce
⅛ *teaspoon each dried oregano, marjoram and powdered thyme*
¼ *cup sliced toasted almonds*

1. In medium skillet, over medium heat, sauté sausage until done, chopping into small granules as it browns. Remove sausage from pan, reserving pan drippings.
2. In same skillet, sauté onion until limp. Add mushrooms. Sauté 2 minutes longer.
3. Cook rice in *furiously* boiling water, to which salt has been added, until done, about 45 minutes. Drain.
4. Preheat oven to 350°F. Grease casserole.
5. In saucepan, combine flour, cream and chicken broth, stirring until sauce is smooth. Cook over medium-low heat until thickened.
6. Combine sausage, rice, onions and mushrooms, and cream sauce. Season with salt and pepper to taste, hot pepper sauce, oregano, marjoram and thyme. Spoon into casserole. Sprinkle with almonds.
7. Bake for 45 minutes.

CHEESE GRITS WITH WATER CHESTNUTS

2 *cups uncooked quick grits*
6 *cups boiling water*
1 *pound sharp cheddar, grated*
1 *teaspoon salt*
  Few drops liquid hot pepper sauce

1 *clove garlic, minced*
4 *eggs, well beaten*
1 *cup dairy sour cream*
½ *cup chopped water chestnuts*
  Paprika

1. Preheat oven to 375°F. Butter 13 × 9 × 2-inch baking dish.
2. In large heavy saucepan, combine grits and *furiously* boiling water. Cook, over medium heat, stirring frequently, for 5 minutes. Add cheese, salt, hot pepper sauce and garlic. Stir until cheese is melted. Cool. Add well-beaten eggs, sour cream and water chestnuts. Pour into prepared dish. Sprinkle with paprika.
3. Bake for 45 minutes to 1 hour, or until center is set.

NOTE: Slice leftover grits. Fry in butter and serve with eggs.

CHEESE AND SAUSAGE GRITS: Before Step 1, cook 1-pound bulk sausage, stirring and chopping with wooden spoon into small granules. In Step 2, add sausage and 1 can (4 ounces) chopped green chilies with cheese.

HOMINY AND GREEN CHILI CASSEROLE

4 SERVINGS

3 cups canned hominy, drained
Salt
Pepper
½ cup grated Monterey Jack

⅓ cup diced green chilies
⅓ cup dairy sour cream
¼ cup milk

1. Preheat oven to 350°F. Butter 1½-quart baking dish.
2. Put hominy in baking dish. Sprinkle with salt and pepper. Sprinkle grated cheese evenly over hominy. Top with green chilies.
3. In small bowl, mix sour cream with milk. Pour over hominy.
4. Bake for 25 minutes.

LASAGNE

8 TO 10 SERVINGS

6 quarts water
1½ teaspoons salt
2 tablespoons cooking oil
1 pound lasagne
2 pounds lean ground beef
4 cups ricotta
4 eggs, slightly beaten
1 cup buttermilk

1 tablespoon salt
1 teaspoon pepper
½ cup fresh, finely chopped
   parsley
1 pound provolone, grated
   Italian Meat Sauce, page 168
1 cup Romano, grated

1. In pan large enough to accommodate lasagne without breaking it, bring water to *furious* boil. Add salt, cooking oil and lasagne. Reduce heat. Cook 10 minutes. Remove from heat.
2. Add cold water until lasagne can be handled. Set aside.
3. In large skillet, over medium heat, sauté meat, chopping into fine granules as it browns. Set aside.
4. Preheat oven to 350°F. Grease one 15 × 9 × 2-inch or two 9 × 9 × 2-inch baking pans or dishes.
5. In mixing bowl, combine ricotta, beaten eggs, buttermilk, salt, pepper and parsley.

6. Cover bottom of prepared pan with layer of lasagne. Spread a layer of ricotta mixture over lasagne, then add a layer of meat. Sprinkle meat liberally with provolone, then cover with Italian Meat Sauce. Sprinkle with Romano. Add another layer of lasagne (there will be four in all) and repeat the procedure of spreading ricotta, meat, provolone, sauce, and Romano, ending with sauce sprinkled with provolone. Cover pan tightly with aluminum foil.

7. Bake 1 hour. Allow to stand 20 minutes. Cut into 6-inch squares. Serve with remaining heated sauce.

MACARONI AND CHEESE WITH WINE

4 TO 6 SERVINGS

1½ cups uncooked elbow macaroni
4 tablespoons finely chopped onion
3 tablespoons butter or margarine
3 tablespoons all-purpose flour
½ teaspoon salt

¼ teaspoon ground pepper
1 cup milk
½ cup dry white wine
¾ cup grated sharp cheddar
¾ cup grated Monterey Jack

1. Cook macaroni according to package directions. Wash in colander under cold water. Set aside.

2. Preheat oven to 350°F. Butter 2-quart casserole.

3. In 2-quart saucepan, over low heat, sauté onion in butter until limp, stirring frequently. Add flour, salt and pepper, stirring constantly. Gradually add milk and wine. Cook over medium-low heat, stirring constantly, until thickened. Add cheeses and stir until melted. Add macaroni. Mix well. Pour into prepared baking dish.

4. Bake about 35 minutes.

BAKED MACARONI, CHEESE AND SPINACH: In Step 3, add 1½ cups cooked, very well drained spinach after macaroni.

ITALIAN MEATBALLS IN TOMATO SAUCE

8 SERVINGS

TOMATO SAUCE

2 tablespoons chopped onion
3 cloves garlic, minced
¼ cup olive oil
4 cups canned Italian pear tomatoes, strained
2 cans (6 ounces each) tomato paste
3 cups water
¼ teaspoon dried oregano

2 tablespoons dried sweet basil
1 tablespoon dried or 3 tablespoons minced fresh parsley
1½ teaspoons salt
¼ teaspoon ground pepper
1 teaspoon granulated sugar

1. In large heavy saucepan with tight-fitting cover, over medium heat, cook onion and garlic in olive oil until lightly browned.
2. Add tomatoes. Cover. Simmer over low heat for 30 minutes. Add tomato paste and water. Re-cover. Simmer 30 minutes, stirring frequently. Add oregano, basil, parsley, salt, pepper and sugar. Re-cover. Simmer 30 minutes.

POLPETTI (MEATBALLS)

1½ pounds ground pork	1 teaspoon dried sweet basil
½ pound ground beef	1 teaspoon dried parsley
½ cup grated Romano	2 tablespoons chopped tomato
4 eggs, beaten	1 teaspoon salt
1 cup finely ground cracker crumbs	¼ teaspoon ground pepper
	2 tablespoons cooking oil
1 large clove garlic, minced	

1. In large mixing bowl, combine all ingredients except oil and mix well. Form into 2-inch balls.
2. In heavy skillet over medium-high heat, brown meatballs in oil. Remove from skillet.
3. Add to Italian Tomato Sauce. Cook over medium-low heat for 30 minutes.

NOTE: Serve over hot cooked spaghetti.

SPAGHETTI PIE

6 SERVINGS

6 ounces spaghetti	1 can (6 ounces) tomato paste
2 tablespoons butter or margarine	1 teaspoon granulated sugar
⅓ cup grated Parmesan	1 teaspoon dried crumbled oregano
2 eggs, well beaten	1 teaspoon dried crumbled sweet
1 pound ground beef	basil
½ cup chopped onion	1 cup cottage cheese
1 clove garlic, minced	½ cup shredded mozzarella
¼ cup chopped green pepper	
1 cup canned tomatoes with juice, coarsely chopped	

1. Have ready 10-inch pie plate.
2. Cook spaghetti following directions on package. Drain.
3. Stir butter or margarine into hot cooked spaghetti. Add Parmesan and beaten eggs.
4. Pour spaghetti into pie plate. Use spoon or fingers to shape in form of pie crust. Set aside.
5. In medium skillet, over medium-high heat, combine ground beef, onion, garlic and green pepper. Cook until onion is limp and meat is brown, chopping meat into small granules as it cooks. Drain off fat.

6. Add tomatoes, tomato paste, sugar, oregano and basil. Heat through.
7. Spoon cottage cheese over spaghetti-pie-crust bottom.
8. Spoon meat-and-tomato mixture over cottage cheese.
9. Bake at 350°F. for 35 minutes. Remove from oven.
10. Sprinkle with mozzarella. Bake 10 minutes more, or until cheese is melted and pie is heated through completely. Cut into wedges to serve.

ZUCCHINI OR EGGPLANT LASAGNE

6 SERVINGS

1 teaspoon cooking oil	sliced lengthwise, or 1 large
½ pound lean ground beef	eggplant, peeled and cut into
⅓ cup chopped onion	½ inch slices
1 can (15 ounces) tomato sauce	1 cup cottage cheese
½ teaspoon salt	2 tablespoons pine nuts, if desired
⅛ teaspoon ground pepper	1 egg, beaten
½ teaspoon crumbled dried oregano	2 tablespoons flour
4 medium zucchini, washed and	¼ cup grated mozzarella

1. Preheat oven to 375°F. Butter shallow baking dish.
2. In large skillet heat oil over medium-high heat, sauté beef and onion until onion is limp and meat is brown, chopping meat into small granules as it cooks. Stir in tomato sauce, salt, pepper and oregano.
3. Meanwhile, parboil zucchini or eggplant for 3 minutes. Drain.
4. In bowl, mix cottage cheese, pine nuts, if desired, and egg.
5. In prepared dish, alternate layers of meat, zucchini or eggplant, and cottage cheese mixture. Sprinkle grated mozzarella on top.
6. Bake 40 minutes, or until well heated through and cheese is melted.

CHILI CON CARNE

ABOUT 8 SERVINGS

1 pound dried chili or kidney beans	1 teaspoon ground cumin
	3 tablespoons chili powder
2 to 3 quarts water	2 cans (6 ounces each) tomato
1½ pounds lean ground chuck or beef	paste
	2 teaspoons salt
1 large onion, finely chopped	½ teaspoon pepper

1. Place beans in colander or sieve. Wash thoroughly.
2. *Stove-top method:* Place beans in large soup kettle with tight-fitting cover. Soak overnight in 6 cups water. Drain. Return to kettle.

Pressure-cooker method: Wash and place beans in pressure cooker.
3. Add 2 to 3 quarts water. Cover. Cook on stove top over medium-low heat for 3 hours or more, adding water when necessary and stirring occasionally. Beans should be tender and somewhat mushy. Or cook in pressure cooker at 15 pounds' pressure for 35 minutes. Let pressure drop of its own accord.
4. In large heavy saucepan with tight-fitting cover, cook meat and onion over medium heat, chopping meat into fine granules, until browned. Add cumin, chili powder, tomato paste, salt and pepper. Mix well. Add to cooked beans. Correct seasoning, if desired. Cover.
5. Cook over low heat for 1 hour, stirring occasionally. If too thick, add water. If too thin, liquid will reduce with cooking.

FLAUTAS

8 SERVINGS

1 can (16 ounces) refried beans
½ teaspoon ground cumin
1 small clove garlic, minced
½ teaspoon salt
⅛ teaspoon ground pepper
1 cup grated Monterey Jack
¾ pound chorizos, casing removed
1½ pounds lean ground beef
2¾ cups canned or bottled green chili salsa

8 white flour tortillas
3 cups grated longhorn cheddar
2 cups peeled and chopped tomatoes
¼ cup chopped green onions
4 cups shredded lettuce
1 cup dairy sour cream

1. Preheat oven to 350°F. Grease large shallow baking dish.
2. In top of double boiler, combine refried beans, cumin, garlic, salt, pepper and Monterey Jack. Cook over boiling water, stirring frequently, until cheese melts.
3. Meanwhile, in large heavy skillet over medium-high heat, sauté sausage and beef, chopping meat into granules as it browns. Pour off fat. Add 2 cups green chili salsa and cook until liquid is reduced and mixture is thick.
4. Spread each tortilla with hot bean mixture. Sprinkle meat over beans. Roll tortillas and place seam side down in prepared baking dish. Pour remaining ¾ cup green chili salsa over top. Sprinkle evenly with longhorn cheddar, tomatoes and green onions.
5. Bake for 25 minutes.
6. Serve each flauta on bed of shredded lettuce topped with dollop of sour cream.

PASTITSIO (GROUND LAMB AND MACARONI CASSEROLE)

6 SERVINGS

1 cup chopped onion
1 pound ground or finely
    chopped lean lamb
1 tablespoon olive oil
1 cup tomato sauce
1½ teaspoons salt
½ teaspoon ground pepper
½ teaspoon dried oregano

¼ teaspoon ground cinnamon
1 cup grated Romano or
    Parmesan
1 pound ziti or elbow macaroni,
    cooked and drained
1 cup White Sauce, page 169
1 egg yolk, beaten

1. Preheat oven to 350°F.
2. In heavy saucepan with tight-fitting cover, over medium-high heat, sauté onion and lamb in oil, chopping meat into granules as it browns. Add tomato sauce, salt, pepper, oregano and cinnamon. Cover. Cook over low heat for about 10 minutes. Add ¾ cup cheese and stir until thoroughly blended.
3. Grease 2½- to 3-quart casserole or baking dish. Arrange half of cooked ziti or macaroni in bottom. Spread lamb mixture over ziti or macaroni. Top with remaining half of ziti or macaroni.
4. Add remaining ¼ cup cheese and egg yolk to white sauce. Pour sauce over macaroni.
5. Bake at 350°F. for about 40 minutes, or until hot and bubbly.

TAGLIARINI

8 SERVINGS

1 cup chopped onion
¾ cup chopped green pepper
2 cloves garlic, minced
2 tablespoons olive or cooking oil
2 pounds lean ground beef
2 cups drained canned pear
    tomatoes, chopped
1½ cups drained canned kernel corn
¼ cup tomato paste
1 teaspoon dried oregano

2 teaspoons salt
1 teaspoon celery seed
½ teaspoon freshly ground pepper
½ teaspoon ground allspice
1 teaspoon dried sweet basil
3 sprigs parsley, chopped
1½ cups grated sharp cheddar
1 cup chopped ripe olives
1 package (1 pound) spaghetti,
    cooked, rinsed, and drained

1. In large skillet with tight-fitting cover, over medium heat, sauté onion, green pepper, and garlic in hot oil until limp. Add ground beef, chopping meat into granules as it browns. Add tomatoes, corn, tomato paste, oregano, salt, celery seed, pepper, allspice, sweet basil and parsley. Cover. Bring to boil. Reduce heat. Simmer for 30 minutes.
2. Stir in grated cheese and chopped olives. Heat until flavors are blended and sauce is bubbly.
3. Serve over hot, cooked spaghetti.

TAMALE PIE

ABOUT 6 SERVINGS

2 pounds ground beef
1 large onion, finely chopped
4 teaspoons chili powder
1½ teaspoons salt
1 tablespoon Worcestershire sauce
1 can (1 pound) tomatoes

1 can (10½ ounces) tomato soup
1 can (1 pound) kidney beans,
   drained
Corn Bread (batter), page 17,
   or 1 package (15 ounces)
   corn-bread mix

1. Preheat oven to 425°F. Lightly grease 2-quart casserole.
2. In large skillet over medium-high heat, sauté ground beef and onion, chopping meat into small granules as it browns. Drain off fat. Add remaining ingredients except corn-bread batter or corn-bread mix. Mix well. Pour into prepared casserole.
3. Spread ready-to-bake corn-bread batter over meat mixture.
4. Bake about 30 minutes, or until corn bread is done.

VEGETABLE PIE WITH WHOLE-WHEAT CRUST

6 SERVINGS

2 tablespoons cooking oil
1 cup chopped zucchini
1 cup chopped celery
½ cup shredded carrot
½ cup sliced fresh mushrooms
½ cup chopped green pepper
1 tomato, seeded and chopped
1 clove garlic, minced
1 can (15 ounces) tomato sauce
½ cup cooked cut-up green beans
½ cup cooked corn
1 tablespoon honey
1 teaspoon crumbled dried oregano

1 teaspoon chili powder
½ teaspoon salt
¼ teaspoon pepper
½ teaspoon crumbled dried sweet
   basil
¼ teaspoon ground allspice
¼ teaspoon dried rosemary
1 cup shredded cheddar
Pastry for 2-crust, 9-inch
   whole-wheat pie, page 223
1 egg, beaten
1 tablespoon water

1. In large heavy skillet with tight-fitting cover, heat oil. Sauté zucchini, celery, carrot, mushrooms, green pepper, tomato, garlic until tender, or about 10 minutes.
2. Stir in tomato sauce, green beans, corn, honey, oregano, chili powder, salt, pepper, basil, allspice, rosemary and cheese. Cover. Simmer 10 minutes.
3. Place bottom crust in 9-inch pie plate.
4. Arrange vegetables in pie shell.
5. Cover with top crust. Seal edges. Prick crust or cut slits or designs to allow steam to escape during baking.

6. Beat egg with water. Brush over crust. Cover edges with foil.
7. Bake at 375°F. for 20 minutes. Remove foil. Bake 30 minutes more. Let stand 5 minutes before serving.

CHICKEN OR TURKEY TETRAZZINI

4 SERVINGS

2 tablespoons butter or margarine
1 cup fresh washed, dried and
  sliced mushrooms **or** 1 can
  (6 ounces) sliced mushrooms,
  drained
¼ *cup slivered blanched almonds*
2 *tablespoons all-purpose flour*
1 *teaspoon salt*
⅛ *teaspoon pepper*

Few grains cayenne pepper
2 *cups chicken broth, bouillon,*
  or consommé
¼ *cup sherry*
½ *cup whipping cream*
2 *cups cooked spaghetti*
2 *to 3 cups cooked diced chicken*
  or turkey
¾ *cup grated Parmesan*

1. Preheat oven to 375°F. Butter 2-quart casserole.
2. In saucepan or skillet, melt butter or margarine over medium-low heat. Sauté mushrooms and almonds until lightly browned.
3. Add flour, salt, pepper and cayenne pepper, stirring until smooth. Stir in chicken broth, bouillon, or consommé. Cook over low heat, stirring constantly, until thickened. Remove from heat. Stir in sherry and cream.
4. Combine sauce, spaghetti, and chicken or turkey. Spoon into casserole. Sprinkle with Parmesan.
5. Bake until lightly browned and bubbly, about 40 minutes.

Salads

BAKED AVOCADO WITH SEAFOOD, CHICKEN OR LAMB

4 SERVINGS

2 *ripe avocados*
2 *tablespoons chopped green onion*
2 *tablespoons butter*
1 *teaspoon dried tarragon*
2 *tablespoons chopped parsley*
⅛ *teaspoon dry mustard*
3 *tablespoons brandy*
2 *cups cubed cooked seafood,*
chicken or lamb

2 *egg yolks, beaten*
½ *cup whipping cream*
1 *tablespoon sherry*
Salt
Paprika
Hollandaise Sauce, page 167

1. Preheat oven to 350°F. Place avocados in oven to warm, but do not allow them to be hot.
2. In skillet over medium heat, sauté green onion in butter until limp. Add tarragon, parsley, mustard and brandy. Cook a few minutes.
3. Add seafood, chicken or lamb, but do not stir. Simmer 5 minutes.
4. Combine egg yolks, cream and sherry. Add to seafood or meat mixture. Shake pan to blend flavors, and cook for 2 minutes, or until heated through. Add salt and paprika to taste. Remove from heat.
5. Cut warmed avocados in half and remove seeds. Stuff with seafood or meat mixture. Top with Hollandaise Sauce.
6. Bake until top is golden brown and avocado is heated through.

FROSTED FRUIT GELATIN

1 package (3 ounces) orange
gelatin
1 package (3 ounces) lemon
gelatin
2 cups boiling water
1½ cups cold water
1 can (1 pound, 14 ounces)
crushed pineapple and juice
1 can (11 ounces) mandarin
oranges, drained

2 large bananas
40 miniature marshmallows
½ cup granulated sugar
2 tablespoons all-purpose flour
1 egg, beaten
1 cup pineapple juice
1 tablespoon orange juice
2 tablespoons butter or margarine
1 cup whipping cream, whipped

1. Dissolve gelatins in boiling water. Add cold water. Stir in undrained pineapple and drained mandarin oranges.
2. Pour into large shallow dish or pan. Slice bananas over top of gelatin. Arrange marshmallows between banana slices. Refrigerate until set.
3. Make topping: Combine remaining ingredients, except whipped cream, in medium-size saucepan. Cook over medium-low heat until thickened. Cool. Spread on set gelatin. Refrigerate.
4. Frost with whipped cream. Cut into squares to serve.

COLESLAW WITH COOKED DRESSING

4 cups finely shredded cabbage
⅓ cup slivered green pepper
1 tablespoon chopped parsley
1 teaspoon celery seed
½ cup white vinegar
½ cup water

3 tablespoons granulated sugar
½ teaspoon salt
1 teaspoon butter or margarine
1 tablespoon all-purpose flour
½ teaspoon dry mustard
1 egg, beaten

1. In large salad bowl, combine cabbage, green pepper, parsley and celery seed. Cover. Refrigerate.
2. In small saucepan, over medium heat, combine vinegar, water, sugar, salt and butter or margarine. Bring to boil.
3. In small bowl, mix together flour, mustard and egg. Add to hot mixture. Cook, stirring constantly, until thickened. If too thick, add a little milk. Cool.
4. Pour dressing over cabbage, tossing lightly but well. Cover. Serve chilled.

TOMATO ASPIC

1 can (1 pound, 13 ounces)
   tomatoes
2 medium onions, thinly sliced
1 bay leaf
1 teaspoon salt
6 whole cloves
6 peppercorns
½ teaspoon paprika

1 teaspoon dried sweet basil or
   tarragon
2 tablespoons unflavored gelatin
Water
2 tablespoons vinegar
1 tablespoon lemon juice
½ teaspoon granulated sugar

1. In saucepan, combine tomatoes, onions, bay leaf, salt, cloves, peppercorns, paprika and basil or tarragon. Bring to boil. Cover. Reduce heat. Simmer for 30 minutes. Press through sieve or food mill, or purée in blender or food processor.
2. Soften gelatin in ½ cup water. Add vinegar, lemon juice and sugar. Add to strained juice. Add enough additional water to make 4 cups liquid.
3. Pour into lightly oiled 1½-quart mold. Refrigerate until set.

MEXICAN SALAD

2 cups shredded lettuce
2 cups canned kidney beans,
   washed and drained
2 tomatoes, chopped
¼ cup chopped ripe olives
2 tablespoons diced green chilies
½ cup chopped green onions
   and tops
½ cup shredded cheddar

1 large avocado, peeled, seeded
   and mashed
½ cup dairy sour cream
1 teaspoon chili powder
2 tablespoons Italian salad dressing
½ teaspoon salt
⅛ teaspoon ground pepper
½ cup crushed corn chips

1. In large salad bowl, mix together lettuce, kidney beans, tomatoes, olives, green chilies, green onions and cheddar. Cover. Chill.
2. In medium mixing bowl, combine mashed avocado, sour cream, chili powder, salad dressing, salt and pepper. Mix well. Cover. Chill.
3. To serve, toss lettuce mixture with sour cream mixture. Sprinkle corn chips over top.

TAOS SALAD: In Step 1, add ½ pound browned, cooked and drained ground beef.

Soups

HIGH ALTITUDE FACTS ABOUT COOKING SOUP

Soups are as near a free form of cookery as there is. Yet even these formula-free gustatory delights are affected by high altitude. Soup ingredients cooking in water or other liquid can get no hotter than the boiling point of that liquid. Beginning at 2,500 feet, the ever-decreasing boiling point cannot be raised by turning the heat higher on the stove. Therefore, soups must be cooked longer or made in a pressure cooker. At elevations of 7,500 feet and above, the pressure cooker is the only recommended method for cooking soups made with legumes (dried peas, beans, lentils).

The longer cooking necessary for soups to reach prime doneness causes more evaporation. To reduce the loss of moisture, always use a heavy pot or kettle with a tight-fitting cover. Take an occasional look to see if the liquids are cooking away, adding more water or other fluids as needed. Adjust the heat to keep a constant simmer or slow boil and stir to prevent scorching.

A bowl of boiling soup at high altitude is not as hot as at sea level.

BORSCH

1 pound beef brisket, cut into
   6 pieces
6 cups water, or 4 cups beef
   stock or diluted canned
   bouillon
1½ cups chopped onion
1½ cups thinly sliced carrots
2 cups thinly sliced beets

1½ cups canned tomatoes, or 1 can
   (6 ounces) tomato paste
1 bay leaf
1 tablespoon salt
2 tablespoons vinegar
1 tablespoon granulated sugar
2 cups finely shredded cabbage
Dairy sour cream

1. In large soup kettle with tight-fitting cover, place beef brisket and water, stock or bouillon. Cover. Simmer over low heat for 2½ hours. Add onion, carrots, beets, tomatoes or tomato paste, bay leaf and salt. Simmer for 30 minutes. Skim off fat.
2. Add vinegar, sugar and cabbage. Cover. Simmer until cabbage is tender.
3. Remove meat to heated platter and thinly slice. Pour soup into bowls. Serve topped with 1 tablespoon sour cream, or refrigerate and serve chilled, topped with sour cream, with meat as a side dish.

QUICK BORSCH: Omit beef brisket. In Step 1, add vegetables and seasonings to beef broth (including vinegar, sugar and cabbage). Bring to boil. Reduce heat. Cover. Cook over low heat 30 minutes.

BEEF STOCK (BROWN STOCK)

3 pounds brisket or stew beef and
   shinbone, or 3 pounds soup
   meat with bone
1 cup chopped onion
1 cup chopped carrots
1 cup chopped celery stalks and
   leaves
½ cup chopped turnips, if desired

½ cup chopped green pepper, if
   desired
1 tablespoon salt
¼ teaspoon ground pepper, or 3
   whole peppercorns
1 bay leaf
2 to 3 quarts water
Beef extract, if desired

1. In large soup kettle with tight-fitting cover, or in pressure cooker, place meat and bones, onion, carrot, celery, turnips and green pepper if desired, salt, pepper or peppercorns, bay leaf and water. Or brown meat and bones in bottom of kettle or pressure cooker, then add vegetables, spices and water. Cover. Simmer 3 hours over medium-low heat, or cook in pressure cooker 30 minutes, letting pressure drop of its own accord.
2. Strain through sieve. Correct seasoning. Add beef extract for color, if desired. Chill. Skim off fat.

JELLIED CONSOMMÉ: Soften 1 tablespoon unflavored gelatin in ½ cup beef stock. Dissolve gelatin in 1½ cups hot beef stock. Flavor with dash Worcestershire sauce and a little sherry, if desired. Refrigerate until set. Serve with lemon slice or sour cream, garnished with chopped chives or parsley.

CHICKEN STOCK (WHITE STOCK)

8 CUPS

3½ to 4 pounds chicken backs, necks and wings, or 1 whole stewing chicken (about 4 pounds)
5 whole peppercorns, preferably white
1 bay leaf
½ teaspoon ground thyme

4 whole cloves
4 sprigs parsley
1 cup chopped onion
1 cup chopped celery and leaves
½ cup chopped carrots
1 clove garlic, if desired
3 to 4 quarts water

1. Wash chicken under running water.
2. In large soup kettle with tight-fitting cover, or in 6-quart pressure cooker, place chicken pieces or chicken and remaining ingredients. Cook in pressure cooker 35 minutes, letting pressure drop of its own accord. Or bring to boil, reduce heat and cover. Cook 1 hour. Uncover. Cook 2 to 3 hours longer, or until liquid is reduced by half.
3. Strain through sieve. Correct seasoning. Chill. Skim off fat.

CREAM SOUP BASE

6 SERVINGS

1½ cups chicken stock, bouillon or broth
1 cup half-and-half
2½ tablespoons butter
1½ tablespoons all-purpose flour
1 teaspoon grated onion, if desired

Salt
Pepper
Paprika, if desired
Alfalfa sprouts, if desired

1. In 1-quart saucepan, combine chicken stock, bouillon or broth, and half-and-half. Heat, but do not boil.
2. Make roux: In small skillet, over low heat, melt butter, but do not brown. Add flour. Stir until smooth. Add onion, if desired. Add a little hot liquid mixture to roux, blending until smooth. Add roux to remaining liquid mixture.

Season to taste with salt and pepper. More half-and-half may be added, if desired. Garnish with paprika and sprouts, if desired.

CHEESE SOUP: After Step 2, add 1 cup grated sharp cheddar. Cook, stirring constantly, until cheese is melted. Add 1½ cups additional chicken broth or milk. Heat through.

CLAM BISQUE: In Step 1, substitute 1 cup clam broth for chicken stock, bouillon or broth. Increase half-and-half to 1½ cups. After Step 2, gradually add 2 beaten egg yolks, 1 tablespoon minced carrot and 1 cup fresh or canned chopped clams. Cook 6 minutes.

CREAM OF ARTICHOKE OF BROCCOLI SOUP: After Step 2, add 2 cups finely chopped or puréed cooked artichoke hearts or broccoli and ½ teaspoon Beau Monde seasoning.

CREAM OF CAULIFLOWER SOUP: Wash and cook small cauliflower head until soft and tender. Drain. Reserve juice. Press cauliflower through sieve or ricer. After Step 2, add cauliflower and 1½ to 2 cups reserved liquid. Heat through.

CREAM OF CELERY SOUP: Cook 2 cups finely chopped celery, including a few leaves, in 1⅓ cups water until tender. After Step 2, add celery pulp or pieces and liquid.

CREAM OF CHICKEN SOUP: In Step 1, add an additional 1½ cups chicken broth, ½ cup chopped celery, 1 tablespoon chopped parsley, ¼ teaspoon paprika and ½ to 1 cup shredded cooked or canned chicken.

CREAM OF CHICKEN SOUP SENEGALESE: Add ½ to 1 teaspoon curry powder (more, if desired), and ¼ cup lemon juice to Cream of Chicken Soup. Garnish with chopped chives or parsley.

CREAM OF MUSHROOM SOUP: Cook ½ pound mushrooms, washed and chopped, in 1⅓ cups water until tender, or about 8 minutes over low heat. After Step 2, add mushrooms and liquid. Add ¼ cup sherry, if desired.

CREAM OF TOMATO SOUP: In Step 1, substitute milk for chicken broth. In saucepan, combine 2½ cups fresh or canned stewed tomatoes with ¼ teaspoon celery seed, ½ teaspoon salt, 1 teaspoon granulated sugar, ½ bay leaf or ¼ teaspoon dried sweet basil, and 1 whole clove. Simmer over low heat for 8 minutes. Press through sieve. Add ⅛ teaspoon baking soda to pulp. *Just before serving*, stir tomato mixture into Cream Soup Base. Heat, but do not boil, stirring constantly. If soup curdles, beat with rotary beater or whisk. Garnish with chopped parsley or chives, grated cheese or sour cream.

CREAM OF WATERCRESS SOUP: After Step 2, add ½ cup finely chopped onion, 1 bunch washed watercress, finely chopped, and ½ teaspoon celery salt. Simmer over low heat 15 minutes.

LOBSTER, CRAB, SHRIMP OR FISH BISQUE: In Step 1, scald half-and-half with 1 slice onion, 2 stalks celery, 1 sprig parsley and 1 bay leaf. Cool. Remove seasonings. After Step 2, add 1½ to 2 cups cooked finely chopped lobster, crab, shrimp, or fish flakes. Add 1 tablespoon vermouth or sherry to each serving, if desired.

VICHYSSOISE: In Step 1, increase chicken stock or broth to 3 cups. Add 1½ cups chopped potatoes and 1½ cups chopped leeks (white part only) to chicken stock or broth. Cook over low heat until vegetables are tender, or about 30 minutes. Press vegetables and liquid through sieve. After Step 2, add strained vegetables and liquid. Chill thoroughly before serving. Garnish with chopped chives.

FRENCH ONION SOUP

6 SERVINGS

4 tablespoons butter or margarine	1 teaspoon salt
4 cups sliced onion	¼ teaspoon ground pepper
6 cups beef stock, or 3 cans	1 teaspoon Worcestershire sauce
(10½ ounces each) beef	1 teaspoon granulated sugar
bouillon and 2 cans water	6 slices French bread, toasted
1 cup dry red wine	¼ cup grated Parmesan

1. In large heavy saucepan with tight-fitting cover, over medium heat, melt butter or margarine. Add onion. Cook over low heat, about 15 minutes or until golden.
2. Add beef stock or bouillon and water, wine, salt, pepper, Worcestershire sauce and sugar. Cover. Simmer 30 minutes.
3. Pour into ovenproof cups or bowls. Place toasted bread on top. Sprinkle with Parmesan. Broil slowly until cheese is melted and lightly browned.

OYSTER STEW

4 SERVINGS

1 *quart oysters*
¼ *cup butter or margarine*
2 *tablespoons Worcestershire sauce*
1 *teaspoon salt*

1 *teaspoon paprika*
⅛ *teaspoon ground pepper*
Milk
Butter

1. Drain oysters, reserving liquid.
2. In saucepan large enough to accommodate all ingredients, melt butter. Add drained oysters, Worcestershire sauce, salt, paprika and pepper. Heat only until edges of oysters begin to curl.
3. Measure liquid from oysters. Add enough milk to make 1 quart. Add to oysters. Heat, but do *not* boil. Top each serving with lump of butter.

FRESH PEA SOUP

4 SERVINGS

2 *cups fresh or fresh-frozen peas*
1 *small onion, sliced*
1 *cup water*
½ *teaspoon salt*
⅛ *teaspoon ground pepper*

3 *cups chicken broth*
2 *tablespoons all-purpose flour*
½ *cup whipping cream*
Fresh mint, finely chopped

1. In saucepan, combine peas, onion, water, salt and pepper. Cook over medium-low heat until peas are tender. Drain peas, reserving liquid. Press peas through sieve.
2. In same saucepan, blend ½ cup chicken broth with flour until smooth. Add remaining chicken broth and liquid from peas. Cook over low heat, stirring constantly, until thickened. Add peas. Bring to boil. Add cream. Serve hot or cold. If cold, serve garnished with chopped mint.

SPLIT PEA SOUP

6 TO 8 SERVINGS

The higher the altitude, the more difficult it is to get dried peas, beans and lentils cooked to that nice soft stage. It was sheer frustration to old prospectors to find that their beans never would get done when they made their camps in the high country. Many homemakers find the pressure cooker the most satisfying solution for faster, thorough cooking of dried legumes, eliminating the hazard of the pot going dry and the need for the cook's continual vigilance.

The following ingredients and amounts are offered as a starting point. The water required is subject to the combination of dried legumes and dry air, so it takes a lot.

2 *cups dried split peas*
2 *to 3 quarts water*
1 *ham bone and meat or turkey carcass, or ½ pound ham pieces, or 1½ pounds ham hocks, or ¼ pound salt pork or bacon, or 2 to 4 frankfurters, sliced*
1 *large onion, chopped*

1 *large carrot, chopped*
1 *cup chopped celery*
1 *bay leaf*
1 *clove garlic, minced, if desired*
1/16 *teaspoon cayenne pepper, if desired*
2 *teaspoons salt*
½ *teaspoon pepper*

1. Place split peas in colander or sieve. Wash thoroughly.
2. *Soup-kettle method:* Place peas in large soup kettle with tight-fitting cover. Soak overnight in 6 cups water. Drain. *Pressure-cooker method:* Wash and place peas in pressure cooker.
3. Add 2 to 3 quarts water, meat or meat and bones (except frankfurters), onion, carrot, celery, bay leaf, garlic and cayenne pepper, if desired. *Do not add salt*, as it toughens, changes flavor and slows cooking process. Cover.
4. Cook over medium-low heat for at least 3 hours, adding water when necessary and stirring occasionally. Peas should be tender and somewhat mushy. Or cook in pressure cooker 35 minutes. Let pressure drop of its own accord.
5. Add salt and pepper. Remove bay leaf.
6. According to personal preference, peas may be slightly mashed and liquid cooked down to consistency for serving. If using frankfurters, add, and heat thoroughly.

LENTIL SOUP: In Step 1, substitute lentils for split peas. In Step 2, lentils do not require soaking. In Step 3, add ¼ teaspoon dried thyme and 1 to 2 cups canned tomatoes, if desired. Excellent made with frankfurters. Decrease cooking time to 1½ hours. Serve with dollop of sour cream, if desired.

NAVY OR PINTO BEAN SOUP: In Step 1, substitute navy or pinto beans for split peas.

PEASANT SOUP

4 *large potatoes, thinly sliced*
2 *large onions, thinly sliced*
1 *carrot, thinly sliced*
2 *stalks celery, thinly sliced*
1 *tomato, thinly sliced*
6 *tablespoons butter*
2 *sprigs parsley, chopped*
1 *tablespoon salt*

1 *teaspoon ground white pepper*
3 *cups water, vegetable liquid, or*
   meat or poultry broth
½ *package (6 ounces) frozen,*
   chopped spinach, thawed
1 *cup cream*
  Croutons

1. In large soup kettle with tight-fitting cover, or pressure cooker, place peeled and thinly sliced potatoes, onions, carrot, celery and tomato. Add butter, parsley, salt, pepper, and water, vegetable liquid or meat or poultry broth. Cover.
2. Cook over low heat about 40 minutes or until vegetables are very soft. Or cook in pressure cooker 5 minutes. Cool cooker quickly in cold water.
3. Stir spinach into kettle or pressure cooker with soup. Cook until spinach is limp, but do not overcook.
4. Press soup through sieve, or purée in blender or food processor, if desired. Add cream. Heat, but do not boil.

POTATO SOUP

4 *large potatoes*
2 *medium onions, finely chopped*
2 *slices bacon, chopped*
3 *large stalks celery, chopped*

2½ *cups water*
1½ *teaspoons salt*
2 *tablespoons butter*
3 *cups milk*

1. Wash, peel and thinly slice potatoes.
2. In large soup kettle with tight-fitting cover or pressure cooker, combine potatoes, onions, bacon, celery and water. Cover. Cook over medium heat until potatoes and onions are tender. Or cook 5 minutes in pressure cooker. Cool cooker quickly in cold water.
3. Mash vegetables with potato masher, or put vegetables in blender or food processor with a little potato water and blend until almost smooth. Return to kettle or pressure cooker and remaining potato water.
4. Add salt, butter and milk. Heat to almost boiling, but do not boil. Serve hot.

VEGETABLE BEEF SOUP

2 *pounds soupbone (one-half*	1 *cup chopped carrots*
meat), or 2 pounds stew beef	½ *cup chopped onion*
2 *tablespoons cooking oil*	1 *cup chopped celery*
2 *quarts water*	1 *cup diced potato*
1½ *tablespoons salt*	2 *cups tomatoes*
3 *whole peppercorns, or* ¼	1 *cup fresh or frozen peas*
teaspoon ground pepper	1 *cup fresh or frozen green beans*
1 *bay leaf*	*Parsley*
¼ *cup barley or uncooked rice*	

1. Remove meat from bones. Cut into ½-inch cubes.
2. In heavy skillet, over medium-high heat, brown meat in hot oil. Place browned meat in large heavy soup kettle with tight-fitting cover or pressure cooker. Or place uncooked meat and bones in soup kettle or pressure cooker.
3. Add water, salt, peppercorns or pepper, and bay leaf. Cover. Cook over medium-low heat for 2 hours in kettle, or cook 17 minutes in pressure cooker. Cool cooker quickly in cold water.
4. Remove bones, bay leaf and peppercorns. Skim off fat. Add barley or rice, carrots, onion, celery, potato, tomatoes, peas and beans. Re-cover. Cook 1 hour longer in kettle, or 3 minutes more in pressure cooker, letting pressure drop of its own accord. Sprinkle parsley on top of soup before serving.

FLAVORFUL ADDITIONS TO VEGETABLE BEEF SOUP:

Substitute frozen mixed vegetables for carrots, peas and beans, adding 30 minutes before end of cooking period.

Add cut-up zucchini, okra, spinach, cabbage, bok choy, or some of each if desired, during the last few minutes of cooking.

Add ½ teaspoon ground oregano, summer savory or sweet basil to meat and water.

To make "Stoup," add more of each vegetable cut in bite-size pieces. Cook down liquid to lesser amount.

Stuffings

HIGH ALTITUDE FACTS ABOUT STUFFINGS

Use flavorful liquids, such as wine, broth, canned soups, bouillon, consommé, butter, cream and eggs, to keep stuffings moist at high altitudes.

The use of stuffings is recommended, as they add moisture to fish, game and game birds, poultry and meats.

BREAD AND BUTTER STUFFING

12 CUPS

1 cup (2 sticks) butter
1 large onion, finely chopped
1 cup finely chopped celery
12 cups dried bread cubes
2 teaspoons poultry seasoning
1 teaspoon salt

¼ teaspoon seasoned or ground pepper
½ teaspoon paprika
2 to 3 eggs, beaten, or 1 can (10½ ounces) consommé, broth or bouillon

1. In skillet large enough to easily accommodate all ingredients, melt ½ cup butter. Add onion and celery. Sauté until golden and limp.
2. Add bread cubes, poultry seasoning, salt, pepper, paprika and eggs or consommé, broth or bouillon. Toss together lightly but well.
3. Add remaining ½ cup butter. Toss with fork until blended.

BURGUNDY STUFFING: Plunge 1 cup golden raisins in boiling water to soften. Drain well. In Step 2, add raisins and 1 cup burgundy. Omit eggs or consommé.

CHESTNUT STUFFING: In Step 2, decrease bread to 2 cups. Add ½ pound large chestnuts, cooked, shelled, skinned and puréed.

CORN BREAD STUFFING: In Step 2, use 6 cups crumbled corn bread and 6 cups white, wheat, or other bread crumbs.

GIBLET STUFFING: In Step 2, add chopped cooked giblets. Substitute juice from cooked giblets for eggs or consommé, if desired.

MUSHROOM STUFFING: In Step 2, add ½ pound fresh chopped, sautéed mushrooms.

NUT STUFFING: In Step 2, add 1 cup chopped Brazil nut, pine nut, pecan, walnut or chestnut meats.

OYSTER STUFFING: In Step 2, add 1 cup chopped or whole oysters and 1 tablespoon capers.

SAGE STUFFING: In Step 2, add 1 teaspoon or more crumbled dried sage.

SAUSAGE STUFFING: In Step 2, add 1 cup browned sausage meat and ½ cup chopped apples.

WINE STUFFING: In Step 2, add ⅓ cup diced lean cooked ham, ½ cup coarsely chopped stuffed olives, ½ teaspoon dried marjoram and ½ teaspoon ground cloves. Substitute dry sherry for eggs.

HERB STUFFING FOR FISH

ABOUT 6 CUPS

2 cups fresh bread cubes	¼ teaspoon dried ground thyme
½ cup finely chopped celery	½ teaspoon dried ground rosemary
½ cup finely chopped carrots	1 teaspoon salt
½ cup finely chopped mushrooms	1 tablespoon chopped fresh parsley
2 tablespoons pine nuts, if desired	⅓ cup melted butter
½ teaspoon dried ground sage	3 tablespoons dry white wine

In large bowl, combine all ingredients. Toss with fork until blended.

STUFFING WITH ANCIENT HERBS

½ cup (1 stick) unsalted butter
¾ pound ground veal
½ pound ground fresh pork or
  pork sausage
5 cloves garlic, finely chopped
4 large onions, chopped
1 cup chopped celery
¼ cup chopped parsley
1 large tart apple, peeled, cored
  and diced
1 large orange, peeled, seeded
  and diced
1 cup drained canned pineapple
  tidbits or crushed pineapple
  Grated rind of 1 small lemon
3 tablespoons chopped preserved
  ginger
2 cans (5 ounces each) sliced water
  chestnuts, drained
2 teaspoons dry mustard
2 teaspoons sesame seeds

2 teaspoons caraway seeds
2 teaspoons celery seeds
2 teaspoons poppy seeds
2 teaspoons dried crumbled
  oregano
1 bay leaf, crumbled
½ teaspoon ground mace
¼ teaspoon ground cloves
½ teaspoon ground turmeric
½ teaspoon dried marjoram
½ teaspoon powdered savory
1 tablespoon poultry seasoning
¾ teaspoon dried crumbled sage
¾ teaspoon powdered thyme
1 teaspoon dried crumbled
  sweet basil
½ teaspoon chili powder
  Few dashes cayenne pepper
2 teaspoons salt
6 cups dried bread cubes

1. In large heavy skillet, melt butter. Sauté veal and pork or pork sausage, garlic, onions, celery and parsley until onions are limp and meats are browned. Set aside.

2. In very large bowl, combine apple, orange, pineapple, lemon rind, ginger and water chestnuts.

3. In small bowl, combine mustard; sesame, caraway, celery and poppy seeds; oregano; bay leaf; mace; cloves; turmeric; marjoram; savory; poultry seasoning; sage; thyme; basil; chili powder; cayenne and salt. Add to fruit mixture. Toss to mix well.

4. Stir in meat mixture and bread cubes. Toss lightly with wooden spoon or fingers until blended.

QUICK WILD AND BROWN RICE STUFFING

ABOUT 4 CUPS

1 *package (6 ounces) fast-cooking*
  long-grain and wild rice
  with herbs
2 *cups chicken bouillon*
¼ *cup butter or margarine*
½ *cup chopped onion*

1 *clove garlic, minced*
½ *cup diced carrots*
⅓ *cup diced celery*
⅓ *cup salted sunflower seeds*
⅓ *cup dry white wine*

1. In 2-quart saucepan with tight-fitting cover, combine rice and bouillon. Cover. Cook over medium-low heat about 25 minutes, removing cover for last 10 minutes to ensure absorption of all liquid.
2. Meanwhile, in small skillet melt butter. Sauté onion, garlic, carrots and celery in butter until limp. Add sunflower seeds and wine. When rice is cooked, add vegetables. Toss with fork until blended.
3. Allow to cool before stuffing meat, fish, poultry or vegetables.

Vegetables

HIGH ALTITUDE FACTS ABOUT VEGETABLE COOKERY

Cooking vegetables at high altitudes requires special attention because of the lower boiling point of water, the rapid rate of evaporation and the distinction between heat and temperature (see Why High Altitude Baking and Cooking Are Different, page xiii). Turning up the burner will not raise the temperature of the water beyond that of its boiling point, so in order to compensate for the lower boiling point at high altitudes and to cook vegetables thoroughly, it is necessary to lengthen the cooking time. Use saucepans with tight-fitting covers to prevent loss of moisture by evaporation, and add additional liquid to sea-level recipes to prevent vegetables from scorching or boiling dry.

HIGH ALTITUDE TIMETABLE FOR COOKING VEGETABLES
For 1 pound fresh (trimmed) or 1 package (9 to 10 ounces)
frozen vegetables

Boiled Fresh Vegetables: Bring water to boil. Add ½ teaspoon salt and prepared vegetables to water. Cover. Reduce heat to medium-low. Begin timing.

Boiled Frozen Vegetables: Bring water to boil. Add ½ teaspoon salt to water. Add vegetables. Allow water to come to second boil. Cover. Reduce heat to medium-low. Begin timing. (If following package directions for frozen vegetables, add a few minutes' cooking time and a little additional liquid.)

Baked Frozen Vegetables: Add 2 tablespoons butter or margarine, ½ teaspoon salt and vegetables to water. Cover baking dish. Stir once or twice during baking. To bake in foil, place frozen vegetables in center of sheet of heavy aluminum foil, add 2 tablespoons butter or margarine and ½ teaspoon salt. Seal package by folding foil tightly. Baking times given are for 350°F. If baking at 325°F., increase time 12 minutes. If baking at 375°F., decrease time 7 minutes.

| | FRESH | | FROZEN | | |
Vegetable	Boiling time (tightly covered) (*minutes*)	Amount of water	Boiling time (*minutes*)	Amount of water	Baking time at 350°F. (tightly covered)
Artichoke (globe)	30 to 45	to depth of 1 inch			
Artichoke hearts	20	1 cup	5 to 10	1 cup	
Asparagus					
cuts	12 to 15	to depth of 1 inch	10	¼ cup	1 hour
spears	14 to 20	to depth of 1 inch	11	¼ cup	1 hour
Beans					
Green, French					
style or cut	25 to 30	1 cup	14	½ cup	1 hour
Green, whole	30 to 40	1 cup	15	½ cup	1 hour
Lima, large	20 to 30	1 cup	15	1 cup	1 hour
Lima, baby	20 to 30	1 cup	15	1 cup	1 hour
Wax	25 to 30	1 cup	12	¼ cup	1 hour
Italian	25 to 30	1 cup	7	½ cup	1 hour
Beets (small whole)					
young	30 to 50	to cover			
old	60 to 90	to cover			
Broccoli					
cuts	20	to depth of 1 inch	7	¼ cup	45 minutes
spears	25	to depth of 1 inch	8	¼ cup	1 hour
Brussels sprouts	15	1 cup	10	¾ cup	1 hour
Cabbage					
shredded	5 to 10	to depth of ¾ inch			
quartered	12 to 20	to depth of ¾ inch			
Carrots					
diced	20	1 cup	10	¼ cup	45 minutes

HIGH ALTITUDE TIMETABLE FOR COOKING VEGETABLES
(CONTINUED)

	FRESH		FROZEN		
Vegetable	Boiling time (tightly covered) (*minutes*)	Amount of water	Boiling time (*minutes*)	Amount of water	Baking time at 350°F. (tightly covered)
Carrots (continued)					
sliced	25	1 cup	14	¼ cup	45 minutes
baby whole	30	1 cup	16	¼ cup	1 hour
Cauliflower					
flowerets	12 to 15	¾ cup	10	½ cup	45 minutes
whole	25	1 cup		½ cup	1¼ hours
Celery, sliced	15 to 25	to depth of 1 inch			
Corn					
kernel	5 to 6	½ cup	8	¼ cup	45 minutes
on the cob	5 to 10	to cover	8 (thawed)	to cover	45 minutes
Eggplant, 1-inch cubes		1 cup			15
Greens					
Spinach	12	to depth of ½ inch	8	½ to 1 cup	1 hour
Beet, mustard, chard, etc.	12 to 18	to depth of ½ inch	16	½ to 1 cup	1 hour
Kohlrabi, ½-inch cubes		to cover			
Leeks, ½-inch slices		1 cup			
Mixed vegetables	Cook and mix		14	½ cup	1 hour
Mushrooms		to depth of 1 inch			5 minutes
Okra	15 to 30	1 cup	10 to 12	¼ cup	1 hour
Onions, small whole or large quartered	25 to 35	to cover			

HIGH ALTITUDE TIMETABLE FOR COOKING VEGETABLES
(CONTINUED)

	FRESH		FROZEN		
Vegetable	Boiling time (tightly covered) (*minutes*)	Amount of water	Boiling time (*min-utes*)	Amount of water	Baking time at 350°F. (tightly covered)
Parsnips, halved or quartered	25 to 35	1 cup			
Peas					
green	15 to 20	½ cup	12	¼ cup	45 minutes
black-eyed	60	1 cup	60	2 cups	1½ hours
Peas and carrots	Cook separately and mix		12	¼ cup	55 minutes
Potatoes					
cut up	25 to 30	to cover			
whole	45	to cover			
sweet (whole, in jackets)	45	to cover			
Rutabagas	See Turnips				
Spinach	See Greens				
Squash					
summer	25	½ cup	15	¼ cup	1 hour
winter: acorn halves or Hubbard pieces	45	1 cup	20 to 30	none (use double boiler)	1 hour
Succotash	Cook separately and mix		15	½ cup	1 hour
Swiss Chard	See Greens				
Tomatoes, quartered	10	¼ cup			
Turnips, sliced or cubed	20 to 30	1 cup			
Zucchini	15 to 20	to depth of 1 inch			

HIGH ALTITUDE TIMETABLE FOR STEAMING FRESH VEGETABLES

Place prepared vegetables in perforated steaming basket or on rack or plate elevated at least ¼ inch above water in bottom of tightly covered pan. Heat water to boiling. Reduce heat to medium. Cover pan. Begin timing. Cook vegetables until tender-crisp. Do not remove lid often to peek or precious steam will escape. If cooking with several layers or tiers, place larger pieces in bottom because they cook faster.

Vegetable	Preparation	Approximate Cooking Time (in minutes)
Artichokes	Whole	40 to 50
	Halved	30 to 35
Asparagus	Whole	8 to 10
Beans, green	Whole	12 to 15
Beets	Peeled, sliced	10 to 15
Broccoli	Stalks, halved	12 to 15
Brussels sprouts	Whole	15 to 20
Cabbage	Quartered	15 to 20
	Chopped	8 to 12
Carrots	Peeled, sliced	12 to 15
Cauliflower	Flowerets	15 to 20
Celery	Sliced	10 to 12
	Ribs	18 to 20
Corn on cob	4-inch pieces	12 to 15
Green peppers	Seeded, halved	8 to 10
	Sliced	5 to 8
Mushrooms	Whole	5 to 8
Onions	Small whole or large quartered	15 to 20
Peas	Shelled	4 to 6
Potatoes	Quartered	30 to 35
Spinach	Stemmed	6 to 8
Tomatoes	Cherry	5 to 7
	Quartered	5 to 7
Yams	Halved	45 to 55
Zucchini	Sliced	5 to 8

ITALIAN ARTICHOKES

4 large artichokes, washed	*1 cup olive oil*
½ bunch parsley, washed and	*Hot water*
shaken dry	*1 teaspoon salt*
12 cloves garlic	

1. Remove small outer leaves around bottoms of artichokes and ½ inch of bottom stem. Cut off spiny tips of leaves. Invert artichokes and push down on them to open out all leaves. Break parsley into clusters and tuck into artichoke center and between leaves.
2. Remove outer skin from garlic cloves and cut each into about 3 slices. Tuck 8 to 10 garlic slices among leaves of each artichoke.
3. Place artichokes close together in pan just large enough to hold them. Pour in olive oil. Marinate in oil 10 minutes.
4. Add hot water to cover. Sprinkle with salt. Cover.
5. Boil for 45 minutes, or until tender.
6. If pressure cooker is used, cook 10 minutes. (See High Altitude Facts about the Pressure Cooker, page xx.) Cool cooker quickly in cold water.
7. Drain and serve hot as a vegetable, or at room temperature as a first course.

STIR-FRY VEGETABLES

2 tablespoons cooking oil	*1 yellow summer squash, sliced*
½ chopped onion	*½ green pepper, seeded and cut*
1 large clove garlic, minced	*into ¼ inch strips*
1 cup broccoli flowerets, cut into	*4 to 6 large mushrooms, washed,*
½ inch pieces	*dried and sliced*
1 cup cauliflower flowerets, cut into	*1 tablespoon lemon juice*
½ inch pieces	*Salt*
1 cup diagonally cut green beans	*Pepper*
3 tablespoons water	*½ cup whole cashews, if desired*
1 cup diagonally cut celery	

1. In heavy skillet with tight-fitting cover, heat oil over medium heat. Add onion and garlic. Cook for 4 minutes.
2. Add broccoli, cauliflower and green beans. Stir-fry for 2 minutes.
3. Add water. Cover. Cook, stirring occasionally, for 4 minutes.
4. Add celery, squash, green pepper and mushrooms. Cover. Cook a few minutes, or until vegetables are tender-crisp.
5. Add lemon juice, salt and pepper to taste.
6. Garnish with cashews, if desired.

STIR-FRIED ASPARAGUS: In Steps 2 and 4, substitute 2 pounds fresh asparagus, washed, woody ends removed and cut into diagonal slices, for vegetables.

GREEN OR WAX BEANS PROVENÇALE

4 SERVINGS

1 pound green or wax beans,
    washed, ends and strings
    removed
4 tablespoons butter
4 green onions (white part only),
    sliced

1 small clove garlic, minced
3 medium tomatoes, peeled, seeded
    and chopped

1. In pan large enough to accommodate beans, cover beans with boiling water. Bring to boil. Cook 5 minutes. Drain.
2. In large skillet, melt butter. Add green onions and garlic. Sauté over medium heat until limp. Add tomatoes and beans. Heat through. Beans should be tender-crisp.

BROCCOLI-CRUNCH CASSEROLE

6 SERVINGS

2 packages (10 ounces each) frozen
    chopped broccoli, cooked
    and drained
½ cup chopped almonds or sliced
    water chestnuts
4 slices bacon, cooked and
    crumbled
2 tablespoons butter

2 tablespoons all-purpose flour
2 cups milk
¾ cup grated Parmesan and
    Romano
1 teaspoon salt
¼ teaspoon ground pepper
½ cup buttered bread crumbs
    Paprika

1. Preheat oven to 350°F. Butter 2-quart casserole.
2. Place broccoli in greased casserole. Sprinkle almonds or chestnuts and bacon over top.
3. In small saucepan, melt butter over medium-low heat. Add flour and stir until blended. Gradually add milk and cook, stirring constantly, until thickened. Add cheese, salt and pepper. Cook until well blended. Pour over broccoli. Sprinkle with crumbs and paprika.
4. Bake for 30 minutes, or until brown and bubbly.

NOTE: Brussels sprouts or various combinations of frozen mixed vegetables may be substituted for broccoli.

CHINESE SNOW PEAS (PEA PODS) WITH WATER CHESTNUTS

3 SERVINGS

1 *package (6 ounces) frozen
or 6 ounces fresh snow peas*
2 *cups chicken stock or bouillon*

9 *canned water chestnuts, thinly
sliced*
1½ *tablespoons cornstarch*

1. If using fresh snow peas, snap off both ends.
2. In saucepan, bring chicken stock or bouillon to boil. Add snow peas to stock. Simmer gently for about 15 minutes. Add sliced water chestnuts. Thicken with cornstarch mixed with a little cold water. Cook, stirring constantly, until sauce has thickened.

MUSHROOMS IN TEQUILA

8 APPETIZER SERVINGS OR 4 MAIN-DISH SERVINGS

6 *tablespoons butter or margarine*
1½ *pounds mushrooms, quickly
washed, dried and sliced*
¾ *cup 80-proof tequila*
¾ *cup dairy sour cream*

¼ *teaspoon ground white pepper*
¼ *teaspoon dried dill weed*
⅛ *teaspoon celery seed*
8 *slices buttered toast, halved*

1. In large skillet, melt butter or margarine. Add mushrooms. Cook over medium-high heat until lightly browned, but not soft.
2. Meanwhile, heat tequila in top of double boiler over boiling water. Pour over mushrooms.
3. Stir in sour cream, pepper, dill and celery seed.
4. To serve, spoon over toast halves.

FRENCH-FRIED ONION RINGS

4 TO 6 SERVINGS

4 *large onions, sliced ¼ inch thick*
Milk
Cooking oil or shortening

1 *cup all-purpose flour*
1 *teaspoon salt*

1. Separate rings of onion slices. Place in 2-quart bowl. Cover with milk. Soak for 4 or more hours.
2. Drain onion rings.
3. In large cooking pan or electric deep-fat fryer, heat cooking oil or shortening

to 350° to 360°F. Have enough oil or shortening to float onion rings, or at least 1½ inches deep.
4. Mix flour and salt together. Dredge onion rings in flour mixture.
5. Fry rings in hot oil until golden brown. Serve very hot.

PEAS WITH LETTUCE AND ONIONS

6 SERVINGS

2 *tablespoons butter*
2 *tablespoons water*
1 *clove garlic, cut in half*
12 *tiny whole onions, peeled*
3 *large lettuce leaves, cut into fourths*

1 *teaspoon granulated sugar*
½ *teaspoon salt or seasoned salt*
   Dash ground or seasoned pepper
3 *cups frozen peas*

1. In large skillet with cover, melt butter over medium heat. Add water, garlic, onions, lettuce leaves, sugar, salt and pepper or seasoned pepper. Cover. Simmer 20 minutes, or until onions are tender.
2. Add peas. Cover. Cook over low heat for 25 minutes, or until peas are tender, stirring occasionally.

BAKED POTATOES

Preheat oven to 400°F. Scrub baking potatoes with vegetable brush. Rub with cooking oil or shortening, if desired. Bake for 1 hour to 1¼ hours, depending on size and maturity of potato. Or, if making oven dinner, bake alongside casserole, roast or other food, adjusting time according to temperature.

FRENCH-FRIED POTATOES

6 SERVINGS

For high altitude deep-fat frying, decrease temperature 2 to 3 degrees for each 1,000 feet.

6 *medium potatoes*

Shortening or cooking oil
Salt

1. Peel potatoes. Cut lengthwise into ¼-inch strips. If time permits, soak in cold water 1 hour or longer. Drain. Pat soaked or unsoaked potatoes dry with paper toweling.
2. In large cooking pan or electric deep-fat fryer, heat shortening or cooking oil to 350°F. to 360°F. Have sufficient oil or shortening to float potato strips.
3. Fry, a few at a time, until well browned and thoroughly cooked, about 5 to 7 minutes. Drain on paper toweling. Sprinkle with salt after cooking. Serve hot.

PARTY MASHED POTATOES

ABOUT **12** SERVINGS

8 to 10 medium potatoes, peeled
    and cut up
Salt or seasoned salt
1 package (8 ounces) cream cheese

⅓ to ½ cup dairy sour cream
Paprika
Butter

1. Preheat oven to 325°F. Generously butter large casserole or baking dish.
2. In large saucepan with cover, cook peeled and cut-up potatoes in water until tender. Drain. Mash. Add salt or seasoned salt to taste.
3. In small bowl, whip cream cheese and sour cream together. Gradually add to potatoes.
4. Pour into prepared casserole or baking dish. Sprinkle with paprika. Dot with butter.
5. Bake for 20 to 25 minutes.

NOTE: 1 cup grated cheddar may be sprinkled over top before baking.

CANDIED SWEET POTATOES WITH BRAZIL NUTS

4 TO **6** SERVINGS

3 sweet potatoes, cooked and
    sliced
½ teaspoon salt
½ cup firmly packed brown sugar

⅓ cup orange juice or water
2½ tablespoons butter
Slivered Brazil nuts or pecan
    meats

1. Preheat oven to 350°F. Butter 1½-quart casserole.
2. Arrange sliced potatoes in bottom of casserole. Sprinkle with salt and sugar. Pour orange juice or water over top. Dot with butter. Sprinkle with slivered nutmeats.
3. Bake for about 30 minutes.

SHERRIED SWEET POTATOES: In Step 2, add ¼ cup sherry and ½ cup chopped pecan meats.

BUTTERED AND BRANDIED LEAVES OF SPINACH

6 SERVINGS

3 packages (12 ounces each)
    frozen spinach leaves
½ pound butter

2 tablespoons brandy
Salt
Pepper

1. Place frozen spinach in colander or on rack of broiler pan. Allow to defrost at room temperature or overnight in refrigerator.
2. Press *all* moisture from spinach. Spinach must be absolutely dry.
3. In heavy saucepan, melt butter. Add spinach. Over low heat, cook spinach *slowly*, turning constantly to absorb melted butter. Add more butter if spinach will absorb more. Do not skimp. The more butter used, the better.
4. Sprinkle brandy over spinach. Add salt and pepper to taste. Serve immediately.

SPRING SQUASH IN WHITE WINE

6 TO 8 SERVINGS

2 tablespoons butter
2 tablespoons olive oil
1 small onion, peeled and finely chopped
½ cup finely chopped celery
1 pound yellow crookneck squash, washed and thinly sliced
1 pound zucchini, washed and thinly sliced

½ cup dry white wine
½ teaspoon dried sweet basil
½ teaspoon salt
¼ teaspoon freshly ground pepper
¼ teaspoon ground nutmeg
¼ teaspoon celery seed

1. In large heavy skillet, heat butter with oil. Add onion and celery. Sauté over medium heat until onion is limp, stirring occasionally.
2. Add remaining ingredients. Cover. Cook over medium heat until tender, about 15 minutes, stirring occasionally.

SAUTÉED CHERRY TOMATOES

6 SERVINGS

2 green onions and tops, sliced
2 small onions, peeled, sliced and separated into rings
½ teaspoon dried sweet basil
3 tablespoons butter

3 cups cherry tomatoes, washed and stems removed
1 teaspoon granulated sugar
½ teaspoon salt
1 tablespoon dry sherry

1. In medium-size skillet, sauté onions and basil in melted butter over medium heat until limp.
2. Add tomatoes. Sprinkle with sugar, salt and sherry. Cook, tossing lightly, just until tomato skins begin to pop, about 3 minutes. Serve at once.

SAUERKRAUT WITH GIN

4 SERVINGS

1 *can (1 pound) sauerkraut, rinsed
  and drained*
¼ *cup gin*
2 *slices bacon, minced*
1 *tablespoon minced onion*
1 *tablespoon peeled and minced
  carrot*

1 *teaspoon caraway seed*
¼ *cup chicken broth or beef
  bouillon*
½ *teaspoon granulated sugar*

1. In bowl, combine and mix sauerkraut and gin.
2. In medium-size skillet, sauté bacon over medium-high heat for 2 minutes. Add onion and carrot. Sauté until onion is limp.
3. Add sauerkraut, caraway seed, broth or bouillon to bacon and vegetable mixture. Mix to blend flavors. Stir in sugar. Cover.
4. Cook over low heat, stirring occasionally, until gin has evaporated, about 40 minutes. Add more broth or bouillon if needed.

VEGETABLES TEMPURA

6 SERVINGS

Vegetables may be prepared, wrapped and stored in refrigerator until needed. If they are cooked ahead, they may be kept warm in oven preheated to 275°F.

1 *pound artichoke hearts, green
  beans, eggplant, large
  mushrooms, turnip slices,
  Jerusalem artichokes, asparagus
  tips and/or green pepper*

1 *cup water*
1 *teaspoon double-acting baking
  powder*
1 *cup sifted all-purpose flour*
  Cooking oil or shortening

1. Wash and/or peel vegetable or vegetables. Cut into 2-inch lengths. Cut eggplant in half lengthwise, then into ½-inch pieces.
2. In mixing bowl, combine water, baking powder and flour. Beat until smooth.
3. In large cooking pan or electric deep-fat fryer, heat cooking oil or shortening to 350°F. to 360°F. Have sufficient oil or shortening to float vegetables, or at least 1½ inches deep.
4. Dip vegetables in batter.
5. Fry until light brown. Turn over once. Do not overcook. Serve hot with Japanese soy sauce or Chinese mustard.

HIGH ALTITUDE TOWNS AND CITIES
OF
THE WORLD

Afghanistan
  Kabul • 5890
  Kandahar • 3462
Algeria
  Telergma • 2484
Andorra
  Andorra • 3376
Australia
  Badgastein • 3323
Austria
  Innsbruck • 2900
Bolivia
  Cochabamba • 8435
  La Paz • 13,402
  Orivo • 12,149
  Potosí • 13,600
  Suere • 8950
Brazil
  Brasilia • 3075
  São Paulo • 2545
Burundi
  Usumbura (Bujumbara) • 2684
Canada
  Aishihik, V.T. • 3176
  Banff, Alb. • 4537
  Beatton River, B.C. • 2743
  Calgary, Alb. • 3557
  Kimberly, B.C. • 3005

Lethbridge, Alb. • 3047
  Penhold, Alb. • 2967
  Swift Current, Sask. • 2680
  Williams Lake, B.C. • 3085
China
  Gartok (Tibet) • 14,240
  Jiachan (Tibet) • 15,870
  Kunming • 6080
  Lanchow • 5185
  Lhassa • 11,800
  Wanchuom (Kalgan) • 2550
Colombia
  Bogotá • 8659
  Cali • 3139
  Cartago • 2950
  Medellín • 5044
Costa Rica
  San José • 3021
Ecuador
  Quito • 9320
Ethiopia
  Addis Ababa • 7749
  Asonara • 7615
France
  Chamonix • 3402
Germany
  Kaufbeuren • 2390

Guatemala
  Guatemala City • 4958
Honduras
  Tegucigalpa • 3250
India
  Bangalore • 2914
  Darjeeling • 6982
  Leh • 11,253
  Simla • 7186
  Srinagar, Kashmir • 5130
Iran
  Hamadan • 5732
  Isfahan • 5207
  Tabriz • 5250
  Tehran • 3950
Israel
  Jerusalem • 4160
Italy
  Cortina d'Ampezzo • 4003
Jordan
  Amman • 2548
Kenya
  Nairobi • 5452
Malaya
  Tonanarive • 4200
Mexico
  Aguascalientes • 6258
  Cananea • 5200
  Chihuahua • 4444
  Cuernavaca • 5058
  Durango • 6200
  León • 6004
  Mexico City • 7340
  Nogales • 4010
  Crizaba • 4028
  Parral • 5990
  Puebla • 7091
  San Luis Potosí • 6156
  Taxco (de Alarcón) • 5756
  Torreón • 3750

Zacatecas • 8010
Mongolia
  Ulan Bator • 4160
Nepal
  Katmandu • 4223
Pakistan
  Lahore • 3270
Peru
  Arequipa • 8460
  Cerro de Pasco • 14,385
  Cuzco • 11,440
  Puno • 12,648
Philippines
  Baguio • 4640
Poland
  Zakopone • 2733
Rwanda
  Kigali • 4806
Rhodesia
  Salisbury • 4780
Saudi Arabia
  Taif • 4500
South Africa
  Germiston • 5478
  Johannesburg • 5689
  Mafeking • 4217
  Pretoria • 4472
South West Africa
  Windhoek • 5543
Spain
  Granada • 2300
  Salamanca • 2602
Switzerland
  Davos • 5062
  Saint Moritz • 6037
  Zug • 6975
  Zermott • 5279
Turkey
  Ankara • 3122
  Ayfas • 3309

Konya • 3366
Malatya • 3015
Murtid • 2755
Uganda
Kampala • 3730

Venezuela
Caracas • 3164
Mérida • 5415
Yemen
San'a • 7700

HIGH ALTITUDE TOWNS AND CITIES
OF
THE UNITED STATES OF AMERICA

Arizona
  Bisbee • 5300
  Douglas • 3955
  Flagstaff • 6895
  Globe • 3509
  Holbrook • 5080
  Kingman • 3328
  Nogales • 3857
  Prescott • 5320
  Winslow • 4836

California
  Alturan • 4370
  Bishop • 4140
  Lake Tahoe Area • 7240
  Mammoth Mountain Ski
    Area • 9110
  Nevada City • 2520
  Quincy • 3405
  Squaw Valley • 8909
  Susanville • 4195
  Yosemite Village • 4000
  Yreka • 2635

Colorado
  Akron • 4654
  Alamosa • 7536
  Aspen • 7844
  Boulder • 5347
  Breckenridge • 9603
  Burlington • 4250

Colorado Springs • 5985
  Craig • 6174
  Del Norte • 7880
  Denver • 5183
  Dillon • 9000
  Durango • 6517
  Estes Park • 7500
  Fort Collins • 4994
  Fort Morgan • 4338
  Georgetown • 8507
  Glenwood Springs • 5758
  Grand Junction • 4579
  Greeley • 4649
  Gunnison • 7820

Montana
  Anaconda • 5288
  Billings • 3117
  Bozeman • 4754
  Butte • 5544
  Deer Lodge • 4519
  Great Falls • 3331
  Helena • 4009
  Lewiston • 3960
  Livingston • 4491
  Missoula • 3197
  Red Lodge • 5537
  Whitefish • 8000

Nebraska
  Alliance • 3958

McCook • 2509
North Platte • 2803
Scottsbluff • 4662
Sidney • 4085
New Mexico
  Albuquerque • 4950
  Carlsbad • 3100
  Clayton • 5050
  Deming • 4335
  Farmington • 5300
  Gallup • 6500
  Hobbs • 3625
  Las Cruces • 3900
  Las Vegas • 6435
  Los Alamos • 7370
  Raton • 6660
  Santa Fe • 7000
  Taos • 6950
Nevada
  Carson City • 4675
  Elko • 5067
  Ely • 6421
  Fallon • 3970
  Reno • 4484
  Tonopah • 6033
  Winnemucca • 4317
Oregon
  Baker • 3449
  Bend • 3623
  Klamath Falls • 4112
  La Grande • 2787
  Lakeview • 4800
South Dakota
  Custer • 5301
  Deadwood • 4543
  Lead • 5089
  Rapid City • 3196

Texas
  Amarillo • 3615
  Dalhart • 3985
  El Paso • 3710
  Lubbock • 3241
  Plainview • 3366
Utah
  Alta • 9265
  Brigham City • 4315
  Eureka • 6464
  Fillmore • 5700
  Heber • 5560
  Lehi • 4550
  Logan • 4507
  Ogden • 4307
  Park City • 6852
  Provo • 4532
  Salt Lake City • 4390
  Vernal • 5331
Washington
  Pullman • 2534
Wyoming
  Buffalo • 4658
  Casper • 5101
  Cody • 5018
  Cheyenne • 6097
  Jackson • 6209
  Kemmerer • 6958
  Lander • 5377
  Laramie • 7153
  Lusk • 5017
  Rawlins • 6787
  Rock Springs • 6265
  Sheridan • 3745
  Torrington • 4098
  Wheatland • 4747
  Worland • 4059

Index

ABOUT THE AUTHORS

BEVERLY M. ANDERSON and DONNA M. HAMILTON are widely recognized authorities on high altitude cooking and baking. They have fifty years of combined culinary experience, and together have spent more than twenty years as professionals in the field of food, testing thousands of recipes over the years, lecturing on cooking and writing food articles and cookbooks, among them *The Complete Book of High Altitude Baking* and *The High Altitude Cookbook*. They live in Denver, Colorado.

Beverly M. Anderson was born in St. Paul, Minnesota. She attended Reed College in Oregon and took her B.A. in journalism at the University of Colorado. A mother of three, she has had a career in teaching, free-lance writing and fashions. She is the author of *The Busy People's Cookbook, The Lunch Box Cookbook* and *Single After 50,* and her food articles have appeared in a number of national magazines.

Donna M. Hamilton comes from a pioneer Colorado family. She was educated in the Denver public schools and attended extensions of the University of Colorado and the University of Denver. She has had a career in advertising, fashions and food and is a member of the board of trustees of the Children's Hospital in Denver. She conducted a weekly cooking show on the PBS television station in Colorado, and is the author of *The After-50 Cookbook*. She has five children.